LK

GEORGE BERKELEY

A Treatise Concerning the Principles of Human Knowledge

1734

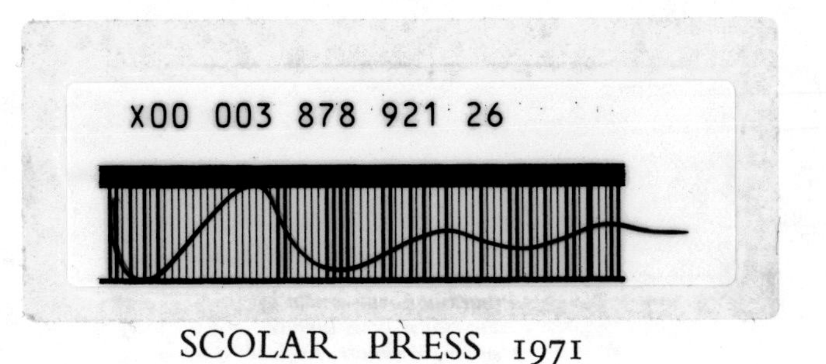

SCOLAR PRESS 1971

NOTE

Reproduced (original size) from a copy in the library of York Minster, by permission of the Librarian.

Printed in Great Britain by
The Scolar Press Limited
Menston, Yorkshire, England

A

TREATISE

Concerning the

PRINCIPLES

OF

HUMAN KNOWLEDGE.

WHEREIN THE

Chief Cauſes of Error and Difficulty in the *Sciences*, with the Grounds of *Scepticiſm*, *Atheiſm*, and *Irreligion*, are inquired into.

Firſt Printed in the Year 1710.

To which are added

THREE DIALOGUES

BETWEEN

Hylas and *Philonous*,

In Oppoſition to

SCEPTICKS *and* ATHEISTS.

Firſt Printed in the Year 1713.

Both written by *GEORGE BERKELEY*, M. A.
Fellow of *Trinity-College*, *Dublin*.

LONDON: Printed for *Jacob Tonſon*, 1734.

INTRODUCTION.

I. PHILOSOPHY being nothing elſe but the ſtudy of Wiſdom and Truth, it may with reaſon be expected, that thoſe who have ſpent moſt Time and Pains in it ſhould enjoy a greater calm and ſerenity of Mind, a greater clearneſs and evidence of Knowledge, and be leſs diſturbed with Doubts and Difficulties than other Men. Yet ſo it is we ſee the Illiterate Bulk of Mankind that walk the High-road of plain, common Senſe, and are governed by the Dictates of Nature, for the moſt part eaſy and undiſturbed. To them nothing that's familiar appears unaccountable or difficult to comprehend. They complain not of any want of Evidence in their Senſes, and are out of all danger of becoming *Sceptics*. But no ſooner do we depart from Senſe and Inſtinct to follow the Light of a Superior Principle, to reaſon, meditate, and reflect on the Nature of Things, but a thouſand Scruples ſpring up in our Minds, concerning thoſe Things which before we ſeemed fully to comprehend. Prejudices and Errors of Senſe do from all Parts diſcover themſelves to our view; and endeavouring to correct theſe by Reaſon we are inſenſibly drawn into uncouth Paradoxes, Difficulties, and Inconſiſtences, which multiply and grow upon us as we advance in Speculation; till at length, having wander'd through many intricate Mazes, we find our ſelves juſt where we were, or, which is worſe, ſit down in a forlorn Scepticiſm.

II. The cauſe of this is thought to be the Obſcurity of things, or the natural Weakneſs and Imperfection of our Underſtandings. It is ſaid the Faculties we have are few, and thoſe deſigned by Nature for the Support and Comfort of Life, and not to penetrate into the inward Eſſence and Conſtitution of Things. Beſides, the Mind of Man being Finite, when it treats of Things which partake of Infinity, it is not to be wondered at, if it run into Abſurdities and Contradictions; out of which it is impoſſible it ſhould ever extricate it ſelf, it being of the nature of Infinite not to be comprehended by that which is Finite.

III. But perhaps we may be too partial to our ſelves in placing the Fault originally in our Faculties, and not rather

in

in the wrong uſe we make of them. It is a hard thing to ſuppoſe, that right Deductions from true Principles ſhould ever end in Conſequences which cannot be maintained or made conſiſtent. We ſhould believe that God has dealt more bountifully with the Sons of Men, than to give them a ſtrong deſire for that Knowledge, which he had placed quite out of their reach. This were not agreeable to the wonted, indulgent Methods of Providence, which, whatever Appetites it may have implanted in the Creatures, doth uſually furniſh them with ſuch means as, if rightly made uſe of, will not fail to ſatisfy them. Upon the whole, I am inclined to think that the far greater Part, if not all, of thoſe Difficulties which have hitherto amus'd Philoſophers, and block'd up the way to Knowledge, are intirely owing to our ſelves. That we have firſt rais'd a Duſt, and then complain, we cannot ſee.

IV. My Purpoſe therefore is, to try if I can diſcover what thoſe Principles are, which have introduced all that Doubtfulneſs and Uncertainty, thoſe Abſurdities and Contradictions into the ſeveral Sects of Philoſophy; inſomuch that the Wiſeſt Men have thought our Ignorance incurable, conceiving it to arise from the natural dulness and limitation of our Faculties. And surely it is a Work well deserving our Pains, to make a strict inquiry concerning the first Principles of *Humane Knowledge*, to sift and examine them on all sides: especially since there may be some Grounds to suspect that those Lets and Difficulties, which stay and embarass the Mind in its search after Truth, do not spring from any Darkness and Intricacy in the Objects, or natural Defect in the Understanding, so much as from false Principles which have been insisted on, and might have been avoided.

V. How difficult and discouraging soever this Attempt may seem, when I consider how many great and extraordinary Men have gone before me in the same Designs: Yet I am not without some Hopes, upon the Consideration that the largest Views are not always the Clearest, and that he who is Short-sighted will be obliged to draw the Object nearer, and may, perhaps, by a close and narrow Survey discern that which had escaped far better Eyes.

VI. In order to prepare the Mind of the Reader for the easier conceiving what follows, it is proper to premise somewhat,

by

by way of Introduction, concerning the Nature and Abuſe of Language. But the unraveling this Matter leads me in ſome meaſure to anticipate my Deſign, by taking notice of what ſeems to have had a chief part in rendering Speculation intricate and perplexed, and to have occaſioned innumerable Errors and Difficulties in almoſt all parts of Knowledge. And that is the opinion that the Mind hath a power of framing *Abſtract Ideas* or Notions of Things. He who is not a perfect Stranger to the Writings and Diſputes of Philoſophers, muſt needs acknowledge that no ſmall part of them are ſpent about abſtract Ideas. Theſe are in a more eſpecial manner, thought to be the Object of thoſe Sciences which go by the name of *Logic* and *Metaphyſics*, and of all that which paſſes under the Notion of the moſt abſtracted and ſublime Learning, in all which one ſhall ſcarce find any Queſtion handled in ſuch a manner, as does not ſuppoſe their Exiſtence in the Mind, and that it is well acquainted with them.

VII. It is agreed on all hands, that the Qualities or Modes of things do never really exiſt each of them apart by it ſelf, and ſeparated from all others, but are mix'd, as it were, and blended together, ſeveral in the ſame Object. But we are told, the Mind being able to consider each Quality singly, or abstracted from those other Qualities with which it is united, does by that means frame to it self abstract Ideas. For example, there is perceived by Sight an Object extended, coloured, and moved: This mix'd or compound Idea the mind resolving into its Simple, constituent Parts, and viewing each by it self, exclusive of the rest, does frame the abstract Ideas of Extension, Colour, and Motion. Not that it is possible for Colour or Motion to exist without Extension: but only that the Mind can frame to it self by *Abstraction* the Idea of Colour exclusive of Extension, and of Motion exclusive of both Colour and Extension.

VIII. Again, the Mind having observed that in the particular Extensions perceiv'd by Sense, there is something common and alike in all, and some other things peculiar, as this or that Figure or Magnitude, which distinguish them one from another; it considers apart or singles out by it self that which is common, making thereof a most abstract Idea of Extension, which is neither Line, Surface, nor Solid, nor has any Figure or Magnitude but is an Idea intirely prescinded from all these. So likewise the Mind by leaving out of the particular

ticular Colours perceived by Senſe, that which diſtinguiſhes them one from another, and retaining that only which is common to all, makes an Idea of Colour in abſtract which is neither Red, nor Blue, nor White, nor any other determinate Colour. And in like manner by conſidering Motion abſtractedly not only from the Body moved, but likewiſe from the Figure it deſcribes, and all particular Directions and Velocities, the abſtract Idea of Motion is framed; which equally correſponds to all particular Motions whatſoever that may be perceived by Senſe.

IX. And as the Mind frames to it ſelf abſtract Ideas of Qualites or Modes, ſo does it, by the ſame preciſion or mental Separation, attain abſtract Ideas of the more compounded Beings, which include ſeveral coexiſtent Qualities. For example, the Mind having obſerved that *Peter*, *James*, and *John*, reſemble each other, in certain common Agreements of Shape and other Qualities, leaves out of the complex or compounded Idea it has of *Peter*, *James*, and any other particular Man, that which is peculiar to each, retaining only what is common to all; and ſo makes an abſtract Idea wherein all the particulars equally partake, abſtracting intirely

tirely from and cutting off all those Circumstances and Differences, which might determine it to any particular Existence. And after this manner it is said we come by the abstract Idea of *Man* or, if you please, Humanity or Humane Nature; wherein it is true there is included Colour, because there is no Man but has some Colour, but then it can be neither White, nor Black, nor any particular Colour; because there is no one particular Colour wherein all Men partake. So likewise there is included Stature, but then it is neither Tall Stature nor Low Stature, nor yet Middle Stature, but something abstracted from all these. And so of the rest. Moreover, there being a great variety of other Creatures that partake in some Parts, but not all, of the complex Idea of *Man*, the Mind leaving out those Parts which are peculiar to Men, and retaining those only which are common to all the living Creatures, frameth the Idea of *Animal*, which abstracts not only from all particular Men, but also all Birds, Beasts, Fishes, and Insects. The constituent Parts of the abstract Idea of Animal are Body, Life, Sense, and Spontaneous Motion. By *Body* is meant, Body without any particular Shape or Figure, there being no one Shape or Figure common

mon to all Animals, without Covering, either of Hair or Feathers, or Scales, &c. nor yet Naked: Hair, Feathers, Scales, and Nakedneſs being the diſtinguiſhing Properties of particular Animals, and for that reaſon left out of the *Abſtract Idea.* Upon the ſame account the ſpontaneous Motion muſt be neither Walking, nor Flying, nor Creeping, it is nevertheleſs a Motion, but what that Motion is, it is not eaſy to conceive.

X. Whether others have this wonderful Faculty of *Abſtracting their Ideas*, they beſt can tell: For my ſelf I find indeed I have a Faculty of imagining, or repreſenting to myſelf the Ideas of thoſe particular things I have perceived and of variouſly compounding and dividing them. I can imagine a Man with Two Heads or the upper parts of a Man joined to the Body of a Horſe. I can conſider the Hand, the Eye, the Noſe, each by it ſelf abſtracted or ſeparated from the reſt of the Body. But then whatever Hand or Eye I imagine, it muſt have ſome particular Shape and Colour. Likewiſe the Idea of Man that I frame to my ſelf, muſt be either of a White, or a Black, or a Tawny, a Straight, or a Crooked, a Tall, or a Low, or a Middle-ſized Man.

I cannot by any effort of Thought conceive the abſtract Idea above deſcribed. And it is equally impoſſible for me to form the abſtract Idea of Motion diſtinct from the Body moving, and which is neither Swift nor Slow, Curvilinear nor Rectilinear; and the like may be ſaid of all other abſtract general Ideas whatſoever. To be plain, I own my ſelf able to abſtract in one Senſe, as when I conſider ſome particular Parts or Qualities ſeparated from others, with which though they are united in ſome Object, yet, it is poſſible they may really Exiſt without them. But I deny that I can abſtract one from another, or conceive ſeparately, thoſe Qualities which it is impoſſible ſhould Exiſt ſo ſeparated; or that I can frame a General Notion by aſtracting from Particulars in the manner aforeſaid. Which two laſt are the proper Acceptations of *Abſtraction.* And there are Grounds to think moſt Men will acknowledge themſelves to be in my Caſe. The Generality of Men which are Simple and Illiterate never pretend to *abſtract Notions.* It is ſaid they are difficult and not to be attained without Pains and Study. We may therefore reaſonably conclude that, if ſuch there be, they are confined only to the Learned.

XI.

XI. I proceed to examine what can be alledged in defence of the Doctrine of Abstraction, and try if I can discover what it is that inclines the Men of Speculation to embrace an Opinion, so remote from common Sense as that seems to be. There has been a late deservedly Esteemed Philosopher, who, no doubt, has given it very much Countenance by seeming to think the having abstract general Ideas is what puts the widest difference in point of Understanding betwixt Man and Beast. "The having of general "Ideas (*saith he*) is that which puts a "perfect distinction betwixt Man and "Brutes, and is an Excellency which the "Faculties of Brutes do by no means "attain unto. For it is evident we ob-"serve no Footsteps in them of making use "of general Signs for universal Ideas; from "which we have reason to imagine that "they have not the Faculty of *abstracting* "or making general Ideas, since they have "no use of Words or any other general "Signs. *And a little after.* Therefore, "I think, we may suppose that it is in "this that the Species of Brutes are dis-"criminated from Men, and 'tis that "proper difference wherein they are "wholly separated, and which at last

"widens

" widens to ſo wide a Diſtance. For if
" they have any Ideas at all, and are
" not bare Machines (as ſome would have
" them) we cannot deny them to have
" ſome Reaſon. It ſeems as evident to
" me that they do ſome of them in cer-
" tain Inſtances reaſon as that they have
" Senſe, but it is only in particular Ideas,
" juſt as they receive them from their
" Senſes. They are the beſt of them tied
" up within thoſe narrow Bounds, and
" have not (as I think) the Faculty to
" enlarge them by any kind of *Abſtraction.*"
Eſſay on Hum. Underſt. B. 2. C. 11. Sect. 10
and 11. I readily agree with this Learned Author, that the Faculties of Brutes
can by no means attain to *Abſtraction.*
But then if this be made the diſtinguiſhing property of that ſort of Animals, I
fear a great many of thoſe that paſs for
Men muſt be reckoned into their number. The reaſon that is here aſſigned
why we have no Grounds to think Brutes
have Abſtract general Ideas, is that we
obſerve in them no uſe of Words or any
other general Signs; which is built on this
Suppoſition, to wit, that the making uſe
of Words, implies the having general Ideas.
From which it follows, that Men who
uſe Language are able to Abſtract or
Generalize their Ideas. That this is the
Senſe

Senſe and Arguing of the Author will further appear by his anſwering the Queſtion he in another place puts. " Since all " things that exiſt are only Particulars, " how come we by general Terms? *His* " *Anſwer is*, Words become general by " being made the Signs of general Ideas." *Eſſay on Hum. Underſt. B.* 3. *C.* 3. *Sect.* 6. But it ſeems that a Word becomes general by being made the Sign, not of an abſtract general Idea but, of ſeveral particular Ideas, any one of which it indifferently ſuggeſts to the Mind. For Example, When it is ſaid *the change of Motion is proportional to the impreſſed force*, or that *whatever has Extenſion is diviſible*; theſe Propoſitions are to be underſtood of Motion and Extenſion in general, and nevertheleſs it will not follow that they ſuggeſt to my Thoughts an Idea of Motion without a Body moved, or any determinate Direction and Velocity, or that I muſt conceive an abſtract general Idea of Extenſion, which is neither Line, Surface nor Solid, neither Great nor Small, Black, White, nor Red, nor of any other determinate Colour. It is only implied that whatever Motion I conſider, whether it be Swift or Slow, Perpendicular, Horizontal or Oblique, or in whatever Object, the Axiom concerning it it holds equally true. As does the other of every particular Extenſion, it matters not whether Line, Surface or Solid, whether of this or that Magnitude or Figure.

XII. By obſerving how Ideas become general, we may the better judge how Words are made ſo. And here it is to be noted that I do not deny abſolutely there are general Ideas, but only that there are any *abſtract general Ideas*: For in the Paſſages above quoted, wherein there is mention of general Ideas, it is always ſuppoſed that they are formed by *Abſtraction*, after the manner ſet forth in *Sect.* VIII and IX. Now if we will annex a meaning to our Words, and ſpeak only of what we can conceive, I believe we ſhall acknowledge, that an Idea, which conſidered in it ſelf is particular, becomes general, by being made to repreſent or ſtand for all other particular Ideas of the ſame ſort. To make this plain by an Example, ſuppoſe a Geometrician is demonſtrating the Method, of cutting a Line in two equal Parts. He draws, for Inſtance, a Black Line of an Inch in Length, this which in it ſelf is a particular Line is nevertheleſs with regard to its ſignification General, ſince as it is there

there uſed, it repreſents all particular Lines whatſoever; ſo that what is demonſtrated of it, is demonſtrated of all Lines, or, in other Words, of a Line in General. And as that particular Line becomes General, by being made a Sign, ſo the name *Line* which taken abſolutely is particular, by being a Sign is made General. And as the former owes its Generality, not to its being the Sign of an abſtract or general Line, but of all particular right Lines that may poſſibly exiſt, ſo the latter muſt be thought to derive its Generality from the ſame Cauſe, namely, the various particular Lines which it indifferently denotes.

XIII. To give the Reader a yet clearer View of the Nature of abſtract Ideas, and the Uſes they are thought neceſſary to, I ſhall add one more Paſſage out of the *Eſſay on Human Underſtanding*, which is as follows. " *Abſtract Ideas* are not ſo ob-" vious or eaſy to Children or the yet " unexerciſed Mind as particular ones. " If they ſeem ſo to grown Men, it is " only becauſe by conſtant and familiar " Uſe they are made ſo. For when we " nicely reflect upon them, we ſhall find " that general Ideas are Fictions and Con-" trivances of the Mind, that carry Dif-" ficulty with them, and do not ſo eaſily

" offer themſelves, as we are apt to ima-
" gine. For Example, Does it not re-
" quire ſome Pains and Skill to form the
" general Idea of a Triangle (which is
" yet none of the moſt abſtract compre-
" henſive and difficult) for it muſt be nei-
" ther Oblique nor Rectangle, neither E-
" quilateral, Equicrural, nor Scalenon, but
" *all and none* of theſe at once. In effect,
" it is ſomething imperfect that cannot ex-
" iſt, an Idea wherein ſome Parts of ſe-
" veral different and *inconſiſtent* Ideas are
" put together. It is true the Mind in this
" imperfect State has need of ſuch Ideas,
" and makes all the haſte to them it can,
" for the conveniency of Communication
" and Enlargement of Knowledge, to both
" which it is naturally very much inclined.
" But yet one has reaſon to ſuſpect ſuch
" Ideas are Marks of our Imperfection.
" At leaſt this is enough to ſhew that the
" moſt abſtract and general Ideas are not
" thoſe that the Mind is firſt and moſt
" eaſily acquainted with, nor ſuch as its
" earlieſt Knowledge is converſant about.
" B. 4. C. 7. Sect. 9." If any Man has the Faculty of framing in his Mind ſuch an Idea of a Triangle as is here deſcribed, it is in vain to pretend to diſpute him out of it, nor would I go about it. All I deſire is, that the Reader would fully and certainly

certainly inform himſelf whether he has ſuch an Idea or no. And this, methinks, can be no hard Task for any one to perform. What more eaſy than for any one to look a little into his own Thoughts, and there try whether he has, or can attain to have, an Idea that ſhall correſpond with the deſcription that is here given of the general Idea of a Triangle, which is, *neither Oblique, nor Rectangle, Equilateral, Equicrural, nor Scalenon, but all and none of theſe at once?*

XIV. Much is here ſaid of the Difficulty that abſtract Ideas carry with them, and the Pains and Skill requiſite to the forming them. And it is on all Hands agreed that there is need of great Toil and Labour of the Mind, to emancipate our Thoughts from particular Objects, and raiſe them to thoſe ſublime Speculations that are converſant about abſtract Ideas. From all which the natural Conſequence ſhould ſeem to be, that ſo difficult a thing as the forming abſtract Ideas was not neceſſary for *Communication*, which is ſo eaſy and familiar to all ſorts of Men. But we are told, if they ſeem obvious and eaſy to grown Men, *It is only becauſe by conſtant and familiar uſe they are made ſo.* Now I would fain know at what time it is, Men are imployed in ſurmounting that Difficulty, and furniſhing themſelves with thoſe neceſſary helps for Diſcourſe. It cannot be when they are grown up, for then it ſeems they are not conſcious of any ſuch Pains-taking; it remains therefore to be the buſineſs of their Childhood. And ſurely, the great and multiplied Labour of framing abſtract Notions, will be found a hard Task for that tender Age. Is it not a hard thing to imagine, that a couple of Children cannot prate together, of their Sugar-plumbs and Rattles and the reſt of their little Trinkets, till they have firſt tacked together numberleſs Inconſiſtencies, and ſo framed in their Minds *abſtract general Ideas*, and annexed them to every common Name they make uſe of?

XV. Nor do I think them a whit more needful for the *Enlargement of Knowledge* than for *Communication*. It is I know a Point much inſiſted on, that all Knowledge and Demonſtration are about univerſal Notions, to which I fully agree: But then it doth not appear to me that thoſe Notions are formed by *Abſtraction* in the manner premiſed; *Univerſality*, ſo far as I can comprehend, not conſiſting in the abſolute, poſitive Nature or Conception of any thing, but in the relation it bears to the

the Particulars ſignified or repreſented by it: By virtue whereof it is that Things, Names, or Notions, being in their own Nature *Particular*, are rendered *Univerſal*. Thus when I demonſtrate any Propoſition concerning Triangles, it is to be ſuppoſed that I have in view the univerſal Idea of a Triangle; which ought not to be underſtood as if I could frame an Idea of a Triangle which was neither Equilateral nor Scalenon nor Equicrural. But only that the particular Triangle I conſider, whether of this or that ſort it matters not, doth equally ſtand for and repreſent all Rectilinear Triangles whatſoever, and is in that ſenſe *Univerſal*. All which ſeems very Plain and not to include any Difficulty in it.

XVI But here it will be demanded, how we can know any Propoſition to be true of all particular Triangles, except we have firſt ſeen it demonſtrated of the abſtract Idea of a Triangle which equally agrees to all? For becauſe a Property may be demonſtrated to agree to ſome one particular Triangle, it will not thence follow that it equally belongs to any other Triangle, which in all reſpects is not the ſame with it. For Example, Having demonſtrated that the three Angles of an Iſoſceles Rectangular Triangle are equal to two right

Ones, I cannot therefore conclude this Affection agrees to all other Triangles, which have neither a right Angle, nor two equal Sides. It seems therefore that, to be certain this Proposition is universally true, we must either make a particular Demonstration for every particular Triangle, which is impossible, or once for all demonstrate it of the *abstract Idea of a Triangle*, in which all the Particulars do indifferently partake, and by which they are all equally represented. To which I answer, that though the Idea I have in view whilst I make the Demonstration, be, for instance, that of an Isosceles Rectangular Triangle, whose Sides are of a determinate Length, I may nevertheless be certain it extends to all other Rectilinear Triangles, of what Sort or Bigness soever. And that, because neither the right Angle, nor the Equality, nor determinate Length of the Sides, are at all concerned in the Demonstration. It is true, the Diagram I have in view includes all these Particulars, but then there is not the least mention made of them in the Proof of the Proposition. It is not said, the three Angles are equal to two right Ones, because one of them is a right Angle, or because the Sides comprehending it are of the same Length. Which sufficiently shews that the right Angle might have been

been Oblique, and the Sides unequal, and for all that the Demonſtration have held good. And for this reaſon it is, that I conclude that to be true of any Obliquangular or Scalenon, which I had demonſtrated of a particular Right-angled, Equicrural Triangle; and not becauſe I demonſtrated the Propoſition of the abſtract Idea of a Triangle. And here it muſt be acknowledged that a Man may conſider a Figure merely as triangular, without attending to the particular Qualities of the Angles, or relations of the Sides. So far he may abſtract: But this will never prove, that he can frame an abſtract general inconſiſtent Idea of a Triangle. In like manner we may conſider *Peter* ſo far forth as Man, or ſo far forth as Animal, without framing the forementioned abſtract Idea, either of Man or of Animal, in as much as all that is perceived is not conſidered.

XVII. It were an endleſs, as well as an uſeleſs Thing, to trace the *Schoolmen*, thoſe great Maſters of Abſtraction, through all the manifold inextricable Labyrinths of Error and Diſpute, which their Doctrine of abſtract Natures and Notions ſeems to have led them into. What Bickerings and Controverſies, and what a learned Duſt have been raiſed about thoſe Matters, and what mighty Advantage hath been from thence derived to Mankind, are things at this Day too clearly known to need being insisted on. And it had been well if the ill Effects of that Doctrine were confined to those only who make the most avowed Profession of it. When Men consider the great Pains, Industry and Parts, that have for so many Ages been laid out on the Cultivation and Advancement of the Sciences, and that notwithstanding all this, the far greater Part of them remain full of Darkness and Uncertainty, and Disputes that are like never to have an end, and even those that are thought to be supported by the most clear and cogent Demonstrations, contain in them Paradoxes which are perfectly irreconcilable to the Understandings of Men, and that taking all together, a small Portion of them doth supply any real Benefit to Mankind, otherwise than by being an innocent Diversion and Amusement: I say, the Consideration of all this is apt to throw them into a Despondency, and perfect Contempt of all Study. But this may perhaps cease, upon a view of the false Principles that have obtained in the World, amongst all which there is none, methinks, hath a more wide Influence over the Thoughts of Speculative Men, than this of abstract general Ideas.

XVIII. I

XVIII. I come now to consider the Source of this prevailing Notion, and that seems to me to be Language. And surely nothing of less extent than Reason it self could have been the Source of an Opinion so universally received. The truth of this appears as from other Reasons, so also from the plain Confession of the ablest Patrons of abstract Ideas, who acknowledge that they are made in order to naming; from which it is a clear Consequence, that if there had been no such thing as Speech or Universal Signs, there never had been any thought of Abstraction. *See* B. 3. C. 6. Sect. 39. *and elsewhere of the Essay on Human Understanding*. Let us therefore examine the manner wherein Words have contributed to the Origin of that Mistake. First then, 'Tis thought that every Name hath, or ought to have, one only precise and settled Signification, which inclines Men to think there are certain *abstract*, *determinate Ideas*, which constitute the true and only immediate Signification of each general Name. And that it is by the mediation of these abstract Ideas, that a general Name comes to signify any particular Thing. Whereas, in truth, there is no such thing as one precise and definite Signification annexed to any general Name,

they

they all ſignifying indifferently a great number of particular Ideas. All which doth evidently follow from what has been already ſaid, and will clearly appear to any one by a little Reflexion. To this it will be objected, that every Name that has a Definition, is thereby reſtrained to one certain Signification. For Example, a *Triangle* is defined to be a *plain Surface comprehended by three right Lines*; by which that Name is limited to denote one certain Idea and no other. To which I anſwer, that in the Definition it is not ſaid whether the Surface be Great or Small, Black or White, nor whether the Sides are Long or Short, Equal or Unequal, nor with what Angles they are inclined to each other; in all which there may be great Variety, and conſequently there is no one ſettled Idea which limits the Signification of the word *Triangle*. 'Tis one thing for to keep a Name conſtantly to the ſame Definition, and another to make it ſtand every where for the ſame Idea: the one is neceſſary, the other uſeleſs and impracticable.

XIX. But to give a farther Account how Words came to produce the Doctrine of abſtract Ideas, it muſt be obſerved that it is a received Opinion, that Language has no other End but the communicating our Ideas,

Ideas, and that every ſignificant Name ſtands for an Idea. This being ſo, and it being withal certain, that Names, which yet are not thought altogether inſignificant, do not always mark out particular conceivable Ideas, it is ſtraightway concluded that they ſtand for abſtract Notions. That there are many Names in uſe amongſt Speculative Men, which do not always ſuggeſt to others determinate particular Ideas, is what no Body will deny. And a little Attention will diſcover, that it is not neceſſary (even in the ſtricteſt Reaſonings) ſignificant Names which ſtand for Ideas ſhould, every time they are uſed, excite in the Underſtanding the Ideas they are made to ſtand for: In Reading and Diſcourſing, Names being for the moſt part uſed as Letters are in *Algebra*, in which though a particular quantity be marked by each Letter, yet to proceed right it is not requiſite that in every ſtep each Letter ſuggeſt to your Thoughts, that particular quantity it was appointed to ſtand for.

XX. Beſides, the communicating of Ideas marked by Words is not the chief and only end of Language, as is commonly ſuppoſed. There are other Ends, as the raiſing of ſome Paſſion, the exciting to, or deterring from an Action, the putting the

the Mind in ſome particular Diſpoſition; to which the former is in many Caſes barely ſubſervient, and ſometimes intirely omitted, when theſe can be obtained without it, as I think doth not infrequently happen in the familiar uſe of Language. I intreat the Reader to reflect with himſelf, and ſee if it doth not often happen either in Hearing or Reading a Diſcourſe, that the Paſſions of Fear, Love, Hatred, Admiration, Diſdain, and the like, ariſe immediately in his Mind upon the Perception of certain Words, without any Ideas coming between. At firſt, indeed, the Words might have occaſioned Ideas that were fit to produce thoſe Emotions; but, if I miſtake not, it will be found that when Language is once grown familiar, the hearing of the Sounds or Sight of the Characters is oft immediately attended with thoſe Paſſions, which at firſt were wont to be produced by the intervention of Ideas, that are now quite omitted. May we not, for Example, be affected with the promiſe of a *good Thing*, though we have not an Idea of what it is? Or is not the being threatned with Danger ſufficient to excite a Dread, though we think not of any particular Evil likely to befal us, nor yet frame to our ſelves an Idea of Danger in Abſtract? If any one ſhall join ever ſo little Reflexion of of his own to what has been ſaid, I believe it will evidently appear to him, that general Names are often uſed in the propriety of Language without the Speaker's deſigning them for Marks of Ideas in his own, which he would have them raiſe in the Mind of the Hearer. Even proper Names themſelves do not ſeem always ſpoken, with a Deſign to bring into our view the Ideas of thoſe Individuals that are ſuppoſed to be marked by them. For Example, when a Schoolman tells me *Ariſtotle hath ſaid it*, all I conceive he means by it, is to diſpoſe me to embrace his Opinion with the Deference and Submiſſion which Cuſtom has annexed to that Name. And this effect may be ſo inſtantly produced in the Minds of thoſe who are accuſtomed to reſign their Judgment to the Authority of that Philoſopher, as it is impoſſible any Idea either of his Perſon, Writings, or Reputation ſhould go before. Innumerable Examples of this kind may be given, but why ſhould I inſiſt on thoſe things, which every one's Experience will, I doubt not, plentifully ſuggeſt unto him?

XXI. We have, I think, ſhewn the Impoſſibility of *abſtract Ideas*. We have conſidered what has been ſaid for them by their ableſt Patrons; and endeavoured to ſhew

ſhew they are of no Uſe for thoſe Ends, to which they are thought neceſſary. And laſtly, we have traced them to the Source from whence they flow, which appears to be Language. It cannot be denied that Words are of excellent Uſe, in that by their means all that Stock of Knowledge which has been purchaſed by the joint Labours of inquiſitive Men in all Ages and Nations, may be drawn into the view and made the poſſeſſion of one ſingle Perſon. But at the ſame time it muſt be owned that moſt parts of Knowledge have been ſtrangely perplexed and darkened by the abuſe of Words, and general ways of Speech wherein they are delivered. Since therefore Words are ſo apt to impoſe on the Underſtanding, whatever Ideas I conſider, I ſhall endeavour to take them bare and naked into my View, keeping out of my Thoughts, ſo far as I am able, thoſe Names which long and conſtant Uſe hath ſo ſtrictly united with them; from which I may expect to derive the following Advantages.

XXII. Firſt, I ſhall be ſure to get clear of all Controverſies purely Verbal; the ſpringing up of which Weeds in almoſt all the Sciences has been a main Hindrance to the Growth of true and ſound Knowledge.

ledge. Secondly, this ſeems to be a ſure way to extricate my ſelf out of that fine and ſubtile Net of *abſtract Ideas*, which has ſo miſerably perplexed and entangled the Minds of Men, and that with this peculiar Circumſtance, that by how much the finer and more curious was the Wit of any Man, by ſo much the deeper was he like to be enſnared, and faſter held therein. Thirdly, ſo long as I confine my Thoughts to my own Ideas diveſted of Words, I do not ſee how I can eaſily be miſtaken. The Objects I conſider, I clearly and adequately know. I cannot be deceived in thinking I have an Idea which I have not. It is not poſſible for me to imagine, that any of my own Ideas are alike or unlike, that are not truly ſo. To diſcern the Agreements or Diſagreements there are between my Ideas, to ſee what Ideas are included in any compound Idea, and what not, there is nothing more requiſite, than an attentive Perception of what paſſes in my own Underſtanding.

XXIII. But the attainment of all theſe Advantages doth preſuppoſe an intire Deliverance from the Deception of Words, which I dare hardly promiſe my ſelf; ſo difficult a thing it is to diſſolve an Union ſo early begun, and confirmed by ſo long a Habit as that betwixt Words and Ideas. Which Difficulty ſeems to have been very much increaſed by the Doctrine of *Abſtraction*. For ſo long as Men thought abſtract Ideas were annexed to their Words, it doth not ſeem ſtrange that they ſhould uſe Words for Ideas: It being found an impracticable thing to lay aſide the Word, and retain the abſtract Idea in the Mind, which in it ſelf was perfectly inconceivable. This ſeems to me the principal Cauſe, why thoſe Men who have ſo emphatically recommended to others, the laying aſide all uſe of Words in their Meditations, and contemplating their bare Ideas, have yet failed to perform it themſelves. Of late many have been very ſenſible of the abſurd Opinions and inſignificant Diſputes, which grow out of the abuſe of Words. And in order to remedy theſe Evils they adviſe well, that we attend to the Ideas ſignified, and draw off our Attention from the Words which ſignify them. But how good ſoever this Advice may be, they have given others, it is plain they could not have a due regard to it themſelves, ſo long as they thought the only immediate uſe of Words was to ſignify Ideas, and that the immediate Signification of every general Name was a *determinate*, *abſtract Idea*.

XXIV. But

XXIV. But theſe being known to be Miſtakes, a Man may with greater Eaſe prevent his being impoſed on by Words. He that knows he has no other than particular Ideas, will not puzzle himſelf in vain to find out and conceive the abſtract Idea, annexed to any Name. And he that knows Names do not always ſtand for Ideas, will ſpare himſelf the labour of looking for Ideas, where there are none to be had. It were therefore to be wiſhed that every one would uſe his utmoſt Endeavours, to obtain a clear View of the Ideas he would conſider, ſeparating from them all that dreſs and incumbrance of Words which ſo much contribute to blind the Judgment and divide the Attention. In vain do we extend our View into the Heavens, and pry into the Entrails of the Earth, in vain do we conſult the Writings of learned Men, and trace the dark Footſteps of Antiquity; we need only draw the Curtain of Words, to behold the faireſt Tree of Knowledge, whoſe Fruit is excellent, and within the reach of our Hand.

XXV. Unleſs we take care to clear the firſt Principles of Knowledge, from the embarras and deluſion of Words, we may make infinite Reaſonings upon them to no purpoſe; we may draw Conſequences from Conſequences, and be never the wiſer. The farther we go, we ſhall only loſe our ſelves the more irrecoverably, and be the deeper entangled in Difficulties and Miſtakes. Whoever therefore deſigns to read the following Sheets, I intreat him to make my Words the Occaſion of his own Thinking, and endeavour to attain the ſame Train of Thoughts in Reading, that I had in writing them. By this means it will be eaſy for him to diſcover the Truth or Falſity of what I ſay. He will be out of all danger of being deceived by my Words, and I do not ſee how he can be led into an Error by conſidering his own naked, undiſguiſed Ideas.

OF

OF THE PRINCIPLES OF Humane Knowledge.

PART I.

I. IT is evident to any one who takes a Survey of the Objects of Humane Knowledge, that they are either Ideas actually imprinted on the Senses, or else such as are perceived by attending to the Passions and Operations of the Mind, or lastly Ideas formed by help of Memory and Imagination, either compounding, dividing, or barely representing those originally perceived in the aforesaid ways. By

Sight I have the Ideas of Light and Colours with their ſeveral Degrees and Variations. By Touch I perceive, for Example, Hard and Soft, Heat and Cold, Motion and Reſiſtance, and of all theſe more and leſs either as to Quantity or Degree. Smelling furniſhes me with Odors; the Palate with Taſtes, and Hearing conveys Sounds to the Mind in all their variety of Tone and Compoſition. And as ſeveral of theſe are obſerved to accompany each other, they come to be marked by one Name, and ſo to be reputed as one Thing. Thus, for Example, a certain Colour, Taſte, Smell, Figure and Conſiſtence having been obſerved to go together, are accounted one diſtinct Thing, ſignified by the Name *Apple*. Other Collections of Ideas conſtitute a Stone, a Tree, a Book, and the like ſenſible Things; which, as they are pleaſing or diſagreeable, excite the Paſſions of Love, Hatred, Joy, Grief, and ſo forth.

II. But beſides all that endleſs variety of Ideas or Objects of Knowledge, there is likewiſe ſomething which knows or perceives them, and exerciſes divers Operations, as Willing, Imagining, Remembering about them. This perceiving, active Being is what I call *Mind*, *Spirit*, *Soul* or *my Self*. By which Words I do not denote any one of my Ideas, but a thing intirely diſtinct

diſtinct from them, wherein they exiſt, or, which is the ſame thing, whereby they are perceived; for the Exiſtence of an Idea conſiſts in being perceived.

III. That neither our Thoughts, nor Paſſions, nor Ideas formed by the Imagination, exiſt without the Mind, is what every Body will allow. And it ſeems no leſs evident that the various Senſations or Ideas imprinted on the Senſe, however blended or combined together (that is, whatever Objects they compoſe) cannot exiſt otherwiſe than in a Mind perceiving them. I think an intuitive Knowledge may be obtained of this, by any one that ſhall attend to what is meant by the Term *Exiſt* when applied to ſenſible Things. The Table I write on, I ſay, exiſts, that is, I ſee and feel it; and if I were out of my Study I ſhould ſay it exiſted, meaning thereby that if I was in my Study I might perceive it, or that ſome other Spirit actually does perceive it. There was an Odor, that is, it was ſmelled; There was a Sound, that is to ſay, it was heard; a Colour or Figure, and it was perceived by Sight or Touch. This is all that I can underſtand by theſe and the like Expreſſions. For as to what is ſaid of the abſolute Exiſtence of unthinking Things without any relation to their being perceived, that ſeems perfectly unintelligible. Their *Eſſe* is *Percipi*, nor is it poſſible they ſhould have any Exiſtence, out of the Minds or thinking Things which perceive them.

IV. It is indeed an Opinion ſtrangely prevailing amongſt Men, that Houſes, Mountains, Rivers, and in a word all ſenſible Objects have an Exiſtence Natural or Real, diſtinct from their being perceived by the Underſtanding. But with how great an Aſſurance and Acquieſcence ſoever this Principle may be entertained in the World; yet whoever ſhall find in his Heart to call it in Queſtion, may, if I miſtake not, perceive it to involve a manifeſt Contradiction. For what are the forementioned Objects but the things we perceive by Senſe, and what do we perceive beſides our own Ideas or Senſations; and is it not plainly repugnant that any one of theſe or any Combination of them ſhould exiſt unperceived?

V. If we throughly examine this Tenet, it will, perhaps, be found at Bottom to depend on the Doctrine of *Abſtract Ideas*. For can there be a nicer Strain of Abſtraction than to diſtinguiſh the Exiſtence of ſenſible Objects from their being perceived, ſo ſo as to conceive them Exiſting unperceived? Light and Colours, Heat and Cold, Extenſion and Figures, in a word the Things we ſee and feel, what are they but ſo many Senſations, Notions, Ideas or Impreſſions on the Senſe; and is it poſſible to ſeparate, even in thought, any of theſe from Perception? For my part I might as eaſily divide a Thing from it Self. I may indeed divide in my Thoughts or conceive apart from each other thoſe Things which, perhaps, I never perceived by Senſe ſo divided. Thus I imagine the Trunk of a Humane Body without the Limbs, or conceive the Smell of a Roſe without thinking on the Roſe it ſelf. So far I will not deny I can abſtract, if that may properly be called *Abſtraction*, which extends only to the conceiving ſeparately ſuch Objects, as it is poſſible may really exiſt or be actually perceived aſunder. But my conceiving or imagining Power does not extend beyond the poſſibility of real Exiſtence or Perception. Hence as it is impoſſible for me to ſee or feel any Thing without an actual Senſation of that Thing, ſo is it impoſſible for me to conceive in my Thoughts any ſenſible Thing or Object diſtinct from the Senſation or Perception of it.

VI. Some Truths there are so near and obvious to the Mind, that a Man need only open his Eyes to see them. Such I take this Important one to be, to wit, that all the Choir of Heaven and Furniture of the Earth, in a word all those Bodies which compose the mighty Frame of the World, have not any Subsistence without a Mind, that their Being is to be perceived or known; that consequently so long as they are not actually perceived by me, or do not exist in my Mind or that of any other created Spirit, they must either have no Existence at all, or else subsist in the Mind of some eternal Spirit; It being perfectly unintelligible and involving all the Absurdity of Abstraction, to attribute to any single part of them an Existence independent of a Spirit. To be convinced of which, the Reader need only reflect and try to separate in his own Thoughts the being of a sensible thing from its being perceived.

VII. From what has been said, it follows, there is not any other Substance than *Spirit*, or that which perceives. But for the fuller proof of this Point, let it be considered, the sensible Qualities are Colour, Figure, Motion, Smell, Taste, and such like, that is, the Ideas perceived by Sense.

Senſe. Now for an Idea to exiſt in an unperceiving Thing, is a manifeſt Contradiction; for to have an Idea is all one as to perceive: that therefore wherein Colour, Figure, and the like Qualities exiſt, muſt perceive them; hence it is clear there can be no unthinking Subſtance or *Subſtratum* of thoſe Ideas.

VIII. But ſay you, though the Ideas themſelves do not exiſt without the Mind, yet there may be Things like them whereof they are Copies or Reſemblances, which Things exiſt without the Mind, in an unthinking Subſtance. I anſwer, an Idea can be like nothing but an Idea; a Colour or Figure can be like nothing but another Colour or Figure. If we look but ever ſo little into our Thoughts, we ſhall find it impoſſible for us to conceive a Likeneſs except only between our Ideas. Again, I ask whether thoſe ſuppoſed Originals or external Things, of which our Ideas are the Pictures or Repreſentations, be themſelves perceivable or no? If they are, then they are Ideas, and we have gained our Point; but if you ſay they are not, I appeal to any one whether it be Senſe, to aſſert a Colour is like ſomething which is inviſible; Hard or Soft, like ſomething which is Intangible; and ſo of the reſt.

IX. Some there are who make a Diſtinction betwixt *Primary* and *Secondary* Qualities: By the former, they mean Extenſion, Figure, Motion, Reſt, Solidity or Impenetrability and Number: By the latter they denote all other ſenſible Qualities, as Colours, Sounds, Taſtes, and ſo forth. The Ideas we have of theſe they acknowledge not to be the Reſemblances of any thing exiſting without the Mind or unperceived; but they will have our Ideas of the primary Qualities to be Patterns or Images of Things which exiſt without the Mind, in an unthinking Subſtance which they call *Matter*. By Matter therefore we are to underſtand an inert, ſenſeleſs Subſtance, in which Extenſion, Figure, and Motion, do actually ſubſiſt. But it is evident from what we have already ſhewn, that Extenſion, Figure and Motion are only Ideas exiſting in the Mind, and that an Idea can be like nothing but another Idea, and that conſequently neither They nor their Archetypes can exiſt in an unperceiving Subſtance. Hence it is plain, that the very Notion of what is called *Matter* or *Corporeal Subſtance*, involves a Contradiction in it.

X. They

X. They who assert that Figure, Motion, and the rest of the Primary or Original Qualities do exist without the Mind, in unthinking Substances, do at the same time acknowledge that Colours, Sounds, Heat, Cold, and such like secondary Qualities, do not, which they tell us are Sensations existing in the Mind alone, that depend on and are occasioned by the different Size, Texture and Motion of the minute Particles of Matter. This they take for an undoubted Truth, which they can demonstrate beyond all Exception. Now if it be certain, that those original Qualities are inseparably united with the other sensible Qualities, and not, even in Thought, capable of being abstracted from them, it plainly follows that they exist only in the Mind. But I desire any one to reflect and try, whether he can by any Abstraction of Thought, conceive the Extension and Motion of a Body, without all other sensible Qualities. For my own part, I see evidently that it is not in my power to frame an Idea of a Body extended and moved, but I must withal give it some Colour or other sensible Quality which is acknowledged to exist only in the Mind. In short, Extension, Figure, and Motion, abstracted from all other Qualities, are inconceivable.

Where

Where therefore the other ſenſible Qualities are, there muſt theſe be alſo, to wit, in the Mind and no where elſe.

XI. Again, *Great* and *Small*, *Swift* and *Slow*, are allowed to exiſt no where without the Mind, being intirely relative, and changing as the Frame or Poſition of the Organs of Senſe varies. The Extenſion therefore which exiſts without the Mind, is neither great nor ſmall, the Motion neither ſwift nor ſlow, that is, they are nothing at all. But ſay you, they are Extenſion in general, and Motion in general: Thus we ſee how much the Tenet of extended, moveable Subſtances exiſting without the Mind, depends on that ſtrange Doctrine of *abſtract Ideas*. And here I cannot but remark, how nearly the Vague and indeterminate Deſcription of Matter or corporeal Subſtance, which the Modern Philoſophers are run into by their own Principles, reſembles that antiquated and ſo much ridiculed Notion of *Materia prima*, to be met with in *Ariſtotle* and his Followers. Without Extenſion Solidity cannot be conceived; ſince therefore it has been ſhewn that Extenſion exiſts not in an unthinking Subſtance, the ſame muſt alſo be true of Solidity.

XII. That

XII. That Number is intirely the Creature of the Mind, even though the other Qualities be allowed to exiſt without, will be evident to whoever conſiders, that the ſame thing bears a different Denomination of Number, as the Mind views it with different reſpects. Thus, the ſame Extenſion is One or Three or Thirty Six, according as the Mind conſiders it with reference to a Yard, a Foot, or an Inch. Number is ſo viſibly relative, and dependent on Mens Underſtanding, that it is ſtrange to think how any one ſhould give it an abſolute Exiſtence without the Mind. We ſay one Book, one Page, one Line; all theſe are equally Unites, though ſome contain ſeveral of the others. And in each Inſtance it is plain, the Unite relates to ſome particular Combination of Ideas arbitrarily put together by the Mind.

XIII. Unity I know ſome will have to be a ſimple or uncompounded Idea, accompanying all other Ideas into the Mind. That I have any ſuch Idea anſwering the Word *Unity*, I do not find; and if I had, methinks I could not miſs finding it; on the contrary it ſhould be the moſt familiar to my Underſtanding, ſince it is ſaid to accompany all other Ideas, and to be perceived

ceived by all the ways of Senſation and Reflexion. To ſay no more, it is an *abſtract Idea.*

XIV. I ſhall farther add, that after the ſame manner, as modern Philoſophers prove certain ſenſible Qualities to have no Exiſtence in Matter, or without the Mind, the ſame thing may be likewiſe proved of all other ſenſible Qualities whatſoever. Thus, for Inſtance, it is ſaid that Heat and Cold are Affections only of the Mind, and not at all Patterns of real Beings, exiſting in the corporeal Subſtances which excite them, for that the ſame Body which appears Cold to one Hand, ſeems Warm to another. Now why may we not as well argue that Figure and Extenſion are not Patterns or Reſemblances of Qualities exiſting in Matter, becauſe to the ſame Eye at different Stations, or Eyes of a different Texture at the ſame Station, they appear various, and cannot therefore be the Images of any thing ſettled and determinate without the Mind? Again, It is proved that Sweetneſs is not really in the ſapid Thing, becauſe the thing remaining unaltered the Sweetneſs is changed into Bitter, as in caſe of a Fever or otherwiſe vitiated Palate. Is it not as reaſonable to ſay, that Motion is not without the Mind, ſince if the

the Succeſſion of Ideas in the Mind become ſwifter, the Motion, it is acknowledged, ſhall appear ſlower without any Alteration in any external Object.

XV. In ſhort, let any one conſider thoſe Arguments, which are thought manifeſtly to prove that Colours and Taſtes exiſt only in the Mind, and he ſhall find they may with equal force, be brought to prove the ſame thing of Extenſion, Figure, and Motion. Though it muſt be confeſſed this Method of arguing doth not ſo much prove that there is no Extenſion or Colour in an outward Object, as that we do not know by Senſe which is the true Extenſion or Colour of the Object. But the Arguments foregoing plainly ſhew it to be impoſſible that any Colour or Extenſion at all, or other ſenſible Quality whatſoever, ſhould exiſt in an unthinking Subject without the Mind, or in truth, that there ſhould be any ſuch thing as an outward Object.

XVI. But let us examine a little the received Opinion. It is ſaid Extenſion is a Mode or Accident of Matter, and that Matter is the *Subſtratum* that ſupports it. Now I deſire that you would explain what is meant by Matter's *ſupporting* Extenſion: Say

Say you, I have no Idea of Matter, and therefore cannot explain it. I anſwer, though you have no poſitive, yet if you have any meaning at all, you muſt at leaſt have a relative Idea of Matter; though you know not what it is, yet you muſt be ſuppoſed to know what Relation it bears to Accidents, and what is meant by its ſupporting them. It is evident *Support* cannot here be taken in its uſual or literal Senſe, as when we ſay that Pillars ſupport a Building: In what Senſe therefore muſt it be taken?

XVII. If we inquire into what the moſt accurate Philoſophers declare themſelves to mean by *Material Subſtance*; we ſhall find them acknowledge, they have no other meaning annexed to thoſe Sounds, but the Idea of Being in general, together with the relative Notion of its ſupporting Accidents. The general Idea of Being appeareth to me the moſt abſtract and incomprehenſible of all other; and as for its ſupporting Accidents, this, as we have juſt now obſerved, cannot be underſtood in the common Senſe of thoſe Words; it muſt therefore be taken in ſome other Senſe, but what that is they do not explain. So that when I conſider the two Parts or Branches which make the ſignification of the Words

Material

Material Subſtance, I am convinced there is no diſtinct meaning annexed to them. But why ſhould we trouble our ſelves any farther, in diſcuſſing this Material *Subſtratum* or Support of Figure and Motion, and other ſenſible Qualities? Does it not ſuppoſe they have an Exiſtence without the Mind? And is not this a direct Repugnancy, and altogether inconceivable?

XVIII. But though it were poſſible that ſolid, figured, moveable Subſtances may exiſt without the Mind, correſponding to the Ideas we have of Bodies, yet how is it poſſible for us to know this? Either we muſt know it by Senſe, or by Reaſon. As for our Senſes, by them we have the Knowledge only of our Senſations, Ideas, or thoſe things that are immediately perceived by Senſe, call them what you will: But they do not inform us that things exiſt without the Mind, or unperceived, like to thoſe which are perceived. This the Materialiſts themſelves acknowledge. It remains therefore that if we have any Knowledge at all of external Things, it muſt be by Reaſon, inferring their Exiſtence from what is immediately perceived by Senſe. But what reaſon can induce us to believe the Exiſtence of Bodies without the Mind, from what we perceive, ſince the very Patrons of Matter themſelves do not pretend, there is any neceſſary Connexion betwixt them and our Ideas? I ſay it is granted on all hands (and what happens in Dreams, Phrenſies, and the like, puts it beyond diſpute) that it is poſſible we might be affected with all the Ideas we have now, though no Bodies exiſted without, reſembling them. Hence it is evident the Suppoſition of external Bodies is not neceſſary for the producing our Ideas: Since it is granted they are produced ſometimes, and might poſſibly be produced always in the ſame Order we ſee them in at preſent, without their Concurrence.

XIX. But though we might poſſibly have all our Senſations without them, yet perhaps it may be thought eaſier to conceive and explain the manner of their Production, by ſuppoſing external Bodies in their likeneſs rather than otherwiſe; and ſo it might be at leaſt probable there are ſuch things as Bodies that excite their Ideas in our Minds. But neither can this be ſaid; for though we give the Materialiſts their external Bodies, they by their own confeſſion are never the nearer knowing how our Ideas are produced: Since they own themſelves unable to comprehend in what manner Body can act upon Spirit, or how it is poſſible

poſſible it ſhould imprint any Idea in the Mind. Hence it is evident the Production of Ideas or Senſations in our Minds, can be no reaſon why we ſhould ſuppoſe Matter or corporeal Subſtances, ſince that is acknowledged to remain equally inexplicable with, or without this Suppoſition. If therefore it were poſſible for Bodies to exiſt without the Mind, yet to hold they do ſo, muſt needs be a very precarious Opinion; ſince it is to ſuppoſe, without any reaſon at all, that God has created innumerable Beings that are intirely uſeleſs, and ſerve to no manner of purpoſe.

XX. In ſhort, if there were external Bodies, it is impoſſible we ſhould ever come to know it; and if there were not, we might have the very ſame Reaſons to think there were that we have now. Suppoſe, what no one can deny poſſible, an Intelligence, without the help of external Bodies, to be affected with the ſame train of Senſations or Ideas that you are, imprinted in the ſame order and with like vividneſs in his Mind. I ask whether that Intelligence hath not all the Reaſon to believe the Exiſtence of corporeal Subſtances, repreſented by his Ideas, and exciting them in his Mind, that you can poſſibly have for believing the ſame thing? Of this there can be no Queſtion; which one Conſideration is enough to make any reaſonable Perſon ſuſpect the ſtrength of whatever Arguments he may think himſelf to have, for the Exiſtence of Bodies without the Mind.

XXI. Were it neceſſary to add any farther Proof againſt the Exiſtence of Matter, after what has been ſaid, I could inſtance ſeveral of thoſe Errors and Difficulties (not to mention Impieties) which have ſprung from that Tenet. It has occaſioned numberleſs Controverſies and Diſputes in Philoſophy, and not a few of far greater moment in Religion. But I ſhall not enter into the detail of them in this Place, as well becauſe I think, Arguments *à Poſteriori* are unneceſſary for confirming what has been, if I miſtake not, ſufficiently demonſtrated *à Priori*, as becauſe I ſhall hereafter find occaſion to ſay ſomewhat of them.

XXII. I am afraid I have given cauſe to think me needleſly prolix in handling this Subject. For to what purpoſe is it to dilate on that which may be demonſtrated with the utmoſt Evidence in a Line or two, to any one that is capable of the leaſt Reflexion? It is but looking into your own Thoughts,

Thoughts, and ſo trying whether you can conceive it poſſible for a Sound, or Figure, or Motion, or Colour, to exiſt without the Mind, or unperceived. This eaſy Trial may make you ſee, that what you contend for, is a downright Contradiction. Inſomuch that I am content to put the whole upon this Iſſue; if you can but conceive it poſſible for one extended moveable Subſtance, or in general, for any one Idea or any thing like an Idea, to exiſt otherwiſe than in a Mind perceiving it, I ſhall readily give up the Cauſe: And as for all that *compages* of external Bodies which you contend for, I ſhall grant you its Exiſtence, though you cannot either give me any Reaſon why you believe it exiſts, or aſſign any uſe to it when it is ſuppoſed to exiſt. I ſay, the bare poſſibility of your Opinion's being true, ſhall paſs for an Argument that it is ſo.

XXIII. But ſay you, ſurely there is nothing eaſier than to imagine Trees, for inſtance, in a Park, or Books exiſting in a Cloſet, and no Body by to perceive them. I anſwer, you may ſo, there is no difficulty in it: But what is all this, I beſeech you, more than framing in your Mind certain Ideas which you call *Books* and *Trees*, and at the ſame time omitting to frame the Idea of any one that may perceive them? But do not you your ſelf perceive or think of them all the while? This therefore is nothing to the purpoſe: It only ſhews you have the Power of imagining or forming Ideas in your Mind; but it doth not ſhew that you can conceive it poſſible, the Objects of your Thought may exiſt without the Mind: To make out this, it is neceſſary that you conceive them exiſting unconceived or unthought of, which is a manifeſt Repugnancy. When we do our utmoſt to conceive the Exiſtence of external Bodies, we are all the while only contemplating our own Ideas. But the Mind taking no notice of it ſelf, is deluded to think it can and doth conceive Bodies exiſting unthought of or without the Mind; though at the ſame time they are apprehended by or exiſt in it ſelf. A little Attention will diſcover to any one the Truth and Evidence of what is here ſaid, and make it unneceſſary to inſiſt on any other Proofs againſt the Exiſtence of material Subſtance.

XXIV. It is very obvious, upon the leaſt Inquiry into our own Thoughts, to know whether it be poſſible for us to underſtand what is meant, by the *abſolute Exiſtence of ſenſible Objects in themſelves, or without the Mind.*

Mind. To me it is evident thoſe Words mark out either a direct Contradiction, or elſe nothing at all. And to convince others of this, I know no readier or fairer way, than to intreat they would calmly attend to their own Thoughts: And if by this Attention, the Emptineſs or Repugnancy of thoſe Expreſſions does appear, ſurely nothing more is requiſite for their Conviction. It is on this therefore that I inſiſt, to wit, that the abſolute Exiſtence of unthinking Things are Words without a Meaning, or which include a Contradiction. This is what I repeat and inculcate, and earneſtly recommend to the attentive Thoughts of the Reader.

XXV. All our Ideas, Senſations, or the things which we perceive, by whatſoever Names they may be diſtinguiſhed, are viſibly inactive, there is nothing of Power or Agency included in them. So that one Idea or Object of Thought cannot produce, or make any Alteration in another. To be ſatisfied of the Truth of this, there is nothing elſe requiſite but a bare Obſervation of our Ideas. For ſince they and every part of them exiſt only in the Mind, it follows that there is nothing in them but what is perceived. But whoever ſhall attend to his Ideas, whether of Senſe or Reflexion, will not perceive in them any Power or Activity; there is therefore no ſuch thing contained in them. A little Attention will diſcover to us that the very Being of an Idea implies Paſſiveneſs and Inertneſs in it, inſomuch that it is impoſſible for an Idea to do any thing, or, ſtrictly ſpeaking, to be the Cauſe of any thing: Neither can it be the Reſemblance or Pattern of any active Being, as is evident from *Sect.* 8. Whence it plainly follows that Extenſion, Figure and Motion, cannot be the Cauſe of our Senſations. To ſay therefore, that theſe are the effects of Powers reſulting from the Configuration, Number, Motion, and Size of Corpuſcles, muſt certainly be falſe.

XXVI. We perceive a continual Succeſſion of Ideas, ſome are anew excited, others are changed or totally diſappear. There is therefore ſome Cauſe of theſe Ideas whereon they depend, and which produces and changes them. That this Cauſe cannot be any Quality or Idea or Combination of Ideas, is clear from the preceding Section. It muſt therefore be a Subſtance; but it has been ſhewn that there is no corporeal or material Subſtance: It remains therefore that the Cauſe of Ideas is an incorporeal active Subſtance or Spirit.

XXVII. A

XXVII. A Spirit is one ſimple, undivided, active Being: as it perceives Ideas, it is called the *Underſtanding*, and as it produces or otherwiſe operates about them, it is called the *Will*. Hence there can be no Idea formed of a Soul or Spirit: For all Ideas whatever, being Paſſive and Inert, *vide Sect.* 25. they cannot repreſent unto us, by way of Image or Likeneſs, that which acts. A little Attention will make it plain to any one, that to have an Idea which ſhall be like that active Principle of Motion and Change of Ideas, is abſolutely impoſſible. Such is the Nature of *Spirit* or that which acts, that it cannot be of it ſelf perceived, but only by the Effects which it produceth. If any Man ſhall doubt of the Truth of what is here delivered, let him but reflect and try if he can frame the Idea of any Power or active Being; and whether he hath Ideas of two principal Powers, marked by the Names *Will* and *Underſtanding*, diſtinct from each other as well as from a third Idea of Subſtance or Being in general, with a relative Notion of its ſupporting or being the Subject of the aforeſaid Powers, which is ſignified by the Name *Soul* or *Spirit*. This is what ſome hold; but ſo far as I can ſee, the Words *Will*, *Soul*, *Spirit*, do not ſtand for

for different Ideas, or in truth, for any Idea at all, but for ſomething which is very different from Ideas, and which being an Agent cannot be like unto, or repreſented by, any Idea whatſoever. Though it muſt be owned at the ſame time, that we have ſome Notion of Soul, Spirit, and the Operations of the Mind, ſuch as Willing, Loving, Hating, in as much as we know or underſtand the meaning of thoſe Words.

XXVIII. I find I can excite Ideas in my Mind at pleaſure, and vary and ſhift the Scene as oft as I think fit. It is no more than Willing, and ſtraightway this or that Idea ariſes in my Fancy: And by the ſame Power it is obliterated, and makes way for another. This making and unmaking of Ideas doth very properly denominate the Mind active. Thus much is certain, and grounded on Experience: But when we talk of unthinking Agents, or of exciting Ideas excluſive of Volition, we only amuſe our ſelves with Words.

XXIX. But whatever Power I may have over my own Thoughts, I find the Ideas actually perceived by Senſe have not a like Dependence on my Will. When in broad Day-light I open my Eyes, it is not in my Power to chooſe whether I ſhall ſee or no,

or

or to determine what particular Objects ſhall preſent themſelves to my View; and ſo likewiſe as to the Hearing and other Senſes, the Ideas imprinted on them are not Creatures of my Will. There is therefore ſome other Will or Spirit that produces them.

XXX. The Ideas of Senſe are more ſtrong, lively, and diſtinct than thoſe of the Imagination; they have likewiſe a Steddineſs, Order, and Coherence, and are not excited at random, as thoſe which are the effects of Humane Wills often are, but in a regular Train or Series, the admirable Connexion whereof ſufficiently teſtifies the Wiſdom and Benevolence of its Author. Now the ſet Rules or eſtabliſhed Methods, wherein the Mind we depend on excites in us the Ideas of Senſe, are called the *Laws of Nature:* And theſe we learn by Experience, which teaches us that ſuch and ſuch Ideas are attended with ſuch and ſuch other Ideas, in the ordinary courſe of Things.

XXXI. This gives us a ſort of Foreſight, which enables us to regulate our Actions for the benefit of Life. And without this we ſhould be eternally at a loſs: We could not know how to act any thing that might

might procure us the leaſt Pleaſure, or remove the leaſt Pain of Senſe. That Food nouriſhes, Sleep refreſhes, and Fire warms us; that to ſow in the Seed-time is the way to reap in the Harveſt, and, in general, that to obtain ſuch or ſuch Ends, ſuch or ſuch Means are conducive, all this we know, not by diſcovering any neceſſary Connexion between our Ideas, but only by the Obſervation of the ſettled Laws of Nature, without which we ſhould be all in Uncertainty and Confuſion, and a grown Man no more know how to manage himſelf in the Affairs of Life, than an Infant juſt born.

XXXII. And yet this conſiſtent uniform working, which ſo evidently diſplays the Goodneſs and Wiſdom of that governing Spirit whoſe Will conſtitutes the Laws of Nature, is ſo far from leading our Thoughts to him, that it rather ſends them a wandering after ſecond Cauſes. For when we perceive certain Ideas of Senſe conſtantly followed by other Ideas, and we know this is not of our own doing, we forthwith attribute Power and Agency to the Ideas themſelves, and make one the Cauſe of another, than which nothing can be more abſurd and unintelligible. Thus, for Example, having obſerved that when

we

we perceive by Sight a certain round luminous Figure, we at the ſame time perceive by Touch the Idea or Senſation called *Heat*, we do from thence conclude the Sun to be the cauſe of Heat. And in like manner perceiving the Motion and Colliſion of Bodies to be attended with Sound, we are inclined to think the latter an effect of the former.

XXXIII. The Ideas imprinted on the Senſes by the Author of Nature are called *real Things:* And thoſe excited in the Imagination being leſs regular, vivid and conſtant, are more properly termed *Ideas*, or *Images of Things*, which they copy and repreſent. But then our Senſations, be they never ſo vivid and diſtinct, are nevertheleſs *Ideas*, that is, they exiſt in the Mind, or are perceived by it, as truly as the Ideas of its own framing. The Ideas of Senſe are allowed to have more reality in them, that is, to be more ſtrong, orderly, and coherent than the Creatures of the Mind; but this is no Argument that they exiſt without the Mind. They are alſo leſs dependent on the Spirit, or thinking Subſtance which perceives them, in that they are excited by the Will of another and more powerful Spirit: yet ſtill they are *Ideas*, and certainly no *Idea*, whether faint or or ſtrong, can exiſt otherwiſe than in a Mind perceiving it.

XXXIV. Before we proceed any farther, it is neceſſary to ſpend ſome Time in anſwering Objections which may probably be made againſt the Principles hitherto laid down. In doing of which, if I ſeem too prolix to thoſe of quick Apprehenſions, I hope it may be pardoned, ſince all Men do not equally apprehend things of this Nature; and I am willing to be underſtood by every one. Firſt then, it will be objected that by the foregoing Principles, all that is real and ſubſtantial in Nature is baniſhed out of the World: And inſtead thereof a chimerical Scheme of Ideas takes place. All things that exiſt, exiſt only in the Mind, that is, they are purely notional. What therefore becomes of the Sun, Moon, and Stars? What muſt we think of Houſes, Rivers, Mountains, Trees, Stones; nay, even of our own Bodies? Are all theſe but ſo many Chimeras and Illuſions on the Fancy? To all which, and whatever elſe of the ſame ſort may be objected, I anſwer, that by the Principles premiſed, we are not deprived of any one thing in Nature. Whatever we ſee, feel, hear, or any wiſe conceive or underſtand, remains as ſecure as ever, and is as real as ever.

There

There is a *rerum natura*, and the Diſtinction between Realities and Chimeras retains its full force. This is evident from *Sect.* 29, 30, and 33, where we have ſhewn what is meant by *real Things* in oppoſition to *Chimeras*, or Ideas of our own framing; but then they both equally exiſt in the Mind, and in that Senſe are alike *Ideas*.

XXXV. I do not argue againſt the Exiſtence of any one thing that we can apprehend, either by Senſe or Reflexion. That the things I ſee with mine Eyes and touch with my Hands do exiſt, really exiſt, I make not the leaſt Queſtion. The only thing whoſe Exiſtence we deny, is that which Philoſophers call Matter or corporeal Subſtance. And in doing of this, there is no Damage done to the reſt of Mankind, who, I dare ſay, will never miſs it. The Atheiſt indeed will want the Colour of an empty Name to ſupport his Impiety; and the Philoſophers may poſſibly find, they have loſt a great Handle for Trifling and Diſputation.

XXXVI. If any Man thinks this detracts from the Exiſtence or Reality of Things, he is very far from underſtanding what hath been premiſed in the plaineſt Terms

Terms I could think of. Take here an Abſtract of what has been ſaid. There are ſpiritual Subſtances, Minds, or humane Souls, which will or excite Ideas in themſelves at pleaſure: but theſe are faint, weak, and unſteady in reſpect of others they perceive by Senſe, which being impreſſed upon them according to certain Rules or Laws of Nature, ſpeak themſelves the Effects of a Mind more powerful and wiſe than humane Spirits. Theſe latter are ſaid to have more *Reality* in them than the former: By which is meant that they are more affecting, orderly, and diſtinct, and that they are not Fictions of the Mind perceiving them. And in this Senſe, the Sun that I ſee by Day is the real Sun, and that which I imagine by Night is the Idea of the former. In the Senſe here given of *Reality*, it is evident that every Vegetable, Star, Mineral, and in general each part of the Mundane Syſtem, is as much a *real Being* by our Principles as by any other. Whether others mean any thing by the Term *Reality* different from what I do, I intreat them to look into their own Thoughts and ſee.

XXXVII. It will be urged that thus much at leaſt is true, to wit, that we take away all corporeal Subſtances. To this my my Anſwer is, That if the word *Subſtance* be taken in the vulgar Senſe, for a Combination of ſenſible Qualities, ſuch as Extenſion, Solidity, Weight, and the like; This we cannot be accuſed of taking away. But if it be taken in a philoſophic Senſe, for the ſupport of Accidents or Qualities without the Mind: Then indeed I acknowledge that we take it away, if one may be ſaid to take away that which never had any Exiſtence, not even in the Imagination.

XXXVIII. But, ſay you, it ſounds very harſh to ſay we eat and drink Ideas, and are clothed with Ideas. I acknowledge it does ſo, the word *Idea* not being uſed in common Diſcourſe to ſignify the ſeveral Combinations of ſenſible Qualities, which are called *Things*: and it is certain that any Expreſſion which varies from the familiar Uſe of Language, will ſeem harſh and ridiculous. But this doth not concern the Truth of the Propoſition, which in other Words is no more than to ſay, we are fed and clothed with thoſe Things which we perceive immediately by our Senſes. The Hardneſs or Softneſs, the Colour, Taſte, Warmth, Figure, and ſuch like Qualities, which combined together conſtitute the ſeveral ſorts of Victuals and

Apparel, have been ſhewn to exiſt only in the Mind that perceives them; and this is all that is meant by calling them *Ideas*; which Word, if it was as ordinarily uſed as *Thing*, would ſound no harſher nor more ridiculous than it. I am not for diſputing about the Propriety, but the Truth of the Expreſſion. If therefore you agree with me that we eat and drink, and are clad with the immediate Objects of Senſe which cannot exiſt unperceived or without the Mind: I ſhall readily grant it is more proper or conformable to Cuſtom, that they ſhould be called Things rather than Ideas.

XXXIX. If it be demanded why I make uſe of the word *Idea*, and do not rather in compliance with Cuſtom call them Things. I anſwer, I do it for two Reaſons: Firſt, becauſe the Term *Thing*, in contradiſtinction to *Idea*, is generally ſuppoſed to denote ſomewhat exiſting without the Mind: Secondly, becauſe *Thing* hath a more comprehenſive Signification than *Idea*, including Spirits or thinking Things as well as Ideas. Since therefore the Objects of Senſe exiſt only in the Mind, and are withal thoughtleſs and inactive, I choſe to mark them by the word *Idea*, which implies thoſe Properties.

XL. But

XL. But ſay what we can, ſome one perhaps may be apt to reply, he will ſtill believe his Senſes, and never ſuffer any Arguments, how plauſible ſoever, to prevail over the Certainty of them. Be it ſo, aſſert the Evidence of Senſe as high as you pleaſe, we are willing to do the ſame. That what I ſee, hear and feel doth exiſt, that is to ſay, is perceived by me, I no more doubt than I do of my own Being. But I do not ſee how the Teſtimony of Senſe can be alledged, as a proof for the Exiſtence of any thing, which is not perceived by Senſe. We are not for having any Man turn *Sceptic*, and disbelieve his Senſes; on the contrary we give them all the Streſs and Aſſurance imaginable; nor are there any Principles more oppoſite to Scepticiſm, than thoſe we have laid down, as ſhall be hereafter clearly ſhewn.

XLI. Secondly, It will be objected that there is a great difference betwixt real Fire, for Inſtance, and the Idea of Fire, betwixt dreaming or imagining ones ſelf burnt, and actually being ſo: This and the like may be urged in oppoſition to our Tenets. To all which the Anſwer is evident from what hath been already ſaid, and I ſhall only add in this place, that if real Fire be very different from the Idea of Fire, ſo alſo is the real Pain that it occaſions, very different from the Idea of the ſame Pain: and yet no Body will pretend that real Pain either is, or can poſſibly be, in an unperceiving Thing or without the Mind, any more than its Idea.

XLII. Thirdly, It will be objected that we ſee Things actually without or at a diſtance from us, and which conſequently do not exiſt in the Mind, it being abſurd that thoſe Things which are ſeen at the diſtance of ſeveral Miles, ſhould be as near to us as our own Thoughts. In anſwer to this, I deſire it may be conſidered, that in a Dream we do oft perceive Things as exiſting at a great diſtance off, and yet for all that, thoſe Things are acknowledged to have their Exiſtence only in the Mind.

XLIII. But for the fuller clearing of this Point, it may be worth while to conſider, how it is that we perceive Diſtance and Things placed at a Diſtance by Sight. For that we ſhould in truth ſee external Space, and Bodies actually exiſting in it, ſome nearer, others farther off, ſeems to carry with it ſome Oppoſition to what hath been ſaid, of their exiſting no where without the Mind. The Conſideration of this Difficulty

ficulty it was, that gave birth to my *Eſſay towards a new Theory of Viſion*, which was publiſhed not long ſince. Wherein it is ſhewn that *Diſtance* or Outneſs is neither immediately of it ſelf perceived by Sight, nor yet apprehended or judged of by Lines and Angles, or any thing that hath a neceſſary Connexion with it: But that it is only ſuggeſted to our Thoughts, by certain viſible Ideas and Senſations attending Viſion, which in their own Nature have no manner of Similitude or Relation, either with Diſtance, or Things placed at a Diſtance. But by a Connexion taught us by Experience, they come to ſignify and ſuggeſt them to us, after the ſame manner that Words of any Language ſuggeſt the Ideas they are made to ſtand for. Inſomuch that a Man born blind, and afterwards made to ſee, would not, at firſt Sight, think the Things he ſaw, to be without his Mind, or at any Diſtance from him. See *Sect.* 41. of the forementioned Treatiſe.

XLIV. The Ideas of Sight and Touch make two Species, intirely diſtinct and heterogeneous. The former are Marks and Prognoſtics of the latter. That the proper Objects of Sight neither exiſt without the Mind, nor are the Images of external

Things, was ſhewn even in that Treatiſe. Though throughout the ſame, the contrary be ſuppoſed true of tangible Objects: Not that to ſuppoſe that vulgar Error, was neceſſary for eſtabliſhing the Notion therein laid down; but becauſe it was beſide my Purpoſe to examine and refute it in a Diſcourſe concerning *Viſion.* So that in ſtrict Truth the Ideas of Sight, when we apprehend by them Diſtance and Things placed at a Diſtance, do not ſuggeſt or mark out to us Things actually exiſting at a Diſtance, but only admoniſh us what Ideas of Touch will be imprinted in our Minds at ſuch and ſuch diſtances of Time, and in conſequence of ſuch or ſuch Actions. It is, I ſay, evident from what has been ſaid in the foregoing Parts of this Treatiſe, and in *Sect.* 147, and elſewhere of the Eſſay concerning Viſion, that viſible Ideas are the Language whereby the governing Spirit, on whom we depend, informs us what tangible Ideas he is about to imprint upon us, in caſe we excite this or that Motion in our own Bodies. But for a fuller Information in this Point, I refer to the Eſſay it ſelf.

XLV. Fourthly, It will be objected that from the foregoing Principles it follows, Things are every moment annihilated and created

created anew. The Objects of Senſe exiſt only when they are perceived: The Trees therefore are in the Garden, or the Chairs in the Parlour, no longer than while there is ſome body by to perceive them. Upon ſhutting my Eyes all the Furniture in the Room is reduced to nothing, and barely upon opening them it is again created. In anſwer to all which, I refer the Reader to what has been ſaid in *Sect.* 3, 4, *&c.* and deſire he will conſider whether he means any thing by the actual Exiſtence of an Idea, diſtinct from its being perceived. For my part, after the niceſt Inquiry I could make, I am not able to diſcover that any thing elſe is meant by thoſe Words. And I once more intreat the Reader to ſound his own Thoughts, and not ſuffer himſelf to be impoſed on by Words. If he can conceive it poſſible either for his Ideas or their Archetypes to exiſt without being perceived, then I give up the Cauſe: But if he cannot, he will acknowledge it is unreaſonable for him to ſtand up in defence of he knows not what, and pretend to charge on me as an Abſurdity, the not aſſenting to thoſe Propoſitions which at Bottom have no meaning in them.

XLVI. It will not be amiſs to obſerve, how far the received Principles of Philoſophy are themſelves chargeable with thoſe pretended Abſurdities. It is thought ſtrangely abſurd that upon cloſing my Eyelids, all the viſible Objects round me ſhould be reduced to nothing; and yet is not this what Philoſophers commonly acknowledge, when they agree on all hands, that Light and Colours, which alone are the proper and immediate Objects of Sight, are mere Senſations that exiſt no longer than they are perceived? Again, it may to ſome perhaps ſeem very incredible, that things ſhould be every moment creating, yet this very Notion is commonly taught in the Schools. For the *Schoolmen*, though they acknowledge the Exiſtence of Matter, and that the whole mundane Fabrick is framed out of it, are nevertheleſs of Opinion that it cannot ſubſiſt without the Divine Conſervation, which by them is expounded to be a continual Creation.

XLVII. Farther, a little Thought will diſcover to us, that though we allow the Exiſtence of Matter or Corporeal Subſtance, yet it will unavoidably follow from the Principles which are now generally admitted, that the particular Bodies of what kind ſoever, do none of them exiſt whilſt they are not perceived. For it is evident from *Sect.* XI. and the following Sections,

that

that the Matter Philoſophers contend for, is an incomprehenſible Somewhat which hath none of thoſe particular Qualities, whereby the Bodies falling under our Senſes are diſtinguiſhed one from another. But to make this more plain, it muſt be remarked, that the infinite Diviſibility of Matter is now univerſally allowed, at leaſt by the moſt approved and conſiderable Philoſophers, who on the received Principles demonſtrate it beyond all Exception. Hence it follows, that there is an infinite Number of Parts in each Particle of Matter, which are not perceived by Senſe. The Reaſon therefore, that any particular Body ſeems to be of a finite Magnitude, or exhibits only a finite Number of Parts to Senſe, is, not becauſe it contains no more, ſince in itſelf it contains an infinite Number of Parts, but becauſe the Senſe is not acute enough to diſcern them. In proportion therefore as the Senſe is rendered more acute, it perceives a greater Number of Parts in the Object, that is, the Object appears greater, and its Figure varies, thoſe Parts in its Extremities which were before unperceivable, appearing now to bound it in very different Lines and Angles from thoſe perceived by an obtuſer Senſe. And at length, after various Changes of Size and Shape, when the Senſe becomes infinitely

nitely acute, the Body ſhall ſeem infinite. During all which there is no Alteration in the Body, but only in the Senſe. Each Body therefore conſidered in it ſelf, is infinitely extended, and conſequently void of all Shape or Figure. From which it follows, that though we ſhould grant the Exiſtence of Matter to be ever ſo certain, yet it is withal as certain, the Materialiſts themſelves are by their own Principles forced to acknowledge, that neither the particular Bodies perceived by Senſe, nor any thing like them exiſts without the Mind. Matter, I ſay, and each Particle thereof is according to them infinite and ſhapeleſs, and it is the Mind that frames all that variety of Bodies which compoſe the viſible World, any one whereof does not exiſt longer than it is perceived.

XLVIII. If we conſider it, the Objection propoſed in *Sect.* 45. will not be found reaſonably charged on the Principles we have premiſed, ſo as in truth to make any Objection at all againſt our Notions. For though we hold indeed the Objects of Senſe to be nothing elſe but Ideas which cannot exiſt unperceived; yet we may not hence conclude they have no Exiſtence except only while they are perceived by us, ſince there may be ſome other Spirit that

that perceives them, though we do not. Wherever Bodies are ſaid to have no Exiſtence without the Mind, I would not be underſtood to mean this or that particular Mind, but all Minds whatſoever. It does not therefore follow from the foregoing Principles, that Bodies are annihilated and created every moment, or exiſt not at all during the Intervals between our Perception of them.

XLIX. Fifthly, It may perhaps be objected, that if Extenſion and Figure exiſt only in the Mind, it follows that the Mind is extended and figured; ſince Extenſion is a Mode or Attribute, which (to ſpeak with the Schools) is predicated of the Subject in which it exiſts. I anſwer, Thoſe Qualities are in the Mind only as they are perceived by it, that is, not by way of *Mode* or *Attribute*, but only by way of *Idea*; and it no more follows, that the Soul or Mind is extended becauſe Extenſion exiſts in it alone, than it does that it is red or blue, becauſe thoſe Colours are on all hands acknowledged to exiſt in it, and no where elſe. As to what Philoſophers ſay of Subject and Mode, that ſeems very groundleſs and unintelligible. For Inſtance, in this Propoſition, a Die is hard, extended and ſquare, they will have it that the Word *Die* de-

notes

notes a Subject or Substance, distinct from the Hardness, Extension and Figure, which are predicated of it, and in which they exist. This I cannot comprehend: To me a Die seems to be nothing distinct from those things which are termed its Modes or Accidents. And to say a Die is hard, extended and square, is not to attribute those Qualities to a Subject distinct from and supporting them, but only an Explication of the meaning of the Word *Die*.

L. Sixthly, You will say there have been a great many things explained by Matter and Motion: Take away these, and you destroy the whole Corpuscular Philosophy, and undermine those mechanical Principles which have been applied with so much Success to account for the *Phænomena*. In short, whatever Advances have been made, either by ancient or modern Philosophers, in the study of Nature, do all proceed on the Supposition, that Corporeal Substance or Matter doth really exist. To this I answer, that there is not any one *Phænomenon* explained on that Supposition, which may not as well be explained without it, as might easily be made appear by an Induction of Particulars. To explain the *Phænomena*, is all one as to shew, why upon such and such

ſuch Occaſions we are affected with ſuch and ſuch Ideas. But how Matter ſhould operate on a Spirit, or produce any Idea in it, is what no Philoſopher will pretend to explain. It is therefore evident, there can be no uſe of Matter in Natural Philoſophy. Beſides, they who attempt to account for Things, do it not by Corporeal Subſtance, but by Figure, Motion, and other Qualities, which are in truth no more than mere Ideas, and therefore cannot be the Cauſe of any thing, as hath been already ſhewn. See *Sect.* 25.

LI. Seventhly, It will upon this be demanded whether it does not ſeem abſurd to take away natural Cauſes, and aſcribe every thing to the immediate Operation of Spirits? We muſt no longer ſay upon theſe Principles that Fire heats, or Water cools, but that a Spirit heats, and ſo forth. Would not a Man be deſervedly laught at, who ſhould talk after this manner? I anſwer, he would ſo; in ſuch things we ought to *think with the Learned, and ſpeak with the Vulgar.* They who to Demonſtration are convinced of the truth of the *Copernican* Syſtem, do nevertheleſs ſay the Sun riſes, the Sun ſets, or comes to the Meridian: And if they affected a contrary Stile in common talk, it would without doubt appear

appear very ridiculous. A little Reflexion on what is here ſaid will make it manifeſt, that the common uſe of Language would receive no manner of Alteration or Diſturbance from the Admiſſion of our Tenets.

LII. In the ordinary Affairs of Life, any Phraſes may be retained, ſo long as they excite in us proper Sentiments, or Diſpoſitions to act in ſuch a manner as is neceſſary for our well-being, how falſe ſoever they may be, if taken in a ſtrict and ſpeculative Senſe. Nay this is unavoidable, ſince Propriety being regulated by Cuſtom, Language is ſuited to the received Opinions, which are not always the trueſt. Hence it is impoſſible, even in the moſt rigid philoſophic Reaſonings, ſo far to alter the Bent and Genius of the Tongue we ſpeak, as never to give a handle for Cavillers to pretend Difficulties and Inconſiſtencies. But a fair and ingenuous Reader will collect the Senſe, from the Scope and Tenor and Connexion of a Diſcourſe, making allowances for thoſe inaccurate Modes of Speech, which uſe has made inevitable.

LIII. As to the Opinion that there are no Corporeal Cauſes, this has been heretofore maintained by ſome of the Schoolmen, as it is of late by others among the modern

modern Philosophers, who though they allow Matter to exist, yet will have GOD alone to be the immediate efficient Cause of all things. These Men saw, that amongst all the Objects of Sense, there was none which had any Power or Activity included in it, and that by Consequence this was likewise true of whatever Bodies they supposed to exist without the Mind, like unto the immediate Objects of Sense. But then, that they should suppose an innumerable Multitude of created Beings, which they acknowledge are not capable of producing any one Effect in Nature, and which therefore are made to no manner of purpose, since God might have done every thing as well without them; this I say, though we should allow it possible, must yet be a very unaccountable and extravagant Supposition.

LIV. In the eighth place, The universal concurrent Assent of Mankind may be thought by some, an invincible Argument in behalf of Matter, or the Existence of external things. Must we suppose the whole World to be mistaken? And if so, what Cause can be assigned of so widespread and predominant an Error? I answer, First, That upon a narrow Inquiry, it will not perhaps be found, so many as

is

is imagined do really believe the Exiſtence of Matter or Things without the Mind. Strictly ſpeaking, to believe that which involves a Contradiction, or has no meaning in it, is impoſſible: And whether the foregoing Expreſſions are not of that ſort, I refer it to the impartial Examination of the Reader. In one ſenſe indeed, Men may be ſaid to believe that Matter exiſts, that is, they act as if the immediate Cauſe of their Senſations, which affects them every moment and is ſo nearly preſent to them, were ſome ſenſeleſs unthinking Being. But that they ſhould clearly apprehend any Meaning marked by thoſe Words, and form thereof a ſettled ſpeculative Opinion, is what I am not able to conceive. This is not the only Inſtance wherein Men impoſe upon themſelves, by imagining they believe thoſe Propoſitions they have often heard, though at bottom they have no meaning in them.

LV. But ſecondly, Though we ſhould grant a Notion to be ever ſo univerſally and ſtedfaſtly adhered to, yet this is but a weak Argument of its Truth, to whoever conſiders what a vaſt number of Prejudices and falſe Opinions are every where embraced with the utmoſt Tenaciouſneſs, by the unreflecting (which are the far greater)

greater) Part of Mankind. There was a time when the *Antipodes* and Motion of the Earth were looked upon as monſtrous Abſurdities, even by Men of Learning: And if it be conſidered what a ſmall proportion they bear to the reſt of Mankind, we ſhall find that at this Day, thoſe Notions have gained but a very inconſiderable footing in the World.

LVI. But it is demanded, that we aſſign a Cauſe of this Prejudice, and account for its obtaining in the World. To this I anſwer, That Men knowing they perceived ſeveral Ideas, whereof they themſelves were not the Authors, as not being excited from within, nor depending on the Operation of their Wills, this made them maintain, thoſe Ideas or Objects of Perception had an Exiſtence independent of, and without the Mind, without ever dreaming that a Contradiction was involved in thoſe Words. But Philoſophers having plainly ſeen, that the immediate Objects of Perception do not exiſt without the Mind, they in ſome degree corrected the miſtake of the Vulgar, but at the ſame time run into another which ſeems no leſs abſurd, to wit, that there are certain Objects really exiſting without the Mind, or having a Subſiſtence diſtinct from being perceived, of which our Ideas are only Images or Resemblances, imprinted by those Objects on the Mind. And this Notion of the Philosophers owes its Origin to the same Cause with the former, namely, their being conscious that they were not the Authors of their own Sensations, which they evidently knew were imprinted from without, and which therefore must have some Cause, distinct from the Minds on which they are imprinted.

LVII. But why they should suppose the Ideas of Sense to be excited in us by things in their likeness, and not rather have recourse to *Spirit* which alone can act, may be accounted for, First, because they were not aware of the Repugnancy there is, as well in supposing things like unto our Ideas existing without, as in attributing to them Power or Activity. Secondly, because the supreme Spirit which excites those Ideas in our Minds, is not marked out and limited to our view by any particular finite Collection of sensible Ideas, as humane Agents are by their Size, Complexion, Limbs, and Motions. And thirdly, because his Operations are regular and uniform. Whenever the Course of Nature is interrupted by a Miracle, Men are ready to own the Presence of a superior Agent.

Agent. But when we ſee things go on in the ordinary Courſe, they do not excite in us any Reflexion; their Order and Concatenation, though it be an Argument of the greateſt Wiſdom, Power, and Goodneſs in their Creator, is yet ſo conſtant and familiar to us, that we do not think them the immediate Effects of a *Free Spirit:* eſpecially ſince Inconſtancy and Mutability in acting, though it be an Imperfection, is looked on as a mark of *Freedom.*

LVIII. Tenthly, It will be objected, that the Notions we advance, are inconſiſtent with ſeveral ſound Truths in Philoſophy and Mathematicks. For Example, The Motion of the Earth is now univerſally admitted by Aſtronomers, as a Truth grounded on the cleareſt and moſt convincing Reaſons; but on the foregoing Principles, there can be no ſuch thing. For Motion being only an Idea, it follows that if it be not perceived, it exiſts not; but the Motion of the Earth is not perceived by Senſe. I anſwer, That Tenet, if rightly underſtood, will be found to agree with the Principles we have premiſed: For the Queſtion, whether the Earth moves or no, amounts in reality to no more than this, to wit, whether we have reaſon to conclude from what hath been obſerved by Aſtronomers, that if we were placed in ſuch and ſuch Circumſtances, and ſuch or ſuch a Poſition and Diſtance, both from the Earth and Sun, we ſhould perceive the former to move among the Choir of the Planets, and appearing in all reſpects like one of them: And this, by the eſtabliſhed Rules of Nature, which we have no reaſon to miſtruſt, is reaſonably collected from the Phænomena.

LIX. We may, from the Experience we have had of the Train and Succeſſion of Ideas in our Minds, often make, I will not ſay uncertain Conjectures, but ſure and well-grounded Predictions, concerning the Ideas we ſhall be affected with, purſuant to a great Train of Actions, and be enabled to paſs a right Judgment of what would have appeared to us, in caſe we were placed in Circumſtances very different from thoſe we are in at preſent. Herein conſiſts the Knowledge of Nature, which may preſerve its Uſe and Certainty very conſiſtently with what hath been ſaid. It will be eaſy to apply this to whatever Objections of the like ſort may be drawn from the Magnitude of the Stars, or any other Diſcoveries in Aſtronomy or Nature.

LX. In

LX. In the eleventh place, It will be demanded to what purpoſe ſerves that curious Organization of Plants, and the admirable Mechaniſm in the Parts of Animals; might not Vegetables grow, and ſhoot forth Leaves and Bloſſoms, and Animals perform all their Motions, as well without as with all that variety of internal Parts ſo elegantly contrived and put together, which being Ideas have nothing powerful or operative in them, nor have any neceſſary Connexion with the Effects aſcribed to them? If it be a Spirit that immediately produces every Effect by a *Fiat*, or Act of his Will, we muſt think all that is fine and artificial in the Works, whether of Man or Nature, to be made in vain. By this Doctrine, though an Artiſt hath made the Spring and Wheels, and every Movement of a Watch, and adjuſted them in ſuch a manner as he knew would produce the Motions he deſigned; yet he muſt think all this done to no purpoſe, and that it is an Intelligence which directs the Index, and points to the Hour of the Day. If ſo, why may not the Intelligence do it, without his being at the pains of making the Movements, and putting them together? Why does not an empty Caſe ſerve as well as another? And how comes it to paſs, that whenever there is any Fault in the going of a Watch, there is ſome correſponding Diſorder to be found in the Movements, which being mended by a skilful Hand, all is right again? The like may be ſaid of all the Clock-work of Nature, great part whereof is ſo wonderfully fine and ſubtile, as ſcarce to be diſcerned by the beſt Microſcope. In ſhort, it will be asked, how upon our Principles any tolerable Account can be given, or any final Cauſe aſſigned of an innumerable multitude of Bodies and Machines framed with the moſt exquiſite Art, which in the common Philoſophy have very appoſite uſes aſſigned them, and ſerve to explain abundance of Phænomena.

LXI. To all which I anſwer, Firſt, That though there were ſome Difficulties relating to the Adminiſtration of Providence, and the uſes by it aſſigned to the ſeveral parts of Nature, which I could not ſolve by the foregoing Principles, yet this Objection could be of ſmall weight againſt the Truth and Certainty of thoſe things which may be proved *à priori*, with the utmoſt Evidence. Secondly, But neither are the received Principles free from the like Difficulties; for it may ſtill be demanded,

manded, to what end God ſhould take thoſe round-about Methods of effecting things by Inſtruments and Machines, which no one can deny might have been effected by the mere Command of his Will, without all that *apparatus*: Nay, if we narrowly conſider it, we ſhall find the Objection may be retorted with greater force on thoſe who hold the Exiſtence of thoſe Machines without the Mind; for it has been made evident, that Solidity, Bulk, Figure, Motion and the like, have no *Activity* or *Efficacy* in them, ſo as to be capable of producing any one Effect in Nature. See *Sect.* 25. Whoever therefore ſuppoſes them to exiſt (allowing the Suppoſition poſſible) when they are not perceived, does it manifeſtly to no purpoſe; ſince the only uſe that is aſſigned to them, as they exiſt unperceived, is that they produce thoſe perceivable Effects, which in truth cannot be aſcribed to any thing but Spirit.

LXII. But to come nearer the Difficulty, it muſt be obſerved, that though the Fabrication of all thoſe Parts and Organs be not abſolutely neceſſary to the producing any Effect, yet it is neceſſary to the producing of things in a conſtant, regular way, according to the Laws of Nature.

There are certain general Laws that run through the whole Chain of natural Effects: These are learned by the Observation and Study of Nature, and are by Men applied as well to the framing artificial things for the Use and Ornament of Life, as to the explaining the various *Phænomena*: Which Explication consists only in shewing the Conformity any particular Phænomenon hath to the general Laws of Nature, or, which is the same thing, in discovering the *Uniformity* there is in the Production of natural Effects; as will be evident to whoever shall attend to the several Instances, wherein Philosophers pretend to account for Appearances. That there is a great and conspicuous Use in these regular constant Methods of working observed by the Supreme Agent, hath been shewn in *Sect.* 31. And it is no less visible, that a particular Size, Figure, Motion and Disposition of Parts are necessary, though not absolutely to the producing any Effect, yet to the producing it according to the standing mechanical Laws of Nature. Thus, for Instance, it cannot be denied that God, or the Intelligence which sustains and rules the ordinary Course of things might, if He were minded to produce a Miracle, cause all the Motions on the Dial-plate of of a Watch, though no Body had ever made the Movements, and put them in it: But yet if he will act agreeably to the Rules of Mechanism, by him for wise ends established and maintained in the Creation, it is necessary that those Actions of the Watchmaker, whereby he makes the Movements and rightly adjusts them, precede the Production of the aforesaid Motions; as also that any Disorder in them be attended with the Perception of some corresponding Disorder in the Movements, which being once corrected all is right again.

LXIII. It may indeed on some Occasions be necessary, that the Author of Nature display his overruling Power in producing some Appearance out of the ordinary Series of things. Such Exceptions from the general Rules of Nature are proper to surprise and awe Men into an Acknowledgment of the Divine Being: But then they are to be used but seldom, otherwise there is a plain Reason why they should fail of that Effect. Besides, God seems to choose the convincing our Reason of his Attributes by the Works of Nature, which discover so much Harmony and Contrivance in their Make, and are such plain Indications of Wisdom

and

and Beneficence in their Author, rather than to aſtoniſh us into a belief of his Being by anomalous and ſurpriſing Events.

LXIV. To ſet this Matter in a yet clearer Light, I ſhall obſerve that what has been objected in *Sect.* 60. amounts in reality to no more than this: Ideas are not any how and at random produced, there being a certain Order and Connexion between them, like to that of Cauſe and Effect: There are alſo ſeveral Combinations of them, made in a very regular and artificial manner, which ſeem like ſo many Inſtruments in the hand of Nature, that being hid as it were behind the Scenes, have a ſecret Operation in producing thoſe Appearances which are ſeen on the Theatre of the World, being themſelves diſcernible only to the curious Eye of the Philoſopher. But ſince one Idea cannot be the Cauſe of another, to what purpoſe is that Connexion? And ſince thoſe Inſtruments, being barely *inefficacious Perceptions* in the Mind, are not ſubſervient to the Production of natural Effects; it is demanded why they are made, or, in other Words, what reaſon can be aſſigned why God ſhould make us, upon a cloſe Inſpection into his Works, behold ſo great Variety

riety of Ideas, ſo artfully laid together, and ſo much according to Rule; it not being credible, that he would be at the Expence (if one may ſo ſpeak) of all that Art and Regularity to no purpoſe?

LXV. To all which my Anſwer is, Firſt, That the Connexion of Ideas does not imply the Relation of *Cauſe* and *Effect*, but only of a Mark or *Sign* with the thing *ſignified*. The Fire which I ſee is not the Cauſe of the Pain I ſuffer upon my approaching it, but the Mark that forewarns me of it. In like manner, the Noiſe that I hear is not the Effect of this or that Motion or Colliſion of the ambient Bodies, but the Sign thereof. Secondly, The Reaſon why Ideas are formed into Machines, that is, artificial and regular Combinations, is the ſame with that for combining Letters into Words. That a few Original Ideas may be made to ſignify a great number of Effects and Actions, it is neceſſary they be variouſly combined together: And to the end their uſe be permanent and univerſal, theſe Combinations muſt be made by *Rule*, and with *wiſe Contrivance*. By this means abundance of Information is conveyed unto us, concerning what we are to expect from ſuch and ſuch Actions, and what Methods

Methods are proper to be taken, for the exciting ſuch and ſuch Ideas: Which in effect is all that I conceive to be diſtinctly meant, when it is ſaid that by diſcerning the Figure, Texture, and Mechaniſm of the inward Parts of Bodies, whether natural or artificial, we may attain to know the ſeveral Uſes and Properties depending thereon, or the Nature of the thing.

LXVI. Hence it is evident, that thoſe things which under the Notion of a Cauſe cooperating or concurring to theProduction of Effects, are altogether inexplicable, and run us into great Abſurdities, may be very naturally explained, and have a proper and obvious uſe aſſigned them, when they are conſidered only as Marks or Signs for our Information. And it is the ſearching after, and endeavouring to underſtand thoſe Signs inſtituted by the Author of Nature, that ought to be the Employment of the Natural Philoſopher, and not the pretending to explain things by Corporeal Cauſes; which Doctrine ſeems to have too much eſtranged the Minds of Men from that active Principle, that ſupreme and wiſe Spirit, *in whom we live, move, and have our being.*

LXVII. It

LXVII. In the twelfth place, it may perhaps be objected, that though it be clear from what has been ſaid, that there can be no ſuch thing as an inert, ſenſeleſs, extended, ſolid, figured, moveable Subſtance, exiſting without the Mind, ſuch as Philoſophers deſcribe Matter: Yet if any Man ſhall leave out of his Idea of *Matter*, the poſitive Idea's of Extenſion, Figure, Solidity and Motion, and ſay that he means only by that Word, an inert ſenſeleſs Subſtance, that exiſts without the Mind, or unperceived, which is the Occaſion of our Ideas, or at the preſence whereof God is pleaſed to excite Ideas in us: It doth not appear, but that Matter taken in this ſenſe may poſſibly exiſt. In Anſwer to which I ſay, Firſt, that it ſeems no leſs abſurd to ſuppoſe a Subſtance without Accidents, than it is to ſuppoſe Accidents without a Subſtance. But Secondly, though we ſhould grant this unknown Subſtance may poſſibly exiſt, yet where can it be ſuppoſed to be? That it exiſts not in the Mind is agreed, and that it exiſts not in Place is no leſs certain; ſince all Extenſion exiſts only in the Mind, as hath been already proved. It remains therefore that it exiſts no where at all.

LXVIII. Let

LXVIII. Let us examine a little the Deſcription that is here given us of *Matter*. It neither acts, nor perceives, nor is perceived: For this is all that is meant by ſaying it is an inert, ſenſeleſs, unknown ſubſtance; which is a Definition intirely made up of Negatives, excepting only the relative Notion of its ſtanding under or ſupporting: But then it muſt be obſerved, that it *ſupports* nothing at all; and how nearly this comes to the Deſcription of a *non-entity*, I deſire may be conſidered. But, ſay you, it is the *unknown Occaſion*, at the preſence of which, Ideas are excited in us by the Will of God. Now I would fain know how any thing can be preſent to us, which is neither perceivable by Senſe nor Reflexion, nor capable of producing any Idea in our Minds, nor is at all extended, nor hath any Form, nor exiſts in any Place. The Words *to be preſent*, when thus applied, muſt needs be taken in ſome abſtract and ſtrange Meaning, and which I am not able to comprehend.

LXIX. Again, let us examine what is meant by *Occaſion*: So far as I can gather from the common uſe of Language, that Word ſignifies, either the Agent which produces

produces any Effect, or else something that is observed to accompany, or go before it, in the ordinary Course of things. But when it is applied to Matter as above described, it can be taken in neither of those senses. For Matter is said to be passive and inert, and so cannot be an Agent or efficient Cause. It is also unperceivable, as being devoid of all sensible Qualities, and so cannot be the Occasion of our Perceptions in the latter Sense: As when the burning my Finger is said to be the Occasion of the Pain that attends it. What therefore can be meant by calling Matter an *Occasion*? This Term is either used in no sense at all, or else in some sense very distant from its received Signification.

LXX. You will perhaps say that Matter, though it be not perceived by us, is nevertheless perceived by GOD, to whom it is the Occasion of exciting Ideas in our Minds. For, say you, since we observe our Sensations to be imprinted in an orderly and constant manner, it is but reasonable to suppose there are certain constant and regular Occasions of their being produced. That is to say, that there are certain permanent and distinct Parcels of Matter, corresponding to our Ideas,

Ideas, which, though they do not excite them in our Minds, or any ways immediately affect us, as being altogether passive and unperceivable to Us, they are nevertheless to GOD, by whom they are perceived, as it were so many Occasions to remind him when and what Ideas to imprint on our Minds: that so things may go on in a constant uniform manner.

LXXI. In answer to this I observe, that as the Notion of Matter is here stated, the Question is no longer concerning the Existence of a thing distinct from *Spirit* and *Idea*, from perceiving and being perceived: But whether there are not certain Ideas, of I know not what sort, in the Mind of GOD, which are so many Marks or Notes that direct him how to produce Sensations in our Minds, in a constant and regular Method: Much after the same manner as a Musician is directed by the Notes of Musick to produce that harmonious Train and Composition of Sound, which is called a *Tune*; though they who hear the Musick do not perceive the Notes, and may be intirely ignorant of them. But this Notion of Matter seems too extravagant to deserve a Confutation. Besides, it is in effect no Objection against what we have advanced, to wit, that there is no senseless, unperceived *Substance*.

LXXII. If

LXXII. If we follow the Light of Reaſon, we ſhall, from the conſtant uniform Method of our Senſations, collect the Goodneſs and Wiſdom of the *Spirit* who excites them in our Minds. But this is all that I can ſee reaſonably concluded from thence. To me, I ſay, it is evident that the Being of a *Spirit infinitely Wiſe, Good, and Powerful* is abundantly ſufficient to explain all the Appearances of Nature. But as for *inert ſenſeleſs Matter*, nothing that I perceive has any the leaſt Connexion with it, or leads to the Thoughts of it. And I would fain ſee any one explain any the meaneſt *Phænomenon* in Nature by it, or ſhew any manner of Reaſon, though in the loweſt Rank of Probability, that he can have for its Exiſtence; or even make any tolerable Senſe or Meaning of that Suppoſition. For as to its being an Occaſion, we have, I think, evidently ſhewn that with regard to us it is no Occaſion: It remains therefore that it muſt be, if at all, the Occaſion to G o d of exciting Ideas in us; and what this amounts to, we have juſt now ſeen.

LXXIII. It is worth while to reflect a little on the Motives which induced Men to ſuppoſe the Exiſtence of material Subſtance; that ſo having obſerved the gradual ceaſing, and Expiration of thoſe Motives or Reaſons, we may proportionably withdraw the Aſſent that was grounded on them. Firſt therefore, it was thought that Colour, Figure, Motion, and the reſt of the ſenſible Qualities or Accidents, did really exiſt without the Mind; and for this reaſon, it ſeemed needful to ſuppoſe ſome unthinking *Subſtratum* or *Subſtance* wherein they did exiſt, ſince they could not be conceived to exiſt by themſelves. Afterwards, in proceſs of time, Men being convinced that Colours, Sounds, and the reſt of the ſenſible ſecondary Qualities had no Exiſtence without the Mind, they ſtripped this *Subſtratum* or material Subſtance of thoſe Qualities, leaving only the primary ones, Figure, Motion, and ſuch like, which they ſtill conceived to exiſt without the Mind, and conſequently to ſtand in need of a material Support. But it having been ſhewn, that none, even of theſe, can poſſibly exiſt otherwiſe than in a Spirit or Mind which perceives them, it follows that we have no longer any reaſon to ſuppoſe the being of *Matter*. Nay, that it is utterly impoſſible there ſhould be any ſuch thing, ſo long as that Word is taken to denote an *unthinking Subſtratum* of Qualities or Accidents, wherein they exiſt without the Mind.

LXXIV.

LXXIV. But though it be allowed by the *Materialists* themselves, that Matter was thought of only for the sake of supporting Accidents; and the reason intirely ceasing, one might expect the Mind should naturally, and without any reluctance at all, quit the belief of what was solely grounded thereon. Yet the Prejudice is riveted so deeply in our Thoughts, that we can scarce tell how to part with it, and are therefore inclined, since the *Thing* it self is indefensible, at least to retain the *Name*; which we apply to I know not what abstracted and indefinite Notions of *Being*, or *Occasion*, though without any shew of Reason, at least so far as I can see. For what is there on our part, or what do we perceive amongst all the Ideas, Sensations, Notions, which are imprinted on our Minds, either by Sense or Reflexion, from whence may be inferred the Existence of an inert, thoughtless, unperceived Occasion? and on the other hand, on the part of an *all-sufficient Spirit*, what can there be that should make us believe, or even suspect, he is *directed* by an inert Occasion to excite Ideas in our Minds?

LXXV. It is a very extraordinary Instance of the force of Prejudice, and much to be lamented, that the Mind of Man retains ſo great a Fondneſs againſt all the evidence of Reaſon, for a ſtupid thoughtleſs *Somewhat*, by the interpoſition whereof it would, as it were, skreen it ſelf from the Providence of God, and remove him farther off from the Affairs of the World. But though we do the utmoſt we can, to ſecure the belief of *Matter*, though when Reaſon forſakes us, we endeavour to ſupport our Opinion on the bare poſſibility of the Thing, and though we indulge our ſelves in the full Scope of an Imagination not regulated by Reaſon, to make out that poor *Poſſibility*, yet the upſhot of all is, that there are certain *unknown Ideas* in the Mind of God; for this, if any thing, is all that I conceive to be meant by *Occaſion* with regard to God. And this, at the Bottom, is no longer contending for the *Thing*, but for the *Name*.

LXXVI. Whether therefore there are ſuch Ideas in the Mind of GOD, and whether they may be called by the name *Matter*, I ſhall not diſpute. But if you ſtick to the Notion of an unthinking Subſtance, or Support of Extenſion, Motion, and other ſenſible Qualities, then to me it is moſt evidently impoſſible there ſhould be any ſuch thing. Since it is a plain Repugnancy, that thoſe

thoſe Qualities ſhould exiſt in or be ſupported by an unperceiving Subſtance.

LXXVII. But ſay you, though it be granted that there is no thoughtleſs ſupport of Extenſion, and the other Qualities or Accidents which we perceive; yet there may, perhaps, be ſome inert unperceiving Subſtance, or *Subſtratum* of ſome other Qualities, as incomprehenſible to us as Colours are to a Man born blind, becauſe we have not a Senſe adapted to them. But if we had a new Senſe, we ſhould poſſibly no more doubt of their Exiſtence, than a Blind-man made to ſee does of the Exiſtence of Light and Colours. I anſwer, Firſt, if what you mean by the word *Matter* be only the unknown Support of unknown Qualities, it is no matter whether there is ſuch a thing or no, ſince it no way concerns us: And I do not ſee the Advantage there is in diſputing about we know not *what*, and we know not *why*.

LXXVIII. But ſecondly, if we had a new Senſe, it could only furniſh us with new Ideas or Senſations; And then we ſhould have the ſame reaſon againſt their exiſting in an unperceiving Subſtance, that has been already offered with relation to Figure, Motion, Colour, and the like. Qualities, as hath been ſhewn, are nothing elſe but *Senſations* or *Ideas*, which exiſt only in a *Mind* perceiving them; and this is true not only of the Ideas we are acquainted with at preſent, but likewiſe of all poſſible Ideas whatſoever.

LXXIX. But you will inſiſt, what if I have no reaſon to believe the Exiſtence of Matter, what if I cannot aſſign any uſe to it, or explain any thing by it, or even conceive what is meant by that Word? Yet ſtill it is no Contradiction to ſay that Matter exiſts, and that this Matter is *in general* a *Subſtance*, or *Occaſion of Ideas*; though, indeed, to go about to unfold the meaning, or adhere to any particular Explication of thoſe Words, may be attended with great Difficulties. I anſwer, when Words are uſed without a Meaning, you may put them together as you pleaſe, without danger of running into a Contradiction. You may ſay, for Example, that *twice Two* is equal to *Seven*, ſo long as you declare you do not take the Words of that Propoſition in their uſual Acceptation, but for Marks of you know not what. And by the ſame reaſon you may ſay, there is an inert thoughtleſs Subſtance without Accidents, which is the occaſion of our Ideas. And we ſhall underſtand juſt as much by one Propoſition, as the other.

LXXX. In

LXXX. In the laſt place, you will ſay, What if we give up the Cauſe of material Subſtance, and aſſert, that Matter is an unknown *Somewhat*, neither Subſtance nor Accident, Spirit nor Idea, inert, thoughtleſs, indiviſible, immoveable, unextended, exiſting in no Place? For, ſay you, Whatever may be urged againſt *Subſtance* or *Occaſion*, or any other poſitive or relative Notion of Matter, hath no place at all, ſo long as this *negative* Definition of Matter is adhered to. I anſwer, you may, if ſo it ſhall ſeem good, uſe the word *Matter* in the ſame Senſe, that other Men uſe *nothing*, and ſo make thoſe Terms convertible in your Style. For after all, this is what appears to me to be the Reſult of that Definition, the Parts whereof when I conſider with Attention, either collectively, or ſeparate from each other, I do not find that there is any kind of Effect or Impreſſion made on my Mind, different from what is excited by the Term *Nothing*.

LXXXI. You will reply perhaps, that in the foreſaid Definition is included, what doth ſufficiently diſtinguiſh it from nothing, the poſitive, abſtract Idea of *Quiddity*, *Entity*, or *Exiſtence*. I own indeed, that thoſe who pretend to the Faculty of framing abſtract general Ideas, do talk as if they had ſuch an Idea, which is, ſay they, the moſt abſtract and general Notion of all, that is to me the moſt incomprehenſible of all others. That there are a great variety of Spirits of different Orders and Capacities, whoſe Faculties, both in Number and Extent, are far exceeding thoſe the Author of my Being has beſtowed on me, I ſee no reaſon to deny. And for me to pretend to determine by my own few, ſtinted, narrow Inlets of Perception, what Ideas the inexhauſtible Power of the SUPREME SPIRIT may imprint upon them, were certainly the utmoſt Folly and Preſumption. Since there may be, for ought that I know, innumerable ſorts of Ideas or Senſations, as different from one another, and from all that I have perceived, as Colours are from Sounds. But how ready ſoever I may be, to acknowledge the Scantineſs of my Comprehenſion, with regard to the endleſs variety of Spirits and Ideas, that might poſſibly exiſt, yet for any one to pretend to a Notion of Entity or Exiſtence, *abſtracted* from *Spirit* and *Idea*, from perceiving and being perceived, is, I ſuſpect, a downright repugnancy and trifling with Words. It remains that we conſider the Objections, which may poſſibly be made on the part of Religion.

LXXXII.

LXXXII. Some there are who think, that though the Arguments for the real Exiſtence of Bodies, which are drawn from Reaſon, be allowed not to amount to Demonſtration, yet the Holy Scriptures are ſo clear in the Point, as will ſufficiently convince every good Chriſtian, that Bodies do really exiſt, and are ſomething more than mere Ideas; there being in Holy Writ innumerable Facts related, which evidently ſuppoſe the reality of Timber, and Stone, Mountains, and Rivers, and Cities, and humane Bodies. To which I anſwer, that no ſort of Writings whatever, ſacred or profane, which uſe thoſe and the like Words in the vulgar Acceptation, or ſo as to have a meaning in them, are in danger of having their Truth called in queſtion by our Doctrine. That all thoſe Things do really exiſt, that there are Bodies, even corporeal Subſtances, when taken in the vulgar Senſe, has been ſhewn to be agreeable to our Principles: And the difference betwixt *Things* and *Ideas*, *Realities* and *Chimeras*, has been diſtinctly explained *. And I do not think, that either what Philoſophers call *Matter*, or the Exiſtence of Objects without the Mind, is any where mentioned in Scripture.

LXXXIII.

* Sect. XXIX, XXX, XXXIII, XXXVI, &c.

LXXXIII. Again, whether there be, or be not external Things, it is agreed on all hands, that the proper Use of Words, is the marking our Conceptions, or Things only as they are known and perceived by us; whence it plainly follows, that in the Tenets we have laid down, there is nothing inconsistent with the right Use and Significancy of *Language*, and that Discourse of what kind soever, so far as it is intelligible, remains undisturbed. But all this seems so manifest, from what hath been set forth in the Premises, that it is needless to insist any farther on it.

LXXXIV. But it will be urged, that Miracles do, at least, lose much of their Stress and Import by our Principles. What must we think of *Moses*'s Rod, was it not *really* turned into a Serpent, or was there only a Change of *Ideas* in the Minds of the Spectators? And can it be supposed, that our Saviour did no more at the Marriage-Feast in *Cana*, than impose on the Sight, and Smell, and Taste of the Guests, so as to create in them the Appearance or Idea only of Wine? The same may be said of all other Miracles: Which, in consequence of the foregoing Principles, must be looked upon only as so many Cheats, or Illusions of of Fancy. To this I reply, that the Rod was changed into a real Serpent, and the Water into real Wine. That this doth not, in the leaſt, contradict what I have elſewhere ſaid, will be evident from *Sect.* 34, and 35. But this Buſineſs of *Real* and *Imaginary* hath been already ſo plainly and fully explained, and ſo often referred to, and the Difficulties about it are ſo eaſily anſwered from what hath gone before, that it were an Affront to the Reader's Underſtanding, to reſume the Explication of it in this place. I ſhall only obſerve, that if at Table all who were preſent ſhould ſee, and ſmell, and taſte, and drink Wine, and find the effects of it, with me there could be no doubt of its Reality. So that, at Bottom, the Scruple conçerning real Miracles hath no place at all on ours, but only on the received Principles, and conſequently maketh rather *for*, than *againſt* what hath been ſaid.

LXXXV. Having done with the Objections, which I endeavoured to propoſe in the cleareſt Light, and gave them all the Force and Weight I could, we proceed in the next place to take a view of our Tenets in their Conſequences. Some of theſe appear at firſt Sight, as that ſeveral difficult and obſcure Queſtions, on which abundance

abundance of Speculation hath been thrown away, are intirely baniſhed from Philoſophy. Whether corporeal Subſtance can think? Whether Matter be infinitely diviſible? And how it operates on Spirit? theſe and the like Inquiries have given infinite Amuſement to Philoſophers in all Ages. But depending on the Exiſtence of *Matter*, they have no longer any place on our Principles. Many other Advantages there are, as well with regard to *Religion* as the *Sciences*, which it is eaſy for any one to deduce from what hath been premiſed. But this will appear more plainly in the Sequel.

LXXXVI. From the Principles we have laid down, it follows, humane Knowledge may naturally be reduced to two Heads, that of *Ideas*, and that of *Spirits*. Of each of theſe I ſhall treat in order. And firſt as to Ideas or unthinking Things, our Knowledge of theſe hath been very much obſcured and confounded, and we have been led into very dangerous Errors, by ſuppoſing a twofold Exiſtence of the Objects of Senſe, the one *intelligible*, or in the Mind, the other *real* and without the Mind: Whereby unthinking Things are thought to have a natural Subſiſtence of their own, diſtinct from being perceived by Spirits. This which, if I miſtake not, hath

hath been ſhewn to be a moſt groundleſs and abſurd Notion, is the very Root of *Scepticiſm*; for ſo long as Men thought that real Things ſubſiſted without the Mind, and that their Knowledge was only ſo far forth *real* as it was conformable to *real Things*, it follows, they could not be certain that they had any real Knowledge at all. For how can it be known, that the Things which are perceived, are conformable to thoſe which are not perceived, or exiſt without the Mind?

LXXXVII. Colour, Figure, Motion, Extenſion and the like, conſidered only as ſo many *Senſations* in the Mind, are perfectly known, there being nothing in them which is not perceived. But if they are looked on as Notes or Images, referred to *Things* or *Archetypes* exiſting without the Mind, then are we involved all in *Scepticiſm*. We ſee only the Appearances, and not the real Qualities of Things. What may be the Extenſion, Figure, or Motion of any thing really and abſolutely, or in it ſelf, it is impoſſible for us to know, but only the proportion or the relation they bear to our Senſes. Things remaining the ſame, our Ideas vary, and which of them, or even whether any of them at all repreſent the true Quality really exiſting in the Thing,

Thing, it is out of our reach to determine. So that, for ought we know, all we ſee, hear, and feel, may be only Phantom and vain Chimera, and not at all agree with the real Things, exiſting in *Rerum Natura*. All this Scepticiſm follows, from our ſuppoſing a difference between *Things* and *Ideas*, and that the former have a Subſiſtence without the Mind, or unperceived. It were eaſy to dilate on this Subject, and ſhew how the Arguments urged by *Sceptics* in all Ages, depend on the Suppoſition of external Objects.

LXXXVIII. So long as we attribute a real Exiſtence to unthinking Things, diſtinct from their being perceived, it is not only impoſſible for us to know with evidence the Nature of any real unthinking Being, but even that it exiſts. Hence it is, that we ſee Philoſophers diſtruſt their Senſes, and doubt of the Exiſtence of Heaven and Earth, of every thing they ſee or feel, even of their own Bodies. And after all their labour and ſtruggle of Thought, they are forced to own, we cannot attain to any ſelf-evident or demonſtrative Knowledge of the Exiſtence of ſenſible Things. But all this Doubtfulneſs, which ſo bewilders and confounds the Mind, and makes *Philoſophy* ridiculous in the Eyes of the World,

World, vaniſhes, if we annex a meaning to our Words, and do not amuſe our ſelves with the Terms *Abſolute*, *External*, *Exiſt*, and ſuch like, ſignifying we know not what. I can as well doubt of my own Being, as of the Being of thoſe Things which I actually perceive by Senſe: It being a manifeſt Contradiction, that any ſenſible Object ſhould be immediately perceived by Sight or Touch, and at the ſame time have no Exiſtence in Nature, ſince the very Exiſtence of an unthinking Being conſiſts in *being perceived*.

LXXXIX. Nothing ſeems of more Importance, towards erecting a firm Syſteme of ſound and real Knowledge, which may be proof againſt the Aſſaults of *Scepticiſm*, than to lay the beginning in a diſtinct Explication of what is meant by *Thing*, *Reality*, *Exiſtence*: For in vain ſhall we diſpute concerning the real Exiſtence of Things, or pretend to any Knowledge thereof, ſo long as we have not fixed the meaning of thoſe Words. *Thing* or *Being* is the moſt general Name of all, it comprehends under it two Kinds intirely diſtinct and heterogeneous, and which have nothing common but the Name, to wit, *Spirits* and *Ideas*. The former are *active*, *indiviſible Subſtances*: The latter are *inert*, *fleeting*,

fleeting, dependent Beings, which ſubſiſt not by themſelves, but are ſupported by, or exiſt in Minds or ſpiritual Subſtances. We comprehend our own Exiſtence by inward Feeling or Reflexion, and that of other Spirits by Reaſon. We may be ſaid to have ſome Knowledge or Notion of our own Minds, of Spirits and active Beings, whereof in a ſtrict Senſe we have not Ideas. In like manner we know and have a Notion of relations between Things or Ideas, which relations are diſtinct from the Ideas or Things related, inaſmuch as the latter may be perceived by us without our perceiving the former. To me it ſeems that Ideas, Spirits and Relations are all in their reſpective kinds, the Object of humane Knowledge and Subject of Diſcourſe: and that the Term *Idea* would be improperly extended to ſignify every thing we know or have any Notion of.

XC. Ideas imprinted on the Senſes are real Things, or do really exiſt; this we do not deny, but we deny they can ſubſiſt without the Minds which perceive them, or that they are Reſemblances of any Archetypes exiſting without the Mind: Since the very Being of a Senſation or Idea conſiſts in being perceived, and an Idea can be like nothing but an Idea. Again, the Things

Things perceived by Senſe may be termed *external*, with regard to their Origin, in that they are not generated from within, by the Mind it ſelf, but imprinted by a Spirit diſtinct from that which perceives them. Senſible Objects may likewiſe be ſaid to be without the Mind, in another ſenſe, namely when they exiſt in ſome other Mind. Thus when I ſhut my Eyes, the Things I ſaw may ſtill exiſt, but it muſt be in another Mind.

XCI. It were a miſtake to think, that what is here ſaid derogates in the leaſt from the Reality of Things. It is acknowledged on the received Principles, that Extenſion, Motion, and in a word all ſenſible Qualities, have need of a Support, as not being able to ſubſiſt by themſelves. But the Objects perceived by Senſe, are allowed to be nothing but Combinations of thoſe Qualities, and conſequently cannot ſubſiſt by themſelves. Thus far it is agreed on all hands. So that in denying the Things perceived by Senſe, an Exiſtence independent of a Subſtance, or Support wherein they may exiſt, we detract nothing from the received Opinion of their *Reality*, and are guilty of no Innovation in that reſpect. All the difference is, that according to us the unthinking Beings perceived by Senſe, have no Exiſtence diſtinct from Being perceived, and cannot therefore exiſt in any other Subſtance, than thoſe unextended, indiviſible Subſtances, or *Spirits*, which act, and think, and perceive them: Whereas Philoſophers vulgarly hold, that the ſenſible Qualities exiſt in an inert, extended, unperceiving Subſtance, which they call *Matter*, to which they attribute a natural Subſiſtence, exterior to all thinking Beings, or diſtinct from Being perceived by any Mind whatſoever, even the eternal Mind of the CREATOR, wherein they ſuppoſe only Ideas of the corporeal Subſtances created by him: If indeed they allow them to be at all created.

XCII. For as we have ſhewn the Doctrine of Matter or corporeal Subſtance, to have been the main Pillar and Support of *Scepticiſm*, ſo likewiſe upon the ſame Foundation have been raiſed all the impious Schemes of *Atheiſm* and Irreligion. Nay ſo great a difficulty hath it been thought, to conceive Matter produced out of nothing, that the moſt celebrated among the ancient Philoſophers, even of theſe who maintained the Being of a GOD, have thought Matter to be uncreated and coeternal with him. How great a Friend material Subſtance hath been to *Atheiſts* in all Ages,

Ages, were needleſs to relate. All their monſtrous Syſtems have ſo viſible and neceſſary a dependence on it, that when this Corner-ſtone is once removed, the whole Fabrick cannot chooſe but fall to the Ground; inſomuch that it is no longer worth while, to beſtow a particular Conſideration on the Abſurdities of every wretched Sect of *Atheiſts.*

XCIII. That impious and profane Perſons ſhould readily fall in with thoſe Syſtems which favour their Inclinations, by deriding immaterial Subſtance, and ſuppoſing the Soul to be diviſible and ſubject to Corruption as the Body; which exclude all Freedom, Intelligence, and Deſign from the Formation of Things, and inſtead thereof make a ſelf-exiſtent, ſtupid, unthinking Subſtance the Root and Origin of all Beings. That they ſhould hearken to thoſe who deny a Providence, or Inſpection of a ſuperior Mind over the Affairs of the World, attributing the whole Series of Events either to blind Chance or fatal Neceſſity, ariſing from the Impulſe of one Body on another. All this is very natural. And on the other hand, when Men of better Principles obſerve the Enemies of Religion lay ſo great a Streſs on *unthinking Matter*, and all of them uſe ſo much Industry and Artifice to reduce every thing to it; methinks they should rejoice to see them deprived of their grand Support, and driven from that only Fortress, without which your *Epicureans*, *Hobbists*, and the like, have not even the Shadow of a Pretence, but become the most cheap and easy Triumph in the World.

XCIV. The Existence of Matter, or Bodies unperceived, has not only been the main Support of *Atheists* and *Fatalists*, but on the same Principle doth *Idolatry* likewise in all its various Forms depend. Did Men but consider that the Sun, Moon, and Stars, and every other Object of the Senses, are only so many Sensations in their Minds, which have no other Existence but barely being perceived, doubtless they would never fall down, and worship their own *Ideas*; but rather address their Homage to that ETERNAL INVISIBLE MIND which produces and sustains all Things.

XCV. The same absurd Principle, by mingling it self with the Articles of our Faith, hath occasioned no small Difficulties to Christians. For Example, about the *Resurrection*, how many Scruples and Objections have been raised by *Socinians* and others? But do not the most plausible of them

them depend on the ſuppoſition, that a Body is denominated the *ſame*, with regard not to the Form or that which is perceived by Senſe, but the material Subſtance which remains the ſame under ſeveral Forms? Take away this *material Subſtance*, about the Identity whereof all the Diſpute is, and mean by *Body* what every plain ordinary Perſon means by that Word, to wit, that which is immediately ſeen and felt, which is only a Combination of ſenſible Qualities, or Ideas: And then their moſt unanſwerable Objections come to nothing.

XCVI. Matter being once expelled out of Nature, drags with it ſo many ſceptical and impious Notions, ſuch an incredible number of Diſputes and puzling Queſtions, which have been Thorns in the Sides of Divines, as well as Philoſophers, and made ſo much fruitleſs Work for Mankind; that if the Arguments we have produced againſt it, are not found equal to Demonſtration (as to me they evidently ſeem) yet I am ſure all Friends to Knowledge, Peace, and Religion, have reaſon to wiſh they were.

XCVII. Beſide the external Exiſtence of the Objects of Perception, another great Source of Errors and Difficulties, with regard to Ideal Knowledge, is the Doctrine of *abstract Ideas*, such as it hath been set forth in the Introduction. The plainest Things in the World, those we are most intimately acquainted with, and perfectly know, when they are considered in an abstract way, appear strangely difficult and incomprehensible. Time, Place, and Motion, taken in particular or concrete, are what every Body knows; but having passed through the Hands of a Metaphysician, they become too abstract and fine, to be apprehended by Men of ordinary Sense. Bid your Servant meet you at such a *Time*, in such a *Place*, and he shall never stay to deliberate on the meaning of those Words: In conceiving that particular Time and Place, or the Motion by which he is to get thither, he finds not the least Difficulty. But if *Time* be taken, exclusive of all those particular Actions and Ideas that diversify the Day, merely for the Continuation of Existence, or Duration in Abstract, then it will perhaps gravel even a Philosopher to comprehend it.

XCVIII. Whenever I attempt to frame a simple Idea of *Time*, abstracted from the succession of Ideas in my Mind, which flows uniformly, and is participated by all Beings, I am lost and embrangled in inextricable

tricable Difficulties. I have no Notion of it at all, only I hear others ſay, it is infinitely diviſible, and ſpeak of it in ſuch a manner as leads me to entertain odd Thoughts of my Exiſtence: Since that Doctrine lays one under an abſolute neceſſity of thinking, either that he paſſes away innumerable Ages without a Thought, or elſe that he is annihilated every moment of his Life: Both which ſeem equally abſurd. Time therefore being nothing, abſtracted from the Succeſſion of Ideas in our Minds, it follows that the Duration of any finite Spirit muſt be eſtimated by the Number of Ideas or Actions ſucceeding each other in that ſame Spirit or Mind. Hence it is a plain conſequence that the Soul always thinks: And in truth whoever ſhall go about to divide in his Thoughts, or abſtract the *Exiſtence* of a Spirit from its *Cogitation*, will, I believe, find it no eaſy Task.

XCIX. So likewiſe, when we attempt to abſtract Extenſion and Motion from all other Qualities, and conſider them by themſelves, we preſently loſe ſight of them, and run into great Extravagancies. All which depend on a two-fold Abſtraction: Firſt, it is ſuppoſed that Extenſion, for Example, may be abſtracted from all other ſenſible Qualities; and Secondly, that the Entity of Extenſion may be abſtracted from its being perceived. But whoever ſhall reflect, and take care to underſtand what he ſays, will, if I miſtake not, acknowledge that all ſenſible Qualities are alike *Senſations*, and alike *real*; that where the Extenſion is, there is the Colour too, to wit, in his Mind, and that their Archetypes can exiſt only in ſome other *Mind*: And that the Objects of Senſe are nothing but thoſe Senſations combined, blended, or (if one may ſo ſpeak) concreted together: None of all which can be ſuppoſed to exiſt unperceived.

C. What it is for a Man to be happy, or an Object good, every one may think he knows. But to frame an abſtract Idea of *Happineſs*, preſcinded from all particular Pleaſure, or of *Goodneſs*, from every thing that is good, this is what few can pretend to. So likewiſe, a Man may be juſt and virtuous, without having preciſe Ideas of *Juſtice* and *Virtue*. The Opinion that thoſe and the like Words ſtand for general Notions abſtracted from all particular Perſons and Actions, ſeems to have rendered Morality difficult, and the Study thereof of leſs uſe to Mankind. And in effect, the Doctrine of *Abſtraction* has not a little con-

contributed towards ſpoiling the moſt uſeful Parts of Knowledge.

CI. The two great Provinces of ſpeculative Science, converſant about Ideas received from Senſe and their Relations, are *natural Philoſophy* and *Mathematics*; with regard to each of theſe I ſhall make ſome Obſervations. And Firſt, I ſhall ſay ſomewhat of natural Philoſophy. On this Subject it is, that the *Sceptics* triumph: All that ſtock of Arguments they produce to depreciate our Faculties, and make Mankind appear ignorant and low, are drawn principally from this Head, to wit, that we are under an invincible Blindneſs as to the *true* and *real* Nature of Things. This they exaggerate, and love to enlarge on. We are miſerably bantered, ſay they, by our Senſes, and amuſed only with the outſide and ſhew of Things. The real Eſſence, the internal Qualities, and Conſtitution of every the meaneſt Object, is hid from our view; ſomething there is in every drop of Water, every grain of Sand, which it is beyond the Power of humane Underſtanding to fathom or comprehend. But it is evident from what has been ſhewn, that all this Complaint is groundleſs, and that we are influenced by falſe Principles to that degree as to miſtruſt our Senſes,

and

and think we know nothing of those Things which we perfectly comprehend.

CII. One great Inducement to our pronouncing our selves ignorant of the Nature of Things, is the current Opinion that every thing includes within it self the Cause of its Properties: Or that there is in each Object an inward Essence, which is the Source whence its discernible Qualities flow, and whereon they depend. Some have pretended to account for Appearances by occult Qualities, but of late they are mostly resolved into mechanical Causes, to wit, the Figure, Motion, Weight, and such like Qualities of insensible Particles: Whereas in truth, there is no other Agent or efficient Cause than *Spirit*, it being evident that Motion, as well as all other *Ideas*, is perfectly inert. See *Sect.* 25. Hence, to endeavour to explain the Production of Colours or Sounds, by Figure, Motion, Magnitude and the like, must needs be labour in vain. And accordingly, we see the Attempts of that kind are not at all satisfactory. Which may be said, in general, of those Instances, wherein one Idea or Quality is assigned for the Cause of another. I need not say, how many *Hypotheses* and Speculations are left out, and how

how much the Study of Nature is abridged by this Doctrine.

CIII. The great mechanical Principle now in Vogue is *Attraction.* That a Stone falls to the Earth, or the Sea ſwells towards the Moon, may to ſome appear ſufficiently explained thereby. But how are we enlightened by being told this is done by Attraction? Is it that that Word ſignifies the manner of the Tendency, and that it is by the mutual drawing of Bodies, inſtead of their being impelled or protruded towards each other? But nothing is determined of the Manner or Action, and it may as truly (for ought we know) be termed *Impulſe* or *Protruſion* as *Attraction.* Again, the Parts of Steel we ſee cohere firmly together, and this alſo is accounted for by Attraction; but in this, as in the other Inſtances, I do not perceive that any thing is ſignified beſides the Effect it ſelf; for as to the manner of the Action whereby it is produced, or the Cauſe which produces it, theſe are not ſo much as aimed at.

CIV. Indeed, if we take a view of the ſeveral *Phænomena*, and compare them together, we may obſerve ſome likeneſs and conformity between them. For Example, in the falling of a Stone to the Ground, in the riſing of the Sea towards the Moon, in Coheſion and Cryſtallization, there is ſomething alike, namely an Union or mutual Approach of Bodies. So that any one of theſe or the like *Phænomena*, may not ſeem ſtrange or ſurpriſing to a Man who hath nicely obſerved and compared the Effects of Nature. For that only is thought ſo which is uncommon, or a thing by it ſelf, and out of the ordinary Courſe of our Obſervation. That Bodies ſhould tend towards the Center of the Earth, is not thought ſtrange, becauſe it is what we perceive every moment of our Lives. But that they ſhould have a like Gravitation towards the Center of the Moon, may ſeem odd and unaccountable to moſt Men, becauſe it is diſcerned only in the Tides. But a Philoſopher, whoſe Thoughts take in a larger compaſs of Nature, having obſerved a certain ſimilitude of Appearances, as well in the Heavens as the Earth, that argue innumerable Bodies to have a mutual Tendency towards each other, which he denotes by the general Name *Attraction*, whatever can be reduced to that, he thinks juſtly accounted for. Thus he explains the Tides by the Attraction of the Terraqueous Globe towards the Moon, which to him doth not appear odd or anomalous, but only

only a particular Example of a general Rule or Law of Nature.

CV. If therefore we consider the difference there is betwixt natural Philosophers and other Men, with regard to their Knowledge of the *Phænomena*, we shall find it consists, not in an exacter Knowledge of the efficient Cause that produces them, for that can be no other than the *Will of a Spirit*, but only in a greater Largeness of Comprehension, whereby Analogies, Harmonies, and Agreements are discovered in the Works of Nature, and the particular Effects explained, that is, reduced to general Rules, see *Sect.* 62. which Rules grounded on the Analogy, and Uniformness observed in the Production of natural Effects, are most agreeable, and sought after by the Mind; for that they extend our Prospect beyond what is present, and near to us, and enable us to make very probable Conjectures, touching Things that may have happened at very great distances of Time and Place, as well as to predict Things to come; which sort of endeavour towards Omniscience, is much affected by the Mind.

CVI. But we should proceed warily in such Things: for we are apt to lay too great

great a Streſs on Analogies, and to the prejudice of Truth, humour that Eagerneſs of the Mind, whereby it is carried to extend its Knowledge into general Theoremes. For Example, Gravitation, or mutual Attraction, becauſe it appears in many Inſtances, ſome are ſtraightway for pronouncing *Univerſal*; and that to *attract, and be attracted by every other Body, is an eſſential Quality inherent in all Bodies whatſoever.* Whereas it appears the fixed Stars have no ſuch Tendency towards each other: and ſo far is that Gravitation, from being *eſſential* to Bodies, that, in ſome Inſtances a quite contrary Principle ſeems to ſhew it ſelf: As in the perpendicular Growth of Plants, and the Elaſticity of the Air. There is nothing neceſſary or eſſential in the Caſe, but it depends intirely on the Will of the *governing Spirit*, who cauſes certain Bodies to cleave together, or tend towards each other, according to various Laws, whilſt he keeps others at a fixed Diſtance; and to ſome he gives a quite contrary Tendency to fly aſunder, juſt as he ſees convenient.

CVII. After what has been premiſed, I think we may lay down the following Concluſions. Firſt, It is plain Philoſophers amuſe themſelves in vain, when they inquire

quire for any natural efficient Cauſe, diſtinct from a *Mind* or *Spirit*. Secondly, Conſidering the whole Creation is the Workmanſhip of a *wiſe and good Agent*, it ſhould ſeem to become Philoſophers, to employ their Thoughts (contrary to what ſome hold) about the final Cauſes of Things: And I muſt confeſs, I ſee no reaſon, why pointing out the various Ends, to which natural Things are adapted, and for which they were originally with unſpeakable Wiſdom contrived, ſhould not be thought one good way of accounting for them, and altogether worthy a Philoſopher. Thirdly, From what hath been premiſed no reaſon can be drawn, why the Hiſtory of Nature ſhould not ſtill be ſtudied, and Obſervations and Experiments made, which, that they are of uſe to Mankind, and enable us to draw any general Concluſions, is not the Reſult of any immutable Habitudes, or Relations between Things themſelves, but only of GOD's Goodneſs and Kindneſs to Men in the Adminiſtration of the World. See *Sect.* 30 and 31. Fourthly, By a diligent Obſervation of the *Phænomena* within our View, we may diſcover the general Laws of Nature, and from them deduce the other *Phænomena*, I do not ſay *demonſtrate*; for all Deductions of that kind depend on a

Suppoſition

Suppoſition that the Author of Nature always operates uniformly, and in a conſtant obſervance of thoſe Rules we take for Principles: Which we cannot evidently know.

CVIII. Thoſe Men who frame general Rules from the *Phænomena*, and afterwards derive the *Phænomena* from thoſe Rules, ſeem to conſider Signs rather than Cauſes. A Man may well underſtand natural Signs without knowing their Analogy, or being able to ſay by what Rule a Thing is ſo or ſo. And as it is very poſſible to write improperly, through too ſtrict an Obſervance of general Grammar-Rules: So in arguing from general Rules of Nature, it is not impoſſible we may extend the Analogy too far, and by that means run into Miſtakes.

CIX. As in reading other Books, a wiſe Man will chooſe to fix his Thoughts on the Senſe and apply it to uſe, rather than lay them out in Grammatical Remarks on the Language; ſo in peruſing the Volume of Nature, it ſeems beneath the Dignity of the Mind to affect an Exactneſs in reducing each particular *Phænomenon* to general Rules, or ſhewing how it follows from them. We ſhould propoſe to our ſelves nobler Views, ſuch as to recreate and exalt

exalt the Mind, with a proſpect of the Beauty, Order, Extent, and Variety of natural Things: Hence, by proper Inferences, to enlarge our Notions of the Grandeur, Wiſdom, and Beneficence of the CREATOR: And laſtly, to make the ſeveral Parts of the Creation, ſo far as in us lies, ſubſervient to the Ends they were deſigned for, GOD's Glory, and the Suſtentation and Comfort of our ſelves and Fellow-Creatures.

CX. The beſt Key for the aforeſaid Analogy, or natural Science, will be eaſily acknowledged to be a certain celebrated Treatiſe of *Mechanics*: In the entrance of which juſtly admired Treatiſe, Time, Space and Motion, are diſtinguiſhed into *Abſolute* and *Relative*, *True* and *Apparent*, *Mathematical* and *Vulgar*: Which Diſtinction, as it is at large explained by the Author, doth ſuppoſe thoſe Quantities to have an Exiſtence without the Mind: And that they are ordinarily conceived with relation to ſenſible Things, to which nevertheleſs in their own Nature, they bear no relation at all.

CXI. As for *Time*, as it is there taken in an abſolute or abſtracted Senſe, for the Duration or Perſeverance of the Exiſtence of Things, I have nothing more to add concerning it, after what hath been already ſaid on that Subject, *Sect.* 97 and 98. For the reſt, this celebrated Author holds there is an *abſolute Space*, which, being unperceivable to Senſe, remains in it ſelf ſimilar and immoveable: And relative Space to be the meaſure thereof, which being moveable, and defined by its Situation in reſpect of ſenſible Bodies, is vulgarly taken for immoveable Space. *Place* he defines to be that part of Space which is occupied by any Body. And according as the Space is abſolute or relative, ſo alſo is the Place. *Abſolute Motion* is ſaid to be the Tranſlation of a Body from abſolute Place to abſolute Place, as relative Motion is from one relative Place to another. And becauſe the Parts of abſolute Space, do not fall under our Senſes, inſtead of them we are obliged to uſe their ſenſible Meaſures: And ſo define both Place and Motion with reſpect to Bodies, which we regard as immoveable. But it is ſaid, in philoſophical Matters we muſt abſtract from our Senſes, ſince it may be, that none of thoſe Bodies which ſeem to be quieſcent, are truly ſo: And the ſame thing which is moved relatively, may be really at reſt. As likewiſe one and the ſame Body may be in relative Reſt and Motion, or even moved with contrary

trary relative Motions at the ſame time, according as its Place is variouſly defined. All which Ambiguity is to be found in the apparent Motions, but not at all in the true or abſolute, which ſhould therefore be alone regarded in Philoſophy. And the true, we are told, are diſtinguiſhed from apparent or relative Motions by the following Properties. Firſt, In true or abſolute Motion, all Parts which preſerve the ſame Poſition with reſpect to the whole, partake of the Motions of the whole. Secondly, The Place being moved, that which is placed therein is alſo moved: So that a Body moving in a Place which is in Motion, doth participate the Motion of its Place. Thirdly, True Motion is never generated or changed, otherwiſe than by Force impreſſed on the Body it ſelf. Fourthly, True Motion is always changed by Force impreſſed on the Body moved. Fifthly, In circular Motion barely relative, there is no centrifugal Force, which nevertheleſs in that which is true or abſolute, is proportional to the Quantity of Motion.

CXII. But notwithſtanding what hath been ſaid, it doth not appear to me, that there can be any Motion other than *relative:* So that to conceive Motion, there muſt be at leaſt conceived two Bodies, whereof the Diſtance or Poſition in regard to each other is varied. Hence if there was one only Body in being, it could not poſſibly be moved. This ſeems evident, in that the Idea I have of Motion doth neceſſarily include Relation.

CXIII. But though in every Motion it be neceſſary to conceive more Bodies than one, yet it may be that one only is moved, namely that on which the Force cauſing the change of diſtance is impreſſed, or in other Words, that to which the Action is applied. For however ſome may define Relative Motion, ſo as to term that Body *moved*, which changes its Diſtance from ſome other Body, whether the Force or Action cauſing that Change were applied to it, or no: Yet as Relative Motion is that which is perceived by Senſe, and regarded in the ordinary Affairs of Life, it ſhould ſeem that every Man of common Senſe knows what it is, as well as the beſt Philoſopher: Now I ask any one, whether in his Senſe of Motion as he walks along the Streets, the Stones he paſſes over may be ſaid to *move*, becauſe they change Diſtance with his Feet? To me it ſeems, that though Motion includes a Relation of one thing to another, yet it is not neceſſary that each Term of the Relation be denominated from

from it. As a Man may think of somewhat which doth not think, so a Body may be moved to or from another Body, which is not therefore it self in Motion.

CXIV. As the Place happens to be variously defined, the Motion which is related to it varies. A Man in a Ship may be said to be quiescent, with relation to the sides of the Vessel, and yet move with relation to the Land. Or he may move Eastward in respect of the one, and Westward in respect of the other. In the common Affairs of Life, Men never go beyond the Earth to define the Place of any Body: And what is quiescent in respect of that, is accounted *absolutely* to be so. But Philosophers who have a greater Extent of Thought, and juster Notions of the System of Things, discover even the Earth it self to be moved. In order therefore to fix their Notions, they seem to conceive the Corporeal World as finite, and the utmost unmoved Walls or Shell thereof to be the Place, whereby they estimate true Motions. If we sound our own Conceptions, I believe we may find all the absolute Motion we can frame an Idea of, to be at bottom no other than relative Motion thus defined. For as hath been already observed, absolute Motion exclusive of all external

Relation is incomprehensible: And to this kind of Relative Motion, all the abovementioned Properties, Causes, and Effects ascribed to absolute Motion, will, if I mistake not, be found to agree. As to what is said of the centrifugal Force, that it doth not at all belong to circular Relative Motion: I do not see how this follows from the Experiment which is brought to prove it. See *Philosophiæ Naturalis Principia Mathematica, in Schol. Def.* VIII. For the Water in the Vessel, at that time wherein it is said to have the greatest relative circular Motion, hath, I think, no Motion at all: As is plain from the foregoing Section.

CXV. For to denominate a Body *moved*, it is requisite, first, that it change its Distance or Situation with regard to some other Body: And secondly, that the Force or Action occasioning that Change be applied to it. If either of these be wanting, I do not think that agreeably to the Sense of Mankind, or the Propriety of Language, a Body can be said to be in Motion. I grant indeed, that it is possible for us to think a Body, which we see change its Distance from some other, to be moved, though it have no force applied to it, (in which Sense there may be apparent Motion,) but then it is, because the Force causing

causing the Change of Distance, is imagined by us to be applied or impressed on that Body thought to move. Which indeed shews we are capable of mistaking a thing to be in Motion which is not, and that is all.

CXVI. From what hath been said, it follows that the Philosophic Consideration of Motion doth not imply the being of an *absolute Space*, distinct from that which is perceived by Sense, and related to Bodies: Which that it cannot exist without the Mind, is clear upon the same Principles, that demonstrate the like of all other Objects of Sense. And perhaps, if we inquire narrowly, we shall find we cannot even frame an Idea of *pure Space*, exclusive of all Body. This I must confess seems impossible, as being a most abstract Idea. When I excite a Motion in some part of my Body, if it be free or without Resistance, I say there is *Space*: But if I find a Resistance, then I say there is *Body*: and in proportion as the Resistance to Motion is lesser or greater, I say the *Space* is more or less *pure*. So that when I speak of pure or empty Space, it is not to be supposed, that the Word *Space* stands for an Idea distinct from, or conceivable without Body and Motion. Though indeed we are apt to think every Noun Subſtantive ſtands for a diſtinct Idea, that may be ſeparated from all others: Which hath occaſioned infinite Miſtakes. When therefore ſuppoſing all the World to be annihilated beſides my own Body, I ſay there ſtill remains *pure Space:* Thereby nothing elſe is meant, but only that I conceive it poſſible, for the Limbs of my Body to be moved on all ſides without the leaſt Reſiſtance: But if that too were annihilated, then there could be no Motion, and conſequently no Space. Some perhaps may think the Senſe of Seeing doth furniſh them with the Idea of pure Space; but it is plain from what we have elſewhere ſhewn, that the Ideas of Space and Diſtance are not obtained by that Senſe. See the *Eſſay concerning Viſion.*

CXVII. What is here laid down, ſeems to put an end to all thoſe Diſputes and Difficulties, which have ſprung up amongſt the Learned concerning the nature of *pure Space.* But the chief Advantage ariſing from it, is, that we are freed from that dangerous *Dilemma,* to which ſeveral who have employed their Thoughts on this Subject, imagine themſelves reduced, to wit, of thinking either that Real Space is God, or elſe that there is ſomething beſide God which

which is Eternal, Uncreated, Infinite, Indivisible, Immutable. Both which may justly be thought pernicious and absurd Notions. It is certain that not a few Divines, as well as Philosophers of great note, have, from the Difficulty they found in conceiving either Limits or Annihilation of Space, concluded it must be *Divine*. And some of late have set themselves particularly to shew, that the incommunicable Attributes of GOD agree to it. Which Doctrine, how unworthy soever it may seem of the Divine Nature, yet I do not see how we can get clear of it, so long as we adhere to the received Opinions.

CXVIII. Hitherto of Natural Philosophy: We come now to make some Inquiry concerning that other great Branch of speculative Knowledge, to wit, *Mathematics*. These, how celebrated soever they may be, for their Clearness and Certainty of Demonstration, which is hardly any where else to be found, cannot nevertheless be supposed altogether free from Mistakes; if in their Principles there lurks some secret Error, which is common to the Professors of those Sciences with the rest of Mankind. Mathematicians, though they deduce their Theoremes from a great height of Evidence, yet their first Principles

ples are limited by the conſideration of Quantity: And they do not aſcend into any Inquiry concerning thoſe tranſcendental Maxims, which influence all the particular Sciences, each Part whereof, Mathematics not excepted, doth conſequently participate of the Errors involved in them. That the Principles laid down by Mathematicians are true, and their way of Deduction from thoſe Principles clear and inconteſtable, we do not deny. But we hold, there may be certain erroneous Maxims of greater Extent than the Object of Mathematics, and for that reaſon not expreſly mentioned, though tacitly ſuppoſed throughout the whole progreſs of that Science; and that the ill Effects of thoſe ſecret unexamined Errors are diffuſed through all the Branches thereof. To be plain, we ſuſpect the Mathematicians are, as well as other Men, concerned in the Errors ariſing from the Doctrine of abſtract general Ideas, and the Exiſtence of Objects without the Mind.

CXIX. *Arithmetic* hath been thought to have for its Object abſtract Ideas of *Number*. Of which to underſtand the Properties and mutual Habitudes is ſuppoſed no mean part of ſpeculative Knowledge. The Opinion of the pure and intellectual Nature

ture of Numbers in Abſtract, hath made them in eſteem with thoſe Philoſophers, who ſeem to have affected an uncommon Fineneſs and Elevation of Thought. It hath ſet a Price on the moſt trifling numerical Speculations which in Practice are of no uſe, but ſerve only for Amuſement: And hath therefore ſo far infected the Minds of ſome, that they have dreamt of mighty *Myſteries* involved in Numbers, and attempted the Explication of natural Things by them. But if we inquire into our own Thoughts, and conſider what hath been premiſed, we may perhaps entertain a low Opinion of thoſe high Flights and Abſtractions, and look on all Inquiries about Numbers, only as ſo many *difficiles nugæ*, ſo far as they are not ſubſervient to practice, and promote the benefit of Life.

CXX. Unity in Abſtract we have before conſidered in *Sect.* 13, from which and what hath been ſaid in the Introduction, it plainly follows there is not any ſuch Idea. But Number being defined a *Collection of Unites*, we may conclude that, if there be no ſuch thing as Unity or Unite in Abſtract, there are no Ideas of Number in Abſtract denoted by the numeral Names and Figures. The Theories therefore in Arithmetic, if they are abſtracted from the

Names

Names and Figures, as likewiſe from all Uſe and Practice, as well as from the particular things numbered, can be ſuppoſed to have nothing at all for their Object. Hence we may ſee, how intirely the Science of Numbers is ſubordinate to Practice, and how jejune and trifling it becomes, when conſidered as a matter of mere Speculation.

CXXI. However ſince there may be ſome, who, deluded by the ſpecious Shew of diſcovering abſtracted Verities, waſte their time in Arithmetical Theoremes and Problemes, which have not any Uſe: It will not be amiſs, if we more fully conſider, and expoſe the Vanity of that Pretence; And this will plainly appear, by taking a view of Arithmetic in its Infancy, and obſerving what it was that originally put Men on the Study of that Science, and to what Scope they directed it. It is natural to think that at firſt, Men, for eaſe of Memory and help of Computation, made uſe of Counters, or in writing of ſingle Strokes, Points or the like, each whereof was made to ſignify an Unite, that is, ſome one thing of whatever Kind they had occaſion to reckon. Afterwards they found out the more compendious ways, of making one Character ſtand in place of ſeveral Strokes,

or

or Points. And laſtly, the Notation of the *Arabians* or *Indians* came into uſe, wherein by the repetition of a few Characters or Figures, and varying the Signification of each Figure according to the place it obtains, all Numbers may be moſt aptly expreſſed: Which ſeems to have been done in Imitation of Language, ſo that an exact Analogy is obſerved betwixt the Notation by Figures and Names, the nine ſimple Figures anſwering the nine firſt numeral Names and Places in the former, correſponding to Denominations in the latter. And agreeably to thoſe Conditions of the ſimple and local Value of Figures, were contrived Methods of finding from the given Figures or Marks of the Parts, what Figures and how placed, are proper to denote the whole or *vice verſa.* And having found the ſought Figures, the ſame Rule or Analogy being obſerved throughout, it is eaſy to read them into Words; and ſo the Number becomes perfectly known. For then the Number of any particular Things is ſaid to be known, when we know the Name or Figures (with their due arangement) that according to the ſtanding Analogy belong to them. For theſe Signs being known, we can by the Operations of Arithmetic, know the Signs of

any

any Part of the particular Sums signified by them; and thus computing in Signs, (because of the Connexion established betwixt them and the distinct multitudes of Things, whereof one is taken for an Unite,) we may be able rightly to sum up, divide, and proportion the things themselves that we intend to number.

CXXII. In *Arithmetic* therefore we regard not the *Things* but the *Signs*, which nevertheless are not regarded for their own sake, but because they direct us how to act with relation to Things, and dispose rightly of them. Now agreeably to what we have before observed, of Words in general (*Sect.* 19. *Introd.*) it happens here likewise, that abstract Ideas are thought to be signified by Numeral Names or Characters, while they do not suggest Ideas of particular Things to our Minds. I shall not at present enter into a more particular Dissertation on this Subject; but only observe that it is evident from what hath been said, those Things which pass for abstract Truths and Theoremes concerning Numbers, are, in reality, conversant about no Object distinct from particular numerable Things, except only Names and Cha-

Characters; which originally came to be considered, on no other account but their being *Signs*, or capable to represent aptly, whatever particular Things Men had need to compute. Whence it follows, that to study them for their own sake would be just as wise, and to as good purpose, as if a Man, neglecting the true Use or original Intention and Subserviency of Language, should spend his time in impertinent Criticisms upon Words, or Reasonings and Controversies purely Verbal.

CXXIII. From Numbers we proceed to speak of *Extension*, which considered as relative, is the Object of Geometry. The *Infinite* Divisibility of *Finite* Extension, though it is not expresly laid down, either as an Axiome or Theoreme in the Elements of that Science, yet is throughout the same every where supposed, and thought to have so inseparable and essential a Connexion with the Principles and Demonstrations in Geometry, that Mathematicians never admit it into Doubt, or make the least Question of it. And as this Notion is the Source from whence do spring all those amusing Geometrical Paradoxes, which have such a direct Repugnancy to the plain common Sense of Mankind,

Mankind, and are admitted with ſo much Reluctance into a Mind not yet debauched by Learning: So is it the principal occaſion of all that nice and extreme Subtilty, which renders the Study of *Mathematics* ſo difficult and tedious. Hence if we can make it appear, that no Finite Extenſion contains innumerable Parts, or is infinitely Diviſible, it follows that we ſhall at once clear the Science of Geometry from a great Number of Difficulties and Contradictions, which have ever been eſteemed a Reproach to Humane Reaſon, and withal make the Attainment thereof a Buſineſs of much leſs Time and Pains, than it hitherto hath been.

CXXIV. Every particular Finite Extenſion, which may poſſibly be the Object of our Thought, is an *Idea* exiſting only in the Mind, and conſequently each Part thereof muſt be perceived. If therefore I cannot perceive innumerable Parts in any Finite Extenſion that I conſider, it is certain they are not contained in it: But it is evident, that I cannot diſtinguiſh innumerable Parts in any particular Line, Surface, or Solid, which I either perceive by Senſe, or Figure to my ſelf in my Mind: Wherefore I conclude they are not contained in it. Nothing can

can be plainer to me, than that the Extenſions I have in View are no other than my own Ideas, and it is no leſs plain, that I cannot reſolve any one of my Ideas into an infinite Number of other Ideas, that is, that they are not infinitely Diviſible. If by *Finite Extenſion* be meant ſomething diſtinct from a Finite Idea, I declare I do not know what that is, and ſo cannot affirm or deny any thing of it. But if the terms *Extenſion*, *Parts*, and the like, are taken in any Senſe conceivable, that is, for Ideas; then to ſay a Finite Quantity or Extenſion conſiſts of Parts infinite in Number, is ſo manifeſt a Contradiction, that every one at firſt ſight acknowledges it to be ſo. And it is impoſſible it ſhould ever gain the Aſſent of any reaſonable Creature, who is not brought to it by gentle and ſlow Degrees, as a converted Gentile to the belief of *Tranſubſtantiation.* Ancient and rooted Prejudices do often paſs into Principles: And thoſe Propoſitions which once obtain the force and credit of a *Principle,* are not only themſelves, but likewiſe whatever is deducible from them, thought privileged from all Examination. And there is no Abſurdity ſo groſs, which by this means the Mind of Man may not be prepared to ſwallow.

CXXV. He whoſe Underſtanding is prepoſſeſt with the Doctrine of abſtract general Ideas, may be perſuaded, that (whatever be thought of the Ideas of Senſe,) Extenſion in *abſtract* is infinitely diviſible. And one who thinks the Objects of Senſe exiſt without the Mind, will perhaps in virtue thereof be brought to admit, that a Line but an Inch long may contain innumerable Parts really exiſting, though too ſmall to be diſcerned. Theſe Errors are grafted as well in the Minds of *Geometricians*, as of other Men, and have a like influence on their Reaſonings; and it were no difficult thing, to ſhew how the Arguments from Geometry made uſe of to ſupport the infinite Diviſibility of Extenſion, are bottomed on them. At preſent we ſhall only obſerve in general, whence it is that the Mathematicians are all ſo fond and tenacious of this Doctrine.

CXXVI. It hath been obſerved in another place, that the Theoremes and Demonſtrations in Geometry are converſant about Univerſal Ideas. *Sect.* 15. *Introd.* Where it is explained in what Senſe this ought to be underſtood, to wit, that the particular Lines and Figures included in the

the Diagram, are ſuppoſed to ſtand for innumerable others of different Sizes: or in other words, the Geometer conſiders them abſtracting from their Magnitude: which doth not imply that he forms an abſtract Idea, but only that he cares not what the particular Magnitude is, whether great or ſmall, but looks on that as a thing indifferent to the Demonſtration: Hence it follows, that a Line in the Scheme, but an Inch long, muſt be ſpoken of, as though it contained ten thouſand Parts, ſince it is regarded not in it ſelf, but as it is univerſal; and it is univerſal only in its Signification, whereby it repreſents innumerable Lines greater than it ſelf, in which may be diſtinguiſhed ten thouſand Parts or more, though there may not be above an Inch in it. After this manner the Properties of the Lines ſignified are (by a very uſual Figure) transferred to the Sign, and thence through Miſtake thought to appertain to it conſidered in its own Nature.

CXXVII. Becauſe there is no Number of Parts ſo great, but it is poſſible there may be a Line containing more, the Inch-line is ſaid to contain Parts more than any aſſignable Number; which is true, not of the Inch taken abſolutely, but only for the Things ſignified by it. But Men not retaining that Diſtinction in their Thoughts, ſlide into a belief that the ſmall particular Line deſcribed on Paper contains in it ſelf Parts innumerable. There is no ſuch thing as the ten-thouſandth Part of an *Inch*; but there is of a *Mile* or *Diameter of the Earth*, which may be ſignified by that Inch. When therefore I delineate a Triangle on Paper, and take one ſide not above an Inch, for Example, in length to be the *Radius*: This I conſider as divided into ten thouſand or an hundred thouſand Parts, or more. For though the ten-thouſandth Part of that Line conſidered in it ſelf, is nothing at all, and conſequently may be neglected without any Error or Inconveniency; yet theſe deſcribed Lines being only Marks ſtanding for greater Quantities, whereof it may be the ten-thouſandth Part is very conſiderable, it follows, that to prevent notable Errors in Practice, the *Radius* muſt be taken of ten thouſand Parts, or more.

CXXVIII. From what hath been ſaid the reaſon is plain why, to the end any Theoreme may become univerſal in its Uſe, it is neceſſary we ſpeak of the Lines deſcribed on Paper, as though they contained Parts which really they do not. In doing of which, if we examine the matter throughly, ly, we ſhall perhaps diſcover that we cannot conceive an Inch it ſelf as conſiſting of, or being diviſible into a thouſand Parts, but only ſome other Line which is far greater than an Inch, and repreſented by it. And that when we ſay a Line is *infinitely diviſible*, we muſt mean a Line which is *infinitely great*. What we have here obſerved ſeems to be the chief Cauſe, why to ſuppoſe the infinite Diviſibility of finite Extenſion hath been thought neceſſary in Geometry.

CXXIX. The ſeveral Abſurdities and Contradictions which flowed from this falſe Principle might, one would think, have been eſteemed ſo many Demonſtrations againſt it. But by I know not what *Logic*, it is held that Proofs *à poſteriori* are not to be admitted againſt Propoſitions relating to Infinity. As though it were not impoſſible even for an infinite Mind to reconcile Contradictions. Or as if any thing abſurd and repugnant could have a neceſſary Connexion with Truth, or flow from it. But whoever conſiders the Weakneſs of this Pretence, will think it was contrived on purpoſe to humour the Lazineſs of the Mind, which had rather acquieſce in an indolent Scepticiſm, than be at the Pains to go through with a ſevere Examination of thoſe Principles it hath ever embraced for true.

CXXX. Of late the Speculations about Infinites have run ſo high, and grown to ſuch ſtrange Notions, as have occaſioned no ſmall Scruples and Diſputes among the Geometers of the preſent Age. Some there are of great Note, who not content with holding that finite Lines may be divided into an infinite Number of Parts, do yet farther maintain, that each of thoſe Infiniteſimals is it ſelf ſubdiviſible into an Infinity of other Parts, or Infiniteſimals of a ſecond Order, and ſo on *ad infinitum*. Theſe, I ſay, aſſert there are Infiniteſimals of Infiniteſimals of Infiniteſimals, without ever coming to an end. So that according to them an Inch doth not barely contain an infinite Number of Parts, but an Infinity of an Infinity of an Infinity *ad infinitum* of Parts. Others there be who hold all Orders of Infiniteſimals below the firſt to be nothing at all, thinking it with good reaſon abſurd, to imagine there is any poſitive Quantity or Part of Extenſion, which though multiplied infinitely, can ever equal the ſmalleſt given Extenſion. And yet on the other hand it ſeems no leſs abſurd, to think the Square, Cube, or other Power of a poſitive real Root, ſhould it ſelf

ſelf be nothing at all; which they who hold Infiniteſimals of the firſt Order, denying all of the ſubſequent Orders, are obliged to maintain.

CXXXI. Have we not therefore reaſon to conclude, that they are *both* in the wrong, and that there is in effect no ſuch thing as Parts infinitely ſmall, or an infinite number of Parts contained in any finite Quantity? But you will ſay, that if this Doctrine obtains, it will follow the very Foundations of Geometry are deſtroyed: And thoſe great Men who have raiſed that Science to ſo aſtoniſhing an height, have been all the while building a Caſtle in the Air. To this it may be replied, that whatever is uſeful in Geometry and promotes the benefit of humane Life, doth ſtill remain firm and unſhaken on our Principles. That Science conſidered as practical, will rather receive Advantage than any Prejudice from what hath been ſaid. But to ſet this in a due Light, may be the Subject of a diſtinct Inquiry. For the reſt, though it ſhould follow that ſome of the more intricate and ſubtile Parts of *Speculative Mathematics* may be pared off without any prejudice to Truth; yet I do not ſee what Damage will be thence derived to Mankind. On the contrary, it were highly to be wiſhed, that Men of great Abilities and obſtinate Application would draw off their Thoughts from thoſe Amuſements, and employ them in the Study of ſuch Things as lie nearer the Concerns of Life, or have a more direct Influence on the Manners.

CXXXII. If it be ſaid that ſeveral Theoremes undoubtedly true, are diſcovered by Methods in which Infiniteſimals are made uſe of, which could never have been, if their Exiſtence included a Contradiction in it. I anſwer, that upon a thorough Examination it will not be found, that in any Inſtance it is neceſſary to make uſe of or conceive infiniteſimal Parts of finite Lines, or even Quantities leſs than the *Minimum Senſibile:* Nay, it will be evident this is never done, it being impoſſible.

CXXXIII. By what we have premiſed, it is plain that very numerous and important Errors have taken their riſe from thoſe falſe Principles, which were impugned in the foregoing Parts of this Treatiſe. And the Oppoſites of thoſe erroneous Tenets at the ſame time appear to be moſt fruitful Principles, from whence do flow innumerable Conſequences highly advantageous to true Philoſophy as well as to Religion. Particularly, *Matter* or *the abſolute Exiſ-*

tence

tence of Corporeal Objects, hath been ſhewn to be that wherein the moſt avowed and pernicious Enemies of all Knowledge, whether humane or divine, have ever placed their chief Strength and Confidence. And ſurely, if by diſtinguiſhing the real Exiſtence of unthinking Things from their being perceived, and allowing them a Subſiſtence of their own out of the Minds of Spirits, no one thing is explained in Nature; but on the contrary a great many inexplicable Difficulties ariſe: If the Suppoſition of Matter is barely precarious, as not being grounded on ſo much as one ſingle Reaſon: If its Conſequences cannot endure the Light of Examination and free Inquiry, but skreen themſelves under the dark and general pretence of *Infinites being incomprehenſible:* If withal the Removal of this *Matter* be not attended with the leaſt evil Conſequence, if it be not even miſſed in the World, but every thing as well, nay much eaſier conceived without it: If laſtly, both *Sceptics* and *Atheiſts* are for ever ſilenced upon ſuppoſing only Spirits and Ideas, and this Scheme of Things is perfectly agreeable both to *Reaſon* and *Religion:* Methinks we may expect it ſhould be admitted and firmly embraced, though it were propoſed only as an *Hypotheſis*, and the Exiſtence of Matter had been allowed

poſſible,

poſſible, which yet I think we have evidently demonſtrated that it is not.

CXXXIV. True it is, that in conſequence of the foregoing Principles, ſeveral Diſputes and Speculations, which are eſteemed no mean Parts of Learning, are rejected as uſeleſs. But how great a Prejudice ſoever againſt our Notions, this may give to thoſe who have already been deeply engaged, and made large Advances in Studies of that Nature: Yet by others, we hope it will not be thought any juſt ground of Diſlike to the Principles and Tenets herein laid down, that they abridge the labour of Study, and make Humane Sciences more clear, compendious, and attainable, than they were before.

CXXXV. Having diſpatched what we intended to ſay concerning the knowledge of *Ideas*, the Method we propoſed leads us, in the next place, to treat of *Spirits*: With regard to which, perhaps Humane Knowledge is not ſo deficient as is vulgarly imagined. The great Reaſon that is aſſigned for our being thought ignorant of the nature of Spirits, is, our not having an Idea of it. But ſurely it ought not to be looked on as a defect in a Humane

mane Underſtanding, that it does not perceive the Idea of *Spirit*, if it is manifeſtly impoſſible there ſhould be any ſuch *Idea*. And this, if I miſtake not, has been demonſtrated in *Sect*. 27: To which I ſhall here add that a Spirit has been ſhewn to be the only Subſtance or Support, wherein the unthinking Beings or Ideas can exiſt: But that this *Subſtance* which ſupports or perceives Ideas ſhould it ſelf be an *Idea* or like an *Idea*, is evidently abſurd.

CXXXVI. It will perhaps be ſaid, that we want a Senſe (as ſome have imagined) proper to know Subſtances withal, which if we had, we might know our own Soul, as we do a Triangle. To this I anſwer, that in caſe we had a new Senſe beſtowed upon us, we could only receive thereby ſome new Senſations or Ideas of Senſe. But I believe no Body will ſay, that what he means by the terms *Soul* and *Subſtance*, is only ſome particular ſort of Idea or Senſation. We may therefore infer, that all things duly conſidered, it is not more reaſonable to think our Faculties defective, in that they do not furniſh us with an Idea of Spirit or active thinking Subſtance, than it would be if we ſhould blame them for not being able to comprehend a *round Square*.

CXXXVII.

CXXXVII. From the opinion that Spirits are to be known after the manner of an Idea or Senſation, have riſen many abſurd and heterodox Tenets, and much Scepticiſm about the Nature of the Soul. It is even probable, that this Opinion may have produced a Doubt in ſome, whether they had any Soul at all diſtinct from their Body, ſince upon inquiry they could not find they had an Idea of it. That an *Idea* which is inactive, and the Exiſtence whereof conſiſts in being perceived, ſhould be the Image or Likeneſs of an Agent ſubſiſting by it ſelf, ſeems to need no other Refutation, than barely attending to what is meant by thoſe Words. But perhaps you will ſay, that tho' an *Idea* cannot reſemble a *Spirit*, in its Thinking, Acting, or Subſiſting by it ſelf, yet it may in ſome other reſpects: And it is not neceſſary that an Idea or Image be in all reſpects like the Original.

CXXXVIII. I anſwer, If it does not in thoſe mentioned, it is impoſſible it ſhould repreſent it in any other thing. Do but leave out the Power of Willing, Thinking, and Perceiving Ideas, and there remains nothing elſe wherein the Idea can be like a Spirit. For by the Word *Spirit*

rit we mean only that which thinks, wills, and perceives; this, and this alone, constitutes the Signification of that Term: If therefore it is impossible that any degree of those Powers should be represented in an Idea, it is evident there can be no Idea of a Spirit.

CXXXIX. But it will be objected, that if there is no Idea signified by the Terms *Soul*, *Spirit*, and *Substance*, they are wholly insignificant, or have no meaning in them. I answer, those Words do mean or signify a real Thing, which is neither an Idea nor like an Idea, but that which perceives Ideas, and Wills, and Reasons about them. What I am my self, that which I denote by the Term I, is the same with what is meant by *Soul* or *Spiritual Substance*. If it be said that this is only quarrelling at a Word, and that since the immediate Significations of other Names are by common consent called *Ideas*, no reason can be assigned, why that which is signified by the Name *Spirit* or *Soul* may not partake in the same Appellation. I answer, All the unthinking Objects of the Mind agree, in that they are intirely passive, and their Existence consists only in being perceived: Whereas a Soul or Spirit is an active Being, whose Existence consists not in being

being perceived, but in perceiving Ideas and Thinking. It is therefore neceſſary, in order to prevent Equivocation and confounding Natures perfectly diſagreeing and unlike, that we diſtinguiſh between *Spirit* and *Idea*. See *Sect.* 27.

CXL. In a large Senſe indeed, we may be ſaid to have an Idea, or rather a Notion of *Spirit*, that is, we underſtand the meaning of the Word, otherwiſe we could not affirm or deny any thing of it. Moreover, as we conceive the Ideas that are in the Minds of other Spirits by means of our own, which we ſuppoſe to be Reſemblances of them: So we know other Spirits by means of our own Soul, which in that Senſe is the Image or Idea of them, it having a like reſpect to other Spirits, that Blueneſs or Heat by me perceived hath to thoſe Ideas perceived by another.

CXLI. It muſt not be ſuppoſed, that they who aſſert the natural Immortality of the Soul are of opinion, that it is abſolutely incapable of Annihilation even by the infinite Power of the CREATOR who firſt gave it Being: But only that it is not liable to be broken or diſſolved by the ordinary Laws of Nature or Motion. They indeed, who hold the Soul of Man to be only

only a thin vital Flame, or Syſtem of animal Spirits, make it periſhing and corruptible as the Body, ſince there is nothing more eaſily diſſipated than ſuch a Being, which it is naturally impoſſible ſhould ſurvive the Ruin of the Tabernacle, wherein it is incloſed. And this Notion hath been greedily embraced and cheriſhed by the worſt part of Mankind, as the moſt effectual Antidote againſt all Impreſſions of Virtue and Religion. But it hath been made evident, that Bodies of what Frame or Texture ſoever, are barely paſſive Ideas in the Mind, which is more diſtant and heterogeneous from them, than Light is from Darkneſs. We have ſhewn that the Soul is Indiviſible, Incorporeal, Unextended, and it is conſequently Incorruptible. Nothing can be plainer, than that the Motions, Changes, Decays, and Diſſolutions which we hourly ſee befal natural Bodies (and which is what we mean by the *Courſe of Nature*) cannot poſſibly affect an active, ſimple, uncompounded Subſtance: Such a Being therefore is indiſſoluble by the force of Nature, that is to ſay, *the Soul of Man is naturally immortal.*

CXLII. After what hath been ſaid, it is I ſuppoſe plain, that our Souls are not to be known in the ſame manner as ſenſeleſs inactive

inactive Objects, or by way of *Idea*. *Spirits* and *Ideas* are Things ſo wholly different, that when we ſay, *they exiſt*, *they are known*, or the like, theſe Words muſt not be thought to ſignify any thing common to both Natures. There is nothing alike or common in them: And to expect that by any Multiplication or Enlargement of our Faculties, we may be enabled to know a Spirit as we do a Triangle, ſeems as abſurd as if we ſhould hope to *ſee a Sound*. This is inculcated becauſe I imagine it may be of Moment towards clearing ſeveral important Queſtions, and preventing ſome very dangerous Errors concerning the Nature of the Soul. We may not I think ſtrictly be ſaid to have an Idea of an active Being, or of an Action, although we may be ſaid to have a Notion of them. I have ſome Knowledge or Notion of my Mind, and its Acts about Ideas, inaſmuch as I know or underſtand what is meant by thoſe Words. What I know, that I have ſome Notion of. I will not ſay, that the Terms *Idea* and *Notion* may not be uſed convertibly, if the World will have it ſo. But yet it conduceth to Clearneſs and Propriety, that we diſtinguiſh Things very different by different Names. It is alſo to be remarked, that all Relations including an Act of the Mind, we cannot ſo properly be be ſaid to have an Idea, but rather a Notion of the Relations or Habitudes between Things. But if in the modern way the Word *Idea* is extended to Spirits, and Relations and Acts; this is after all an Affair of verbal Concern.

CXLIII. It will not be amiſs to add, that the Doctrine of *Abſtract Ideas* hath had no ſmall ſhare in rendering thoſe Sciences intricate and obſcure, which are particularly converſant about ſpiritual Things. Men have imagined they could frame abſtract Notions of the Powers and Acts of the Mind, and conſider them preſcinded, as well from the Mind or Spirit it ſelf, as from their reſpective Objects and Effects. Hence a great number of dark and ambiguous Terms preſumed to ſtand for abſtract Notions, have been introduced into Metaphyſics and Morality, and from theſe have grown infinite Diſtractions and Diſputes amongſt the Learned.

CXLIV. But nothing ſeems more to have contributed towards engaging Men in Controverſies and Miſtakes, with regard to the Nature and Operations of the Mind, than the being uſed to ſpeak of thoſe Things, in Terms borrowed from ſenſible Ideas. For Example, the Will is termed the *Motion* of the Soul: This infuſes a Belief, that the Mind of Man is as a Ball in Motion, impelled and determined by the Objects of Senſe, as neceſſarily as that is by the Stroke of a Racket. Hence ariſe endleſs Scruples and Errors of dangerous conſequence in Morality. All which I doubt not may be cleared, and Truth appear plain, uniform, and conſiſtent, could but Philoſophers be prevailed on to retire into themſelves, and attentively conſider their own meaning.

CXLV. From what hath been ſaid, it is plain that we cannot know the Exiſtence of other Spirits, otherwiſe than by their Operations, or the Ideas by them excited in us. I perceive ſeveral Motions, Changes, and Combinations of Ideas, that inform me there are certain particular Agents like my ſelf, which accompany them, and concur in their Production. Hence the Knowledge I have of other Spirits is not immediate, as is the Knowledge of my Ideas; but depending on the Intervention of Ideas, by me referred to Agents or Spirits diſtinct from my ſelf, as Effects or concomitant Signs.

CXLVI. But though there be ſome Things which convince us, humane Agents are

are concerned in producing them; yet it is evident to every one, that thoſe Things which are called the Works of Nature, that is, the far greater part of the Ideas or Senſations perceived by us, are not produced by, or dependent on the Wills of Men. There is therefore ſome other Spirit that cauſes them, ſince it is repugnant that they ſhould ſubſiſt by themſelves. See *Sect.* 29. But if we attentively conſider the conſtant Regularity, Order, and Concatenation of natural Things, the ſurpriſing Magnificence, Beauty, and Perfection of the larger, and the exquiſite Contrivance of the ſmaller Parts of the Creation, together with the exact Harmony and Correſpondence of the whole, but above all, the never enough admired Laws of Pain and Pleaſure, and the Inſtincts or natural Inclinations, Appetites, and Paſſions of Animals; I ſay if we conſider all theſe Things, and at the ſame time attend to the meaning and import of the Attributes, One, Eternal, infinitely Wiſe, Good, and Perfect, we ſhall clearly perceive that they belong to the aforeſaid Spirit, *who works all in all*, and *by whom all things conſiſt*.

CXLVII. Hence it is evident, that God is known as certainly and immediately as any other Mind or Spirit whatſoever, diſtinct from our ſelves. We may even aſſert, that the Exiſtence of GOD is far more evidently perceived than the Exiſtence of Men; becauſe the Effects of Nature are infinitely more numerous and conſiderable, than thoſe aſcribed to humane Agents. There is not any one Mark that denotes a Man, or Effect produced by him, which doth not more ſtrongly evince the Being of that Spirit who is the *Author of Nature.* For it is evident that in affecting other Perſons, the Will of Man hath no other Object, than barely the Motion of the Limbs of his Body; but that ſuch a Motion ſhould be attended by, or excite any Idea in the Mind of another, depends wholly on the Will of the CREATOR. He alone it is who *upholding all Things by the Word of his Power*, maintains that Intercourſe between Spirits, whereby they are able to perceive the Exiſtence of each other. And yet this pure and clear Light which enlightens every one, is it ſelf inviſible.

CXLVIII. It ſeems to be a general Pretence of the unthinking Herd, that they cannot ſee GOD. Could we but ſee him, ſay they, as we ſee a Man, we ſhould believe that he is, and believing obey his Commands. But alas we need only open our

our Eyes to ſee the ſovereign Lord of all Things with a more full and clear View, than we do any one of our Fellow-Creatures. Not that I imagine we ſee GOD (as ſome will have it) by a direct and immediate View, or ſee Corporeal Things, not by themſelves, but by ſeeing that which repreſents them in the Eſſence of GOD, which Doctrine is I muſt confeſs to me incomprehenſible. But I ſhall explain my Meaning. A humane Spirit or Perſon is not perceived by Senſe, as not being an Idea; when therefore we ſee the Colour, Size, Figure, and Motions of a Man, we perceive only certain Senſations or Ideas excited in our own Minds: And theſe being exhibited to our View in ſundry diſtinct Collections, ſerve to mark out unto us the Exiſtence of finite and created Spirits like our ſelves. Hence it is plain, we do not ſee a Man, if by *Man* is meant that which lives, moves, perceives, and thinks as we do: But only ſuch a certain Collection of Ideas, as directs us to think there is a diſtinct Principle of Thought and Motion like to our ſelves, accompanying and repreſented by it. And after the ſame manner we ſee GOD; all the difference is, that whereas ſome one finite and narrow Aſſemblage of Ideas denotes a particular humane Mind, whitherſoever we direct our View, we do at all Times and in all Places perceive manifest Tokens of the Divinity: Every thing we see, hear, feel, or any wise perceive by Sense, being a Sign or Effect of the Power of GOD; as is our Perception of those very Motions, which are produced by Men.

CXLIX. It is therefore plain, that nothing can be more evident to any one that is capable of the least Reflexion, than the Existence of GOD, or a Spirit who is intimately present to our Minds, producing in them all that variety of Ideas or Sensations, which continually affect us, on whom we have an absolute and intire Dependence, in short, *in whom we live, and move, and have our Being*. That the Discovery of this great Truth which lies so near and obvious to the Mind, should be attained to by the Reason of so very few, is a sad instance of the Stupidity and Inattention of Men, who, though they are surrounded with such clear Manifestations of the Deity, are yet so little affected by them, that they seem as it were blinded with excess of Light.

CL. But you will say, Hath Nature no share in the Production of natural Things, and must they be all ascribed to the immediate and sole Operation of GOD? I answer,

ſwer, If by *Nature* is meant only the viſible *Series* of Effects, or Senſations imprinted on our Minds according to certain fixed and general Laws: Then it is plain, that Nature taken in this Senſe cannot produce any thing at all. But if by *Nature* is meant ſome Being diſtinct from GOD, as well as from the Laws of Nature, and Things perceived by Senſe, I muſt confeſs that Word is to me an empty Sound, without any intelligible Meaning annexed to it. Nature in this Acceptation is a vain *Chimera* introduced by thoſe Heathens, who had not juſt Notions of the Omnipreſence and infinite Perfection of GOD. But it is more unaccountable, that it ſhould be received among *Chriſtians* profeſſing Belief in the Holy Scriptures, which conſtantly aſcribe thoſe Effects to the immediate Hand of GOD, that Heathen Philoſophers are wont to impute to *Nature*. *The LORD, he cauſeth the Vapours to aſcend; he maketh Lightnings with Rain; he bringeth forth the Wind out of his Treaſures,* Jerem. Chap. 10. ver. 13. *He turneth the ſhadow of Death into the Morning, and maketh the Day dark with Night,* Amos Chap. 5. ver. 8. *He viſiteth the Earth, and maketh it ſoft with Showers: He bleſſeth the ſpringing thereof, and crowneth the Year with his Goodneſs; ſo that the Paſtures are clothed with Flocks, and the Valleys are covered over with Corn.* See *Psalm* 65. But notwithstanding that this is the constant Language of Scripture; yet we have I know not what Aversion from believing, that GOD concerns himself so nearly in our Affairs. Fain would we suppose him at a great distance off, and substitute some blind unthinking Deputy in his stead, though (if we may believe Saint *Paul*) *he be not far from every one of us.*

CLI. It will I doubt not be objected, that the slow and gradual Methods observed in the Production of natural Things, do not seem to have for their Cause the immediate Hand of an *almighty Agent.* Besides, Monsters, untimely Births, Fruits blasted in the Blossom, Rains falling in desert Places, Miseries incident to humane Life, are so many Arguments that the whole Frame of Nature is not immediately actuated and superintended by a Spirit of infinite Wisdom and Goodness. But the Answer to this Objection is in a good measure plain from *Sect.* 62, it being visible, that the aforesaid Methods of Nature are absolutely necessary, in order to working by the most simple and general Rules, and after a steady and consistent Manner; which argues both the *Wisdom* and *Goodness* of GOD. Such is the artificial Contrivance of of this mighty Machine of Nature, that whilſt its Motions and various Phænomena ſtrike on our Senſes, the Hand which actuates the whole is it ſelf unperceivable to Men of Fleſh and Blood. *Verily* (ſaith the Prophet) *thou art a GOD that hideſt thy ſelf*, Iſaiah Chap. 45. ver. 15. But though GOD conceal himſelf from the Eyes of the *Senſual* and *Lazy*, who will not be at the leaſt Expence of Thought; yet to an unbiaſſed and attentive Mind, nothing can be more plainly legible, than the intimate Preſence of an *All-wiſe Spirit*, who faſhions, regulates, and ſuſtains the whole Syſteme of Being. It is clear from what we have elſewhere obſerved, that the operating according to general and ſtated Laws, is ſo neceſſary for our Guidance in the Affairs of Life, and letting us into the Secret of Nature, that without it, all Reach and Compaſs of Thought, all humane Sagacity and Deſign could ſerve to no manner of purpoſe: It were even impoſſible there ſhould be any ſuch Faculties or Powers in the Mind. See *Sect.* 31. Which one Conſideration abundantly out-balances whatever particular Inconveniences may thence ariſe.

CLII. We ſhould further conſider, that the very Blemiſhes and Defects of Nature are

are not without their Uſe, in that they make an agreeable ſort of Variety, and augment the Beauty of the reſt of the Creation, as Shades in a Picture ſerve to ſet off the brighter and more enlightened Parts. We would likewiſe do well to examine, whether our taxing the Waſte of Seeds and Embryos, and accidental Deſtruction of Plants and Animals, before they come to full Maturity, as an Imprudence in the Author of Nature, be not the effect of Prejudice contracted by our Familiarity with impotent and ſaving Mortals. In *Man* indeed a thrifty Management of thoſe Things, which he cannot procure without much Pains and Induſtry, may be eſteemed *Wiſdom.* But we muſt not imagine, that the inexplicably fine Machine of an Animal or Vegetable, coſts the great CREATOR any more Pains or Trouble in its Production than a Pebble doth: nothing being more evident, than that an omnipotent Spirit can indifferently produce every thing by a mere *Fiat* or Act of his Will. Hence it is plain, that the ſplendid Profuſion of natural Things ſhould not be interpreted, Weakneſs or Prodigality in the Agent who produces them, but rather be looked on as an Argument of the Riches of his Power.

CLIII. As

CLIII. As for the mixture of Pain or Uneasineſs which is in the World, purſuant to the general Laws of Nature, and the Actions of finite imperfect Spirits: This, in the State we are in at preſent, is indiſpenſibly neceſſary to our well-being. But our Proſpects are too narrow: We take, for Inſtance, the Idea of ſome one particular Pain into our Thoughts, and account it *Evil*; whereas if we enlarge our View, ſo as to comprehend the various Ends, Connexions, and Dependencies of Things, on what Occaſions and in what Proportions we are affected with Pain and Pleaſure, the Nature of humane Freedom, and the Deſign with which we are put into the World; we ſhall be forced to acknowledge that thoſe particular Things, which conſidered in themſelves appear to be *Evil*, have the Nature of *Good*, when conſidered as linked with the whole Syſteme of Beings.

CLIV. From what hath been ſaid it will be manifeſt to any conſidering Perſon, that it is merely for want of Attention and Comprehenſiveneſs of Mind, that there are any Favourers of *Atheiſm* or the *Manichean Hereſy* to be found. Little and unreflecting Souls may indeed burleſque the Works of Providence, the Beauty and Order whereof of they have not Capacity, or will not be at the Pains to comprehend. But those who are Masters of any Justness and Extent of Thought, and are withal used to reflect, can never sufficiently admire the divine Traces of Wisdom and Goodness that shine throughout the Oeconomy of Nature. But what Truth is there which shineth so strongly on the Mind, that by an Aversion of Thought, a wilful shutting of the Eyes, we may not escape seeing it? Is it therefore to be wondered at, if the generality of Men, who are ever intent on Business or Pleasure, and little used to fix or open the Eye of their Mind, should not have all that Conviction and Evidence of the Being of GOD, which might be expected in reasonable Creatures?

CLV. We should rather wonder, that Men can be found so stupid as to neglect, than that neglecting they should be unconvinced of such an evident and momentous Truth. And yet it is to be feared that too many of Parts and Leisure, who live in Christian Countries, are merely through a supine and dreadful Negligence sunk into a sort of *Atheism*. Since it is downright impossible, that a Soul pierced and enlightened with a thorough Sense of the Omnipresence, Holiness, and Justice of that *Almighty*

mighty Spirit, ſhould perſiſt in a remorſeleſs Violation of his Laws. We ought therefore earneſtly to meditate and dwell on thoſe important Points; that ſo we may attain Conviction without all Scruple, *that the Eyes of the LORD are in every place beholding the Evil and the Good*; *that he is with us and keepeth us in all places whither we go, and giveth us Bread to eat, and Raiment to put on*; that he is preſent and conſcious to our innermoſt Thoughts; and that we have a moſt abſolute and immediate dependence on him. A clear View of which great Truths cannot chooſe but fill our Hearts with an awful Circumſpection and holy Fear, which is the ſtrongeſt Incentive to *Virtue*, and the beſt Guard againſt *Vice*.

CLVI. For after all, what deſerves the firſt place in our Studies, is the Conſideration of *GOD*, and our *Duty*; which to promote, as it was the main drift and deſign of my Labours, ſo ſhall I eſteem them altogether uſeleſs and ineffectual, if by what I have ſaid I cannot inſpire my Readers with a pious Senſe of the Preſence of GOD: And having ſhewn the Falſeneſs or Vanity of thoſe barren Speculations, which make the chief Employment of learned Men,

Men, the better diſpoſe them to reverence and embrace the ſalutary Truths of the GOSPEL, which to know and to practiſe is the higheſt Perfection of humane Nature.

THREE
DIALOGUES
BETWEEN
Hylas and *Philonous*.
In OPPOSITION to
SCEPTICS and ATHEISTS.

By *GEORGE BERKELEY*, M. A.
Fellow of *Trinity College*, *Dublin*.

First Printed in the Year 1713.

THE FIRST DIALOGUE.

PHILONOUS.

GOOD Morrow, *Hylas*: I did not expect to find you abroad so early.

Hylas. It is indeed something unusual; but my Thoughts were so taken up with a Subject I was discoursing of last Night, that finding I could not sleep, I resolved to rise and take a turn in the Garden.

Phil. It happened well, to let you see what innocent and agreeable Pleasures you lose every Morning. Can there be a pleasanter time of the Day, or a more delightful Season of the Year? That purple Sky, these wild but sweet Notes of Birds, the fragrant Bloom upon the Trees and Flowers,

ers, the gentle Influence of the riſing Sun, theſe and a thouſand nameleſs Beauties of Nature inſpire the Soul with ſecret Tranſports; its Faculties too being at this time freſh and lively, are fit for thoſe Meditations, which the Solitude of a Garden and Tranquillity of the Morning naturally diſpoſe us to. But I am afraid I interrupt your Thoughts: for you ſeemed very intent on ſomething.

Hyl. It is true, I was, and ſhall be obliged to you if you will permit me to go on in the ſame Vein; not that I would by any means deprive my ſelf of your Company, for my Thoughts always flow more eaſily in Converſation with a Friend, than when I am alone: But my Requeſt is, that you would ſuffer me to impart my Reflexions to you.

Phil. With all my heart, it is what I ſhould have requeſted my ſelf, if you had not prevented me.

Hyl. I was conſidering the odd Fate of thoſe Men who have in all Ages, through an Affectation of being diſtinguiſhed from the Vulgar, or ſome unaccountable Turn of Thought, pretended either to believe nothing at all, or to believe the moſt extravagant Things in the World. This however might be born, if their Paradoxes and Scepticiſm did not draw after them ſome Con-

Consequences of general Disadvantage to Mankind. But the Mischief lieth here; that when Men of less Leisure see them who are supposed to have spent their whole time in the Pursuits of Knowledge, professing an intire Ignorance of all Things, or advancing such Notions as are repugnant to plain and commonly received Principles, they will be tempted to entertain Suspicions concerning the most important Truths, which they had hitherto held sacred and unquestionable.

Phil. I intirely agree with you, as to the ill Tendency of the affected Doubts of some Philosophers, and fantastical Conceits of others. I am even so far gone of late in this way of Thinking, that I have quitted several of the sublime Notions I had got in their Schools for vulgar Opinions. And I give it you on my Word, since this Revolt from Metaphysical Notions to the plain Dictates of Nature and common Sense, I find my Understanding strangely enlightened, so that I can now easily comprehend a great many Things which before were all Mystery and Riddle.

Hyl. I am glad to find there was nothing in the Accounts I heard of you.

Phil. Pray, what were those?

Hyl. You were represented in last Night's Conversation, as one who maintained the moſt extravagant Opinion that ever entered into the Mind of Man, to wit, That there is no ſuch Thing as *material Subſtance* in the World.

Phil. That there is no ſuch Thing as what Philoſophers call *Material Subſtance*, I am ſeriouſly perſuaded: But if I were made to ſee any thing abſurd or ſceptical in this, I ſhould then have the ſame Reaſon to renounce this, that I imagine I have now to reject the contrary Opinion.

Hyl. What! can any Thing be more fantaſtical, more repugnant to common Senſe, or a more manifeſt Piece of Scepticiſm, than to believe there is no ſuch Thing as *Matter?*

Phil. Softly, good *Hylas.* What if it ſhould prove, that you, who hold there is, are by virtue of that Opinion a greater *Sceptic*, and maintain more Paradoxes and Repugnancies to common Senſe, than I who believe no ſuch Thing?

Hyl. You may as ſoon perſuade me, The Part is greater than the Whole, as that, in order to avoid Abſurdity and Scepticiſm, I ſhould ever be obliged to give up my Opinion in this Point.

Phil. Well then, are you content to admit that Opinion for true, which upon Examination ſhall appear moſt agreeable to common Senſe, and remote from Scepticiſm?

Hyl.

Hyl. With all my Heart. Since you are for raiſing Diſputes about the plaineſt Things in Nature, I am content for once to hear what you have to ſay.

Phil. Pray, *Hylas*, what do you mean by a *Sceptic?*

Hyl. I mean what all Men mean, one that doubts of every Thing.

Phil. He then who entertains no Doubt concerning ſome particular Point, with regard to that Point cannot be thought a *Sceptic*.

Hyl. I agree with you.

Phil. Whether doth Doubting conſiſt in embracing the Affirmative or Negative Side of a Queſtion?

Hyl. In neither; for whoever underſtands *Engliſh*, cannot but know that *Doubting* ſignifies a Suſpenſe between both.

Phil. He then that denieth any Point, can no more be ſaid to doubt of it, than he who affirmeth it with the ſame Degree of Aſſurance.

Hyl. True.

Phil. And conſequently, for ſuch his Denial is no more to be eſteemed a *Sceptic* than the other.

Hyl. I acknowledge it.

Phil. How cometh it to paſs then, *Hylas*, that you pronounce me a *Sceptic*, becauſe I deny what you affirm, to wit, the Exiſtence of Matter? Since, for ought you can tell, I am as peremptory in my Denial, as you in your Affirmation.

Hyl. Hold, *Philonous*, I have been a little out in my Definition; but every false Step a Man makes in Discourse is not to be insisted on. I said indeed, that a *Sceptic* was one who doubted of every Thing; but I should have added, or who denies the Reality and Truth of Things.

Phil. What Things? Do you mean the Principles and Theoremes of Sciences? But these you know are universal intellectual Notions, and consequently independent of Matter; the Denial therefore of this doth not imply the denying them.

Hyl. I grant it. But are there no other Things? What think you of distrusting the Senses, of denying the real Existence of sensible Things, or pretending to know nothing of them. Is not this sufficient to denominate a Man a *Sceptic*?

Phil. Shall we therefore examine which of us it is that denies the Reality of Sensible Things, or professes the greatest Ignorance of them; since, if I take you rightly, he is to be esteemed the greatest *Sceptic*?

Hyl. That is what I desire.

Phil. What mean you by Sensible Things?

Hyl.

Hyl. Those Things which are perceived by the Senses. Can you imagine that I mean any thing else?

Phil. Pardon me, *Hylas*, if I am desirous clearly to apprehend your Notions, since this may much shorten our Inquiry. Suffer me then to ask you this farther Question. Are those Things only perceived by the Senses which are perceived immediately? Or may those Things properly be said to be *Sensible*, which are perceived mediately, or not without the Intervention of others?

Hyl. I do not sufficiently understand you.

Phil. In reading a Book, what I immediately perceive are the Letters, but mediately, or by means of these, are suggested to my Mind the Notions of God, Virtue, Truth, *&c.* Now, that the Letters are truly Sensible Things, or perceived by Sense, there is no doubt: But I would know whether you take the Things suggested by them to be so too.

Hyl. No certainly, it were absurd to think *God* or *Virtue* Sensible Things, though they may be signified and suggested to the Mind by Sensible Marks, with which they have an arbitrary Connexion.

Phil. It seems then, that by *Sensible Things* you mean those only which can be perceived immediately by Sense.

Hyl. Right.

Phil. Doth it not follow from this, that though I see one part of the Sky Red, and another Blue, and that my Reason doth thence evidently conclude there must be some Cause of that Diversity of Colours, yet that Cause cannot be said to be a Sensible Thing, or perceived by the Sense of Seeing?

Hyl. It doth.

Phil. In like manner, though I hear Variety of Sounds, yet I cannot be said to hear the Causes of those Sounds.

Hyl. You cannot.

Phil. And when by my Touch I perceive a Thing to be hot and heavy, I cannot say with any Truth or Propriety, that I feel the Cause of its Heat or Weight.

Hyl. To prevent any more Questions of this kind, I tell you once for all, that by *Sensible Things* I mean those only which are perceived by Sense, and that in truth the Senses perceive nothing which they do not perceive immediately: for they make no Inferences. The deducing therefore of Causes or Occasions from Effects and Appearances, which alone are perceived by Sense, intirely relates to Reason.

Phil. This Point then is agreed between us, That *Sensible Things are those only which are immediately perceived by Sense.* You will

will farther inform me, whether we immediately perceive by Sight any thing beside Light, and Colours, and Figures: or by Hearing, any thing but Sounds: by the Palate, any thing beside Tastes: by the Smell, beside Odors: or by the Touch, more than tangible Qualities.

Hyl. We do not.

Phil. It seems therefore, that if you take away all sensible Qualities, there remains nothing sensible.

Hyl. I grant it.

Phil. Sensible Things therefore are nothing else but so many sensible Qualities, or Combinations of sensible Qualities.

Hyl. Nothing else.

Phil. Heat then is a sensible Thing.

Hyl. Certainly.

Phil. Doth the Reality of sensible Things consist in being perceived? or, is it something distinct from their being perceived, and that bears no relation to the Mind?

Hyl. To *exist* is one thing, and to be *perceived* is another.

Phil. I speak with regard to sensible Things only: And of these I ask, Whether by their real Existence you mean a Subsistence exterior to the Mind, and distinct from their being perceived?

Hyl. I mean a real absolute Being, distinct from, and without any relation to their being perceived.

Phil.

Phil. Heat therefore, if it be allowed a real Being, muſt exiſt without the Mind.

Hyl. It muſt.

Phil. Tell me, *Hylas*, is this real Exiſtence equally compatible to all Degrees of Heat, which we perceive: or is there any Reaſon why we ſhould attribute it to ſome, and deny it others? And if there be, pray let me know that Reaſon.

Hyl. Whatever Degree of Heat we perceive by Senſe, we may be ſure the ſame exiſts in the Object that occaſions it.

Phil. What, the greateſt as well as the leaſt?

Hyl. I tell you, the Reaſon is plainly the ſame in reſpect of both: They are both perceived by Senſe; nay, the greater Degree of Heat is more ſenſibly perceived; and conſequently, if there is any Difference, we are more certain of its real Exiſtence than we can be of the Reality of a leſſer Degree.

Phil. But is not the moſt vehement and intenſe Degree of Heat a very great Pain?

Hyl. No one can deny it.

Phil. And is any unperceiving Thing capable of Pain or Pleaſure?

Hyl. No certainly.

Phil. Is your material Subſtance a ſenſeleſs Being, or a Being endowed with Senſe and Perception?

Hyl.

Hyl. It is ſenſeleſs, without doubt.

Phil. It cannot therefore be the Subject of Pain.

Hyl. By no means.

Phil. Nor conſequently of the greateſt Heat perceived by Senſe, ſince you acknowledge this to be no ſmall Pain.

Hyl. I grant it.

Phil. What ſhall we ſay then of your external Object; is it a material Subſtance, or no?

Hyl. It is a material Subſtance with the ſenſible Qualities inhering in it.

Phil. How then can a great Heat exiſt in it, ſince you own it cannot in a material Subſtance? I deſire you would clear this Point.

Hyl. Hold, *Philonous*, I fear I was out in yielding intenſe Heat to be a Pain. It ſhould ſeem rather, that Pain is ſomething diſtinct from Heat, and the Conſequence or Effect of it.

Phil. Upon putting your Hand near the Fire, do you perceive one ſimple uniform Senſation, or two diſtinct Senſations?

Hyl. But one ſimple Senſation.

Phil. Is not the Heat immediately perceived?

Hyl. It is.

Phil. And the Pain?

Hyl. True.

Phil.

Phil. Seeing therefore they are both immediately perceived at the ſame time, and the Fire affects you only with one ſimple, or uncompounded Idea, it follows that this ſame ſimple Idea is both the intenſe Heat immediately perceived, and the Pain ; and conſequently, that the intenſe Heat immediately perceived, is nothing diſtinct from a particular ſort of Pain.

Hyl. It ſeems ſo.

Phil. Again, try in your Thoughts, *Hylas*, if you can conceive a vehement Senſation to be without Pain, or Pleaſure.

Hyl. I cannot.

Phil. Or can you frame to yourſelf an Idea of ſenſible Pain or Pleaſure in general, abſtracted from every particular Idea of Heat, Cold, Taſtes, Smells ? *&c.*

Hyl. I do not find that I can.

Phil. Doth it not therefore follow, that ſenſible Pain is nothing diſtinct from thoſe Senſations or Ideas, in an intenſe Degree ?

Hyl. It is undeniable ; and to ſpeak the Truth, I begin to ſuſpect a very great Heat cannot exiſt but in a Mind perceiving it.

Phil. What ! are you then in that *Sceptical* State of Suſpenſe, between Affirming and Denying ?

Hyl.

Hyl. I think I may be poſitive in the Point. A very violent and painful Heat cannot exiſt without the Mind.

Phil. It hath not therefore, according to you, any real Being.

Hyl. I own it.

Phil. Is it therefore certain, that there is no body in Nature really hot?

Hyl. I have not denied there is any real Heat in Bodies. I only ſay, there is no ſuch thing as an intenſe real Heat.

Phil. But did you not ſay before, that all Degrees of Heat were equally real: or if there was any difference, that the Greater were more undoubtedly real than the Leſſer?

Hyl. True: But it was, becauſe I did not then conſider the Ground there is for diſtinguiſhing between them, which I now plainly ſee. And it is this: Becauſe intenſe Heat is nothing elſe but a particular kind of painful Senſation; and Pain cannot exiſt but in a perceiving Being; it follows that no intenſe Heat can really exiſt in an unperceiving corporeal Subſtance. But this is no Reaſon why we ſhould deny Heat in an inferior Degree to exiſt in ſuch a Subſtance.

Phil. But how ſhall we be able to diſcern thoſe Degrees of Heat which exiſt only in the Mind, from thoſe which exiſt without it?

Hyl.

Hyl. That is no difficult matter. You know, the least Pain cannot exist unperceived; whatever therefore Degree of Heat is a Pain, exists only in the Mind. But as for all other Degrees of Heat, nothing obliges us to think the same of them.

Phil. I think you granted before, that no unperceiving Being was capable of Pleasure, any more than of Pain.

Hyl. I did.

Phil. And is not Warmth, or a more gentle Degree of Heat than what causes Uneasiness, a Pleasure?

Hyl. What then?

Phil. Consequently it cannot exist without the Mind in any unperceiving Substance, or Body.

Hyl. So it seems.

Phil. Since therefore, as well those Degrees of Heat that are not painful, as those that are, can exist only in a Thinking Substance; may we not conclude that external Bodies are absolutely incapable of any Degree of Heat whatsoever?

Hyl. On second Thoughts, I do not think it so evident that Warmth is a Pleasure, as that a great Degree of Heat is a Pain.

Phil. I do not pretend that Warmth is as great a Pleasure as Heat is a Pain. But if you grant it to be even a small Pleasure, it serves to make good my Conclusion.

Hyl.

Hyl. I could rather call it an *Indolence.* It ſeems to be nothing more than a Privation of both Pain and Pleaſure. And that ſuch a Quality or State as this may agree to an unthinking Subſtance, I hope you will not deny.

Phil. If you are reſolved to maintain that Warmth, or a gentle Degree of Heat, is no Pleaſure, I know not how to convince you otherwiſe, than by appealing to your own Senſe. But what think you of Cold?

Hyl. The ſame that I do of Heat. An intenſe Degree of Cold is a Pain; for to feel a very great Cold, is to perceive a great Uneaſineſs: It cannot therefore exiſt without the Mind; but a leſſer Degree of Cold may, as well as a leſſer Degree of Heat.

Phil. Thoſe Bodies therefore, upon whoſe Application to our own, we perceive a moderate Degree of Heat, muſt be concluded to have a moderate Degree of Heat or Warmth in them: And thoſe, upon whoſe Application we feel a like Degree of Cold, muſt be thought to have Cold in them.

Hyl. They muſt.

Phil. Can any Doctrine be true that neceſſarily leads a Man into an Abſurdity?

Hyl. Without doubt it cannot.

Phil.

Phil. Is it not an Abſurdity to think that the ſame thing ſhould be at the ſame time both cold and warm?

Hyl. It is.

Phil. Suppoſe now one of your Hands hot, and the other cold, and that they are both at once put into the ſame Veſſel of Water, in an intermediate State; will not the Water ſeem cold to one Hand, and warm to the other?

Hyl. It will.

Phil. Ought we not therefore by your Principles to conclude, it is really both cold and warm at the ſame time, that is, according to your own Conceſſion, to believe an Abſurdity.

Hyl. I confeſs it ſeems ſo.

Phil. Conſequently, the Principles themſelves are falſe, ſince you have granted that no true Principle leads to an Abſurdity.

Hyl. But after all, can any thing be more abſurd than to ſay, *there is no Heat in the Fire?*

Phil. To make the Point ſtill clearer; tell me, whether in two Caſes exactly alike, we ought not to make the ſame Judgment?

Hyl. We ought.

Phil. When a Pin pricks your Finger, doth it not rend and divide the Fibres of your Fleſh?

Hyl.

Hyl. It doth.

Phil. And when a Coal burns your Finger, doth it any more?

Hyl. It doth not.

Phil. Since therefore you neither judge the Senſation itſelf occaſioned by the Pin, nor any thing like it to be in the Pin; you ſhould not, conformably to what you have now granted, judge the Senſation occaſioned by the Fire, or any thing like it, to be in the Fire.

Hyl. Well, ſince it muſt be ſo, I am content to yield this Point, and acknowledge, that Heat and Cold are only Senſations exiſting in our Minds: But there ſtill remain Qualities enough to ſecure the Reality of external Things.

Phil. But what will you ſay, *Hylas*, if it ſhall appear that the Caſe is the ſame with regard to all other ſenſible Qualities, and that they can no more be ſuppoſed to exiſt without the Mind, than Heat and Cold?

Hyl. Then indeed you will have done ſomething to the purpoſe; but that is what I deſpair of ſeeing proved.

Phil. Let us examine them in order. What think you of Taſtes, do they exiſt without the Mind, or no?

Hyl. Can any Man in his Senſes doubt whether Sugar is ſweet, or Wormwood bitter?

Phil. Inform me, *Hylas.* Is a ſweet Taſte a particular kind of Pleaſure or pleaſant Senſation, or is it not?

Hyl. It is.

Phil. And is not Bitterneſs ſome kind of Uneaſineſs or Pain?

Hyl. I grant it.

Phil. If therefore Sugar and Wormwood are unthinking corporeal Subſtances exiſting without the Mind, how can Sweetneſs and Bitterneſs, that is, Pleaſure and Pain, agree to them?

Hyl. Hold, *Philonous,* I now ſee what it was deluded me all this time. You asked whether Heat and Cold, Sweetneſs and Bitterneſs, were not particular Sorts of Pleaſure and Pain; to which I anſwered ſimply, that they were. Whereas I ſhould have thus diſtinguiſhed: Thoſe Qualities, as perceived by us, are Pleaſures or Pains, but not as exiſting in the external Objects. We muſt not therefore conclude abſolutely, that there is no Heat in the Fire, or Sweetneſs in the Sugar, but only that Heat or Sweetneſs, as perceived by us, are not in the Fire or Sugar. What ſay you to this?

Phil. I ſay it is nothing to the Purpoſe. Our Diſcourſe proceeded altogether concerning Senſible Things, which you defined to be the Things we *immediately perceive by our*

our Senſes. Whatever other Qualities therefore you ſpeak of, as diſtinct from theſe, I know nothing of them, neither do they at all belong to the Point in Diſpute. You may indeed pretend to have diſcovered certain Qualities which you do not perceive, and aſſert thoſe inſenſible Qualities exiſt in Fire and Sugar. But what Uſe can be made of this to your preſent Purpoſe, I am at a loſs to conceive. Tell me then once more, do you acknowledge that Heat and Cold, Sweetneſs and Bitterneſs, (meaning thoſe Qualities which are perceived by the Senſes) do not exiſt without the Mind?

Hyl. I ſee it is to no purpoſe to hold out, ſo I give up the Cauſe as to thoſe mentioned Qualities. Though I profeſs it ſounds odly, to ſay that Sugar is not ſweet.

Phil. But for your farther Satisfaction, take this along with you: That which at other times ſeems ſweet, ſhall to a diſtempered Palate appear bitter. And nothing can be plainer, than that divers Perſons perceive different Taſtes in the ſame Food, ſince that which one Man delights in, another abhors. And how could this be, if the Taſte was ſomething really inherent in the Food?

Hyl. I acknowledge I know not how.

Phil. In the next place, Odours are to be conſidered. And with regard to theſe,

I would fain know, whether what hath been ſaid of Taſtes doth not exactly agree to them? Are they not ſo many pleaſing or diſpleaſing Senſations?

Hyl. They are.

Phil. Can you then conceive it poſſible that they ſhould exiſt in an unperceiving Thing?

Hyl. I cannot.

Phil. Or can you imagine, that Filth and Ordure affect thoſe brute Animals that feed on them out of Choice, with the ſame Smells which we perceive in them?

Hyl. By no means.

Phil. May we not therefore conclude of Smells, as of the other forementioned Qualities, that they cannot exiſt in any but a perceiving Subſtance or Mind?

Hyl. I think ſo.

Phil. Then as to Sounds, what muſt we think of them: Are they Accidents really inherent in external Bodies, or not?

Hyl. That they inhere not in the ſonorous Bodies, is plain from hence; becauſe a Bell ſtruck in the exhauſted Receiver of an Air-Pump, ſends forth no Sound. The Air therefore muſt be thought the Subject of Sound.

Phil. What Reaſon is there for that, *Hylas?*

Hyl.

Hyl. Becauſe when any Motion is raiſed in the Air, we perceive a Sound greater or leſſer, in Proportion to the Air's Motion; but without ſome Motion in the Air, we never hear any Sound at all.

Phil. And granting that we never hear a Sound but when ſome Motion is produced in the Air, yet I do not ſee how you can infer from thence, that the Sound itſelf is in the Air.

Hyl. It is this very Motion in the external Air, that produces in the Mind the Senſation of *Sound*. For, ſtriking on the Drum of the Ear, it cauſeth a Vibration, which by the Auditory Nerves being communicated to the Brain, the Soul is thereupon affected with the Senſation called *Sound*.

Phil. What! is Sound then a Senſation?

Hyl. I tell you, as perceived by us, it is a particular Senſation in the Mind.

Phil. And can any Senſation exiſt without the Mind?

Hyl. No certainly.

Phil. How then can Sound, being a Senſation exiſt in the Air, if by the *Air* you mean a ſenſeleſs Subſtance exiſting without the Mind?

Hyl. You muſt diſtinguiſh, *Philonous*, between Sound as it is perceived by us, and as it is in itſelf; or (which is the ſame

 thing)

thing) between the Sound we immediately perceive, and that which exiſts without us. The former indeed is a particular kind of Senſation, but the latter is merely a Vibrative or Undulatory Motion in the Air.

Phil. I thought I had already obviated that Diſtinction by the Anſwer I gave when you were applying it in a like Caſe before. But to ſay no more of that; Are you ſure then that Sound is really nothing but Motion?

Hyl. I am.

Phil. Whatever therefore agrees to real Sound, may with Truth be attributed to Motion.

Hyl. It may.

Phil. It is then good Senſe to ſpeak of *Motion*, as of a thing that is *loud*, *ſweet*, *acute*, or *grave*.

Hyl. I ſee you are reſolved not to underſtand me. Is it not evident, thoſe Accidents or Modes belong only to ſenſible Sound, or *Sound* in the common Acceptation of the Word, but not to *Sound* in the Real and Philoſophic Senſe, which, as I juſt now told you, is nothing but a certain Motion of the Air?

Phil. It ſeems then there are two Sorts of Sound, the one Vulgar, or that which is heard, the other Philoſophical and Real.

Hyl.

Hyl. Even ſo.

Phil. And the latter conſiſts in Motion.

Hyl. I told you ſo before.

Phil. Tell me, *Hylas*, to which of the Senſes think you, the Idea of Motion belongs: To the Hearing?

Hyl. No certainly, but to the Sight and Touch.

Phil. It ſhould follow then, that according to you, real Sounds may poſſibly be *ſeen* or *felt*, but never *heard*.

Hyl. Look you, *Philonous*, you may if you pleaſe make a Jeſt of my Opinion, but that will not alter the Truth of Things. I own indeed, the Inferences you draw me into, ſound ſomething odly; but common Language, you know, is framed by, and for the Uſe of the Vulgar: we muſt not therefore wonder, if Expreſſions adapted to exact Philoſophic Notions, ſeem uncouth and out of the way.

Phil. Is it come to that? I aſſure you, I imagine myſelf to have gained no ſmall Point, ſince you make ſo light of departing from common Phraſes and Opinions; it being a main Part of our Inquiry, to examine whoſe Notions are wideſt of the common Road, and moſt repugnant to the general Senſe of the World. But can you think it no more than a Philoſophical Paradox, to ſay that *real Sounds are never*

 heard,

heard, and that the Idea of them is obtained by ſome other Senſe. And is there nothing in this contrary to Nature and the Truth of Things?

Hyl. To deal ingenuouſly, I do not like it. And after the Conceſſions already made, I had as well grant that Sounds too have no real Being without the Mind.

Phil. And I hope you will make no Difficulty to acknowledge the ſame of Colours.

Hyl. Pardon me: the Caſe of Colours is very different. Can any thing be plainer, than that we ſee them on the Objects?

Phil. The Objects you ſpeak of are, I ſuppoſe, corporeal Subſtances exiſting without the Mind.

Hyl. They are.

Phil. And have true and real Colours inhering in them?

Hyl. Each viſible Object hath that Colour which we ſee in it.

Phil. How! Is there any thing viſible but what we perceive by Sight.

Hyl. There is not.

Phil. And do we perceive any thing by Senſe, which we do not perceive immediately?

Hyl. How often muſt I be obliged to repeat the ſame thing? I tell you, we do not.

Phil.

Phil. Have Patience, good *Hylas*; and tell me once more, whether there is any thing immediately perceived by the Senſes, except ſenſible Qualities. I know you aſſerted there was not: But I would now be informed, whether you ſtill perſiſt in the ſame Opinion.

Hyl. I do.

Phil. Pray, is your corporeal Subſtance either a ſenſible Quality, or made up of ſenſible Qualities?

Hyl. What a Queſtion that is! who ever thought it was?

Phil. My Reaſon for asking was, becauſe in ſaying, *each viſible Object hath that Colour which we ſee in it*, you make viſible Objects to be corporeal Subſtances; which implies either that corporeal Subſtances are ſenſible Qualities, or elſe that there is ſomething beſide ſenſible Qualities perceived by Sight: But as this Point was formerly agreed between us, and is ſtill maintained by you, it is a clear Conſequence, that your corporeal Subſtance is nothing diſtinct from ſenſible Qualities.

Hyl. You may draw as many abſurd Conſequences as you pleaſe, and endeavour to perplex the plaineſt Things; but you ſhall never perſuade me out of my Senſes. I clearly underſtand my own Meaning.

Phil.

Phil. I wiſh you would make me underſtand it too. But ſince you are unwilling to have your Notion of corporeal Subſtance examined, I ſhall urge that Point no farther. Only be pleaſed to let me know, whether the ſame Colours which we ſee, exiſt in external Bodies, or ſome other.

Hyl. The very ſame.

Phil. What! are then the beautiful Red and Purple we ſee on yonder Clouds, really in them? Or do you imagine they have in themſelves any other Form, than that of a dark Miſt or Vapour?

Hyl. I muſt own, *Philonous*, thoſe Colours are not really in the Clouds as they ſeem to be at this Diſtance. They are only apparent Colours.

Phil. *Apparent* call you them? how ſhall we diſtinguiſh theſe apparent Colours from real?

Hyl. Very eaſily. Thoſe are to be thought apparent, which appearing only at a diſtance, vaniſh upon a nearer Approach.

Phil. And thoſe I ſuppoſe are to be thought real, which are diſcovered by the moſt near and exact Survey.

Hyl. Right.

Phil. Is the neareſt and exacteſt Survey made by the help of a Microſcope, or by the naked Eye?

Hyl.

Hyl. By a Microſcope, doubtleſs.

Phil. But a Microſcope often diſcovers Colours in an Object different from thoſe perceived by the unaſſiſted Sight. And in caſe we had Microſcopes magnifying to any aſſigned Degree; it is certain, that no Object whatſoever viewed through them, would appear in the ſame Colour which it exhibits to the naked Eye.

Hyl. And what will you conclude from all this? You cannot argue that there are really and naturally no Colours on Objects: becauſe by artificial Managements they may be altered, or made to vaniſh.

Phil. I think it may evidently be concluded from your own Conceſſions, that all the Colours we ſee with our naked Eyes, are only apparent as thoſe on the Clouds, ſince they vaniſh upon a more cloſe and accurate Inſpection, which is afforded us by a Microſcope. Then as to what you ſay by way of Prevention: I aſk you, whether the real and natural State of an Object is better diſcovered by a very ſharp and piercing Sight, or by one which is leſs ſharp?

Hyl. By the former without doubt.

Phil. Is it not plain from *Dioptrics*, that Microſcopes make the Sight more penetrating, and repreſent Objects as they would appear to the Eye, in caſe it were naturally

naturally endowed with a moſt exquiſite Sharpneſs?

Hyl. It is.

Phil. Conſequently the Microſcopical Repreſentation is to be thought that which beſt ſets forth the real Nature of the Thing, or what it is in itſelf. The Colours therefore by it perceived, are more genuine and real, than thoſe perceived otherwiſe.

Hyl. I confeſs there is ſomething in what you ſay.

Phil. Beſides, it is not only poſſible but manifeſt, that there actually are Animals, whoſe Eyes are by Nature framed to perceive thoſe Things, which by reaſon of their Minuteneſs eſcape our Sight. What think you of thoſe inconceivably ſmall Animals perceived by Glaſſes? Muſt we ſuppoſe they are all ſtark blind? Or, in caſe they ſee, can it be imagined their Sight hath not the ſame Uſe in preſerving their Bodies from Injuries, which appears in That of all other Animals? And if it hath, is it not evident, they muſt ſee Particles leſs than their own Bodies, which will preſent them with a far different View in each Object, from that which ſtrikes our Senſes? Even our own Eyes do not always repreſent Objects to us after the ſame manner. In the *Jaundice*, every one knows that all Things ſeem yellow. Is it not therefore highly

highly probable, thoſe Animals in whoſe Eyes we diſcern a very different Texture from that of ours, and whoſe Bodies abound with different Humours, do not ſee the ſame Colours in every Object that we do? From all which, ſhould it not ſeem to follow, that all Colours are equally apparent, and that none of thoſe which we perceive are really inherent in any outward Object?

Hyl. It ſhould.

Phil. The Point will be paſt all doubt, if you conſider, that in caſe Colours were real Properties or Affections inherent in external Bodies, they could admit of no Alteration, without ſome Change wrought in the very Bodies themſelves: But is it not evident from what hath been ſaid, that upon the Uſe of Microſcopes, upon a Change happening in the Humours of the Eye, or a Variation of Diſtance, without any manner of real Alteration in the Thing itſelf, the Colours of any Object are either changed, or totally diſappear? Nay all other Circumſtances remaining the ſame, change but the Situation of ſome Objects, and they ſhall preſent different Colours to the Eye. The ſame thing happens upon viewing an Object in various Degrees of Light. And what is more known, than that the ſame Bodies appear differently coloured by Candle-light, dle-light, from what they do in the open Day? Add to these the Experiment of a Prism, which separating the heterogeneous Rays of Light, alters the Colour of any Object; and will cause the Whitest to appear of a deep Blue or Red to the naked Eye. And now tell me, whether you are still of Opinion, that every Body hath its true real Colour inhering in it; and if you think it hath, I would fain know farther from you, what certain Distance and Position of the Object, what peculiar Texture and Formation of the Eye, what Degree or Kind of Light is necessary for ascertaining that true Colour, and distinguishing it from apparent ones.

Hyl. I own myself intirely satisfied, that they are all equally apparent; and that there is no such thing as Colour really inhering in external Bodies, but that it is altogether in the Light. And what confirms me in this Opinion is, that in proportion to the Light, Colours are still more or less vivid; and if there be no Light, then are there no Colours perceived. Besides, allowing there are Colours on external Objects, yet how is it possible for us to perceive them? For no external Body affects the Mind, unless it act first on our Organs of Sense. But the only Action of Bodies is Motion; and Motion cannot be communicated

cated otherwiſe than by Impulſe. A diſtant Object therefore cannot act on the Eye, nor conſequently make itſelf or its Properties perceivable to the Soul. Whence it plainly follows, that it is immediately ſome contiguous Subſtance, which operating on the Eye occaſions a Perception of Colours: And ſuch is Light.

Phil. How! is Light then a Subſtance?

Hyl. I tell you, *Philonous*, external Light is nothing but a thin fluid Subſtance, whoſe minute Particles being agitated with a brisk Motion, and in various Manners reflected from the different Surfaces of outward Objects to the Eyes, communicate different Motions to the Optick Nerves; which being propagated to the Brain, cauſe therein various Impreſſions: And theſe are attended with the Senſations of Red, Blue, Yellow, &c.

Phil. It ſeems then, the Light doth no more than ſhake the Optick Nerves.

Hyl. Nothing elſe.

Phil. And conſequent to each particular Motion of the Nerves the Mind is affected with a Senſation, which is ſome particular Colour.

Hyl. Right.

Phil. And theſe Senſations have no Exiſtence without the Mind.

Hyl. They have not.

Phil.

Phil. How then do you affirm that Colours are in the Light, ſince by *Light* you underſtand a corporeal Subſtance external to the Mind?

Hyl. Light and Colours, as immediately perceived by us, I grant cannot exiſt without the Mind. But in themſelves they are only the Motions and Configurations of certain inſenſible Particles of Matter.

Phil. Colours then in the vulgar Senſe, or taken for the immediate Objects of Sight, cannot agree to any but a perceiving Subſtance.

Hyl. That is what I ſay.

Phil. Well then, ſince you give up the Point as to thoſe ſenſible Qualities, which are alone thought Colours by all Mankind beſide, you may hold what you pleaſe with regard to thoſe inviſible ones of the Philoſophers. It is not my Buſineſs to diſpute about them; only I would adviſe you to bethink your ſelf, whether conſidering the Inquiry we are upon, it be prudent for you to affirm, *The Red and Blue which we ſee are not real Colours, but certain unknown Motions and Figures which no Man ever did or can ſee, are truly ſo.* Are not theſe ſhocking Notions, and are not they ſubject to as many ridiculous Inferences, as thoſe you were obliged to renounce before in the Caſe of Sounds?

Hyl.

Hyl. I frankly own, *Philonous*, that it is in vain to ſtand out any longer. Colours, Sounds, Taſtes, in a word, all thoſe termed *Secondary Qualities*, have certainly no Exiſtence without the Mind. But by this Acknowledgment I muſt not be ſuppoſed to derogate any thing from the Reality of Matter or external Objects, ſeeing it is no more than ſeveral Philoſophers maintain, who nevertheleſs are the fartheſt imaginable from denying Matter. For the clearer Underſtanding of this, you muſt know ſenſible Qualities are by Philoſophers divided into *Primary* and *Secondary*. The former are Extenſion, Figure, Solidity, Gravity, Motion, and Reſt. And theſe they hold exiſt really in Bodies. The latter are thoſe above enumerated; or briefly, all ſenſible Qualities beſide the Primary, which they aſſert are only ſo many Senſations or Ideas exiſting no where but in the Mind. But all this, I doubt not, you are already appriſed of. For my part, I have been a long time ſenſible there was ſuch an Opinion current among Philoſophers, but was never thoroughly convinced of its Truth till now.

Phil. You are ſtill then of Opinion, that Extenſion and Figures are inherent in external unthinking Subſtances.

Hyl. I am.

Phil. But what if the ſame Arguments which are brought againſt Secondary Qualities, will hold good againſt theſe alſo?

Hyl. Why then I ſhall be obliged to think, they too exiſt only in the Mind.

Phil. Is it your Opinion, the very Figure and Extenſion which you perceive by Senſe, exiſt in the outward Object or material Subſtance?

Hyl. It is.

Phil. Have all other Animals as good Grounds to think the ſame of the Figure and Extenſion which they ſee and feel?

Hyl. Without doubt, if they have any Thought at all.

Phil. Anſwer me, *Hylas.* Think you the Senſes were beſtowed upon all Animals for their Preſervation and Well-being in Life? or were they given to Men alone for this End?

Hyl. I make no queſtion but they have the ſame Uſe in all other Animals.

Phil. If ſo, is it not neceſſary they ſhould be enabled by them to perceive their own Limbs, and thoſe Bodies which are capable of harming them?

Hyl. Certainly.

Phil. A Mite therefore muſt be ſuppoſed to ſee his own Foot, and Things equal or even leſs than it, as Bodies of ſome conſiderable Dimenſion; though at the ſame time

time they appear to you ſcarce diſcernible, or at beſt as ſo many viſible Points.

Hyl. I cannot deny it.

Phil. And to Creatures leſs than the Mite they will ſeem yet larger.

Hyl. They will.

Phil. Inſomuch that what you can hardly diſcern, will to another extremely minute Animal appear as ſome huge Mountain.

Hyl. All this I grant.

Phil. Can one and the ſame thing be at the ſame time in itſelf of different Dimenſions?

Hyl. That were abſurd to imagine.

Phil. But from what you have laid down it follows, that both the Extenſion by you perceived, and that perceived by the Mite itſelf, as likewiſe all thoſe perceived by leſſer Animals, are each of them the true Extenſion of the Mite's Foot, that is to ſay, by your own Principles you are led into an Abſurdity.

Hyl. There ſeems to be ſome Difficulty in the Point.

Phil. Again, have you not acknowledged that no real inherent Property of any Object can be changed, without ſome Change in the thing itſelf?

Hyl. I have.

Phil. But as we approach to or recede from an Object, the visible Extension varies, being at one Distance ten or an hundred times greater than at another. Doth it not therefore follow from hence likewise, that it is not really inherent in the Object?

Hyl. I own I am at a loss what to think.

Phil. Your Judgment will soon be determined, if you will venture to think as freely concerning this Quality, as you have done concerning the rest. Was it not admitted as a good Argument, that neither Heat nor Cold was in the Water, because it seemed warm to one Hand, and cold to the other?

Hyl. It was.

Phil. Is it not the very same Reasoning to conclude, there is no Extension or Figure in an Object, because to one Eye it shall seem little, smooth, and round, when at the same time it appears to the other, great, uneven, and angular?

Hyl. The very same. But doth this latter Fact ever happen?

Phil. You may at any time make the Experiment, by looking with one Eye bare, and with the other through a Microscope.

Hyl.

Hyl. I know not how to maintain it, and yet I am loth to give up *Extension*, I see so many odd Consequences following upon such a Concession.

Phil. Odd, say you? After the Concessions already made, I hope you will stick at nothing for its Oddness. But on the other hand should it not seem very odd, if the general reasoning which includes all other sensible Qualities did not also include Extension? If it be allowed that no Idea nor any thing like an Idea can exist in an unperceiving Substance, then surely it follows, that no Figure or Mode of Extension, which we can either perceive or imagine, or have any Idea of, can be really inherent in Matter; not to mention the peculiar Difficulty there must be, in conceiving a material Substance, prior to and distinct from Extension, to be the *Substratum* of Extension. Be the sensible Quality what it will, Figure, or Sound, or Colour; it seems alike impossible it should subsist in that which doth not perceive it.

Hyl. I give up the Point for the present, reserving still a Right to retract my Opinion, in case I shall hereafter discover any false Step in my Progress to it.

Phil. That is a Right you cannot be denied. Figures and Extension being dis-

O 3 patched,

patched, we proceed next to *Motion.* Can a real Motion in any external Body be at the ſame time both very ſwift and very ſlow?

Hyl. It cannot.

Phil. Is not the Motion of a Body ſwift in a reciprocal Proportion to the time it takes up in deſcribing any given Space? Thus a Body that deſcribes a Mile in an Hour, moves three times faſter than it would in caſe it deſcribed only a Mile in three Hours.

Hyl. I agree with you.

Phil. And is not Time meaſured by the Succeſſion of Ideas in our Minds?

Hyl. It is.

Phil. And is it not poſſible Ideas ſhould ſucceed one another twice as faſt in your Mind, as they do in mine, or in that of ſome Spirit of another kind.

Hyl. I own it.

Phil. Conſequently the ſame Body may to another ſeem to perform its Motion over any Space in half the time that it doth to you. And the ſame Reaſoning will hold as to any other Proportion: That is to ſay, according to your Principles (ſince the Motions perceived are both really in the Object) it is poſſible one and the ſame Body ſhall be really moved the ſame way at once, both

both very ſwift and very ſlow. How is this conſiſtent either with common Senſe, or with what you juſt now granted?

Hyl. I have nothing to ſay to it.

Phil. Then as for *Solidity*; either you do not mean any ſenſible Quality by that Word, and ſo it is beſide our Inquiry: Or if you do, it muſt be either Hardneſs or Reſiſtance. But both the one and the other are plainly relative to our Senſes: It being evident, that what ſeems hard to one Animal, may appear ſoft to another, who hath greater Force and Firmneſs of Limbs. Nor is it leſs plain, that the Reſiſtance I feel is not in the Body.

Hyl. I own the very Senſation of Reſiſtance, which is all you immediately perceive, is not in the *Body*, but the Cauſe of that Senſation is.

Phil. But the Cauſes of our Senſations are not Things immediately perceived, and therefore not ſenſible. This Point I thought had been already determined.

Hyl. I own it was; but you will pardon me if I ſeem a little embaraſſed: I know not how to quit my old Notions.

Phil. To help you out, do but conſider, that if Extenſion be once acknowledged to have no Exiſtence without the Mind, the ſame muſt neceſſarily be granted of Motion, Solidity, and Gravity, ſince they all evidently ſuppoſe Extenſion. It is therefore ſuperfluous to inquire particularly concerning each of them. In denying Extenſion, you have denied them all to have any real Exiſtence.

Hyl. I wonder, *Philonous*, if what you ſay be true, why thoſe Philoſophers who deny the Secondary Qualities any real Exiſtence, ſhould yet attribute it to the Primary. If there is no Difference between them, how can this be accounted for?

Phil. It is not my buſineſs to account for every Opinion of the Philoſophers. But among other Reaſons which may be aſſigned for this, it ſeems probable, that Pleaſure and Pain being rather annexed to the former than the latter, may be one. Heat and Cold, Taſtes and Smells, have ſomething more vividly pleaſing or diſagreeable than the Ideas of Extenſion, Figure, and Motion, affect us with. And it being too viſibly abſurd to hold, that Pain or Pleaſure can be in an unperceiving Subſtance, Men are more eaſily weaned from believing the external Exiſtence of the Secondary, than the Primary Qualities. You will be ſatisfied there is ſomething in this, if you recollect the Difference you made between an intenſe and more moderate Degree of Heat, allowing the one a real Exiſtence, while you denied it to the other. But after

ter all, there is no rational Ground for that Diſtinction; for ſurely an indifferent Senſation is as truly *a Senſation*, as one more pleaſing or painful; and conſequently ſhould not any more than they be ſuppoſed to exiſt in an unthinking Subject.

Hyl. It is juſt come into my Head, *Philonous*, that I have ſomewhere heard of a Diſtinction between abſolute and ſenſible Extenſion. Now though it be acknowledged that *great* and *ſmall*, conſiſting merely in the Relation which other extended Beings have to the Parts of our own Bodies, do not really inhere in the Subſtances themſelves; yet nothing obliges us to hold the ſame with regard to *abſolute Extenſion*, which is ſomething abſtracted from *great* and *ſmall*, from this or that particular Magnitude or Figure. So likewiſe as to Motion, *ſwift* and *ſlow* are altogether relative to the Succeſſion of Ideas in our own Minds. But it doth not follow, becauſe thoſe Modifications of Motion exiſt not without the Mind, that therefore abſolute Motion abſtracted from them doth not.

Phil. Pray what is it that diſtinguiſhes one Motion, or one Part of Extenſion from another? Is it not ſomething ſenſible, as ſome Degree of Swiftneſs or Slowneſs, ſome certain Magnitude or Figure peculiar to each?

Hyl.

Hyl. I think ſo.

Phil. Theſe Qualities therefore ſtripped of all ſenſible Properties, are without all ſpecific and numerical Differences, as the Schools call them.

Hyl. They are.

Phil. That is to ſay, they are Extenſion in general, and Motion in general.

Hyl. Let it be ſo.

Phil. But it is an univerſally received Maxim, That *Every thing which exiſts, is particular*. How then can Motion in general, or Extenſion in general exiſt in any corporeal Subſtance?

Hyl. I will take time to ſolve your Difficulty.

Phil. But I think the Point may be ſpeedily decided. Without doubt you can tell, whether you are able to frame this or that Idea. Now I am content to put our Diſpute on this Iſſue. If you can frame in your Thoughts a diſtinct abſtract Idea of Motion or Extenſion, diveſted of all thoſe ſenſible Modes, as ſwift and ſlow, great and ſmall, round and ſquare, and the like, which are acknowledged to exiſt only in the Mind, I will then yield the Point you contend for. But if you cannot, it will be unreaſonable on your Side to inſiſt any longer upon what you have no Notion of.

Hyl. To confeſs ingenuouſly, I cannot.

Phil.

Phil. Can you even ſeparate the Ideas of Extenſion and Motion, from the Ideas of all thoſe Qualities which they who make the Diſtinction, term *Secondary*.

Hyl. What! is it not an eaſy Matter, to conſider Extenſion and Motion by themſelves, abſtracted from all other ſenſible Qualities? Pray how do the Mathematicians treat of them?

Phil. I acknowledge, *Hylas*, it is not difficult to form general Propoſitions and Reaſonings about thoſe Qualities, without mentioning any other; and in this Senſe to conſider or treat of them abſtractedly. But how doth it follow that becauſe I can pronounce the Word *Motion* by itſelf, I can form the Idea of it in my Mind excluſive of Body? Or becauſe Theoremes may be made of Extenſion and Figures, without any mention of *great* or *ſmall*, or any other ſenſible Mode or Quality; that therefore it is poſſible ſuch an abſtract Idea of Extenſion, without any particular Size or Figure, or ſenſible Quality, ſhould be diſtinctly formed, and apprehended by the Mind? Mathematicians treat of Quantity, without regarding what other ſenſible Qualities it is attended with, as being altogether indifferent to their Demonſtrations. But when laying aſide the Words, they contemplate the bare Ideas, I believe you will

will find, they are not the pure abstracted Ideas of Extension.

Hyl. But what say you to *pure Intellect?* May not abstracted Ideas be framed by that Faculty?

Phil. Since I cannot frame abstract Ideas at all, it is plain, I cannot frame them by the help of *pure Intellect*, whatsoever Faculty you understand by those Words. Besides, not to inquire into the Nature of pure Intellect and its spiritual Objects, as *Virtue*, *Reason*, *God*, or the like; thus much seems manifest, that sensible Things are only to be perceived by Sense, or represented by the Imagination. Figures therefore and Extension being originally perceived by Sense, do not belong to pure Intellect. But for your farther Satisfaction, try if you can frame the Idea of any Figure, abstracted from all Particularities of Size, or even from other sensible Qualities.

Hyl. Let me think a little——I do not find that I can.

Phil. And can you think it possible, that should really exist in Nature, which implies a Repugnancy in its Conception?

Hyl. By no means.

Phil. Since therefore it is impossible even for the Mind to disunite the Ideas of Extension and Motion from all other sensible

ſible Qualities, doth it not follow, that where the one exiſt, there neceſſarily the other exiſt likewiſe?

Hyl. It ſhould ſeem ſo.

Phil. Conſequently the very ſame Arguments which you admitted, as concluſive againſt the Secondary Qualities, are without any farther Application of Force againſt the Primary too. Beſides, if you will truſt your Senſes, is it not plain all ſenſible Qualities coexiſt, or to them, appear as being in the ſame Place? Do they ever repreſent a Motion, or Figure, as being diveſted of all other viſible and tangible Qualities?

Hyl. You need ſay no more on this Head. I am free to own, if there be no ſecret Error or Overſight in our Proceedings hitherto, that all ſenſible Qualities are alike to be denied Exiſtence without the Mind. But my Fear is, that I have been too liberal in my former Conceſſions, or overlooked ſome Fallacy or other. In ſhort, I did not take time to think.

Phil. For that matter, *Hylas*, you may take what time you pleaſe in reviewing the Progreſs of our Inquiry. You are at liberty to recover any Slips you might have made, or offer whatever you have omitted, which makes for your firſt Opinion.

Hyl.

Hyl. One great Overſight I take to be this: That I did not ſufficiently diſtinguiſh the *Object* from the *Senſation.* Now though this latter may not exiſt without the Mind, yet it will not thence follow that the former cannot.

Phil. What Object do you mean? the Object of the Senſes?

Hyl. The ſame.

Phil. It is then immediately perceived.

Hyl. Right.

Phil. Make me to underſtand the Difference between what is immediately perceived, and a Senſation.

Hyl. The Senſation I take to be an Act of the Mind perceiving; beſide which, there is ſomething perceived; and this I call the *Object.* For Example, there is Red and Yellow on that Tulip. But then the Act of perceiving thoſe Colours is in me only, and not in the Tulip.

Phil. What Tulip do you ſpeak of? is it that which you ſee?

Hyl. The ſame.

Phil. And what do you ſee beſide Colour, Figure, and Extenſion?

Hyl. Nothing.

Phil. What you would ſay then is, that the Red and Yellow are coexiſtent with the Extenſion; is it not?

Hyl.

Hyl. That is not all; I would ſay, They have a real Exiſtence without the Mind, in ſome unthinking Subſtance.

Phil. That the Colours are really in the Tulip which I ſee, is manifeſt. Neither can it be denied, that this Tulip may exiſt independent of your Mind or mine; but that any immediate Object of the Senſes, that is, any Idea, or Combination of Ideas, ſhould exiſt in an unthinking Subſtance, or exterior to all Minds, is in itſelf an evident Contradiction. Nor can I imagine how this follows from what you ſaid juſt now, to wit that the Red and Yellow were on the Tulip *you ſaw*, ſince you do not pretend to *ſee* that unthinking Subſtance.

Hyl. You have an artful way, *Philonous*, of diverting our Inquiry from the Subject.

Phil. I ſee you have no mind to be preſſed that way. To return then to your Diſtinction between *Senſation* and *Object*; if I take you right, you diſtinguiſh in every Perception two Things, the one an Action of the Mind, the other not.

Hyl. True.

Phil. And this Action cannot exiſt in, or belong to any unthinking thing; but whatever beſide is implied in a Perception, may.

Hyl. That is my Meaning.

Phil.

Phil. So that if there was a Perception without any Act of the Mind, it were possible such a Perception should exist in an unthinking Substance.

Hyl. I grant it. But it is impossible there should be such a Perception.

Phil. When is the Mind said to be active?

Hyl. When it produces, puts an end to, or changes any thing.

Phil. Can the Mind produce, discontinue, or change any thing but by an Act of the Will?

Hyl. It cannot.

Phil. The Mind therefore is to be accounted active in its Perceptions, so far forth as Volition is included in them.

Hyl. It is.

Phil. In plucking this Flower, I am active, because I do it by the Motion of my Hand, which was consequent upon my Volition; so likewise in applying it to my Nose. But is either of these Smelling?

Hyl. No.

Phil. I act too in drawing the Air through my Nose; because my Breathing so rather than otherwise, is the Effect of my Volition. But neither can this be called *Smelling:* For if it were, I should smell every time I breathed in that manner.

Hyl.

Hyl. True.

Phil. Smelling then is ſomewhat conſequent to all this.

Hyl. It is.

Phil. But I do not find my Will concerned any farther. Whatever more there is, as that I perceive ſuch a particular Smell or any Smell at all, this is independent of my Will, and therein I am altogether paſſive. Do you find it otherwiſe with you, *Hylas?*

Hyl. No, the very ſame.

Phil. Then as to Seeing, is it not in your Power to open your Eyes, or keep them ſhut; to turn them this or that way?

Hyl. Without doubt.

Phil. But doth it in like manner depend on your Will, that in looking on this Flower, you perceive *White* rather than any other Colour? Or directing your open Eyes toward yonder Part of the Heaven, can you avoid ſeeing the Sun? Or is Light or Darkneſs the Effect of your Volition?

Hyl. No certainly.

Phil. You are then in theſe Reſpects altogether paſſive.

Hyl. I am.

Phil. Tell me now, whether *Seeing* conſiſts in perceiving Light and Colours, or in opening and turning the Eyes?

Hyl. Without doubt, in the former.

Phil. Since therefore you are in the very Perception of Light and Colours altogether passive, what is become of that Action you were speaking of, as an Ingredient in every Sensation? And doth it not follow from your own Concessions, that the Perception of Light and Colours, including no Action in it, may exist in an unperceiving Substance? And is not this a plain Contradiction?

Hyl. I know not what to think of it.

Phil. Besides, since you distinguish the *Active* and *Passive* in every Perception, you must do it in that of Pain. But how is it possible that Pain, be it as little active as you please, should exist in an unperceiving Substance? In short, do but consider the Point, and then confess ingenuously, whether Light and Colours, Tastes, Sounds, &c. are not all equally Passions or Sensations in the Soul. You may indeed call them *external Objects*, and give them in Words what Subsistence you please. But examine your own Thoughts, and then tell me whether it be not as I say?

Hyl. I acknowledge, *Philonous*, that upon a fair Observation of what passes in my Mind, I can discover nothing else, but that I am a thinking Being, affected with Variety of Sensations; neither is it possible to conceive how a Sensation should exist in

an

an unperceiving Subſtance. But then on the other hand, when I look on ſenſible Things in a different View, conſidering them as ſo many Modes and Qualities, I find it neceſſary to ſuppoſe a material *Subſtratum*, without which they cannot be conceived to exiſt.

Phil. *Material Subſtratum* call you it? Pray, by which of your Senſes came you acquainted with that Being?

Hyl. It is not itſelf ſenſible; its Modes and Qualities only being perceived by the Senſes.

Phil. I preſume then, it was by Reflexion and Reaſon you obtained the Idea of it.

Hyl. I do not pretend to any proper poſitive Idea of it. However I conclude it exiſts, becauſe Qualities cannot be conceived to exiſt without a Support.

Phil. It ſeems then you have only a relative Notion of it, or that you conceive it not otherwiſe than by conceiving the Relation it bears to ſenſible Qualities.

Hyl. Right.

Phil. Be pleaſed therefore to let me know wherein that Relation conſiſts.

Hyl. Is it not ſufficiently expreſſed in the Term *Subſtratum*, or *Subſtance*?

Phil. If ſo, the Word *Subſtratum* ſhould import, that it is ſpread under the ſenſible Qualities or Accidents.

Hyl. True.

Phil. And consequently under Extension.

Hyl. I own it.

Phil. It is therefore somewhat in its own Nature intirely distinct from Extension.

Hyl. I tell you, Extension is only a Mode, and Matter is something that supports Modes. And is it not evident the Thing supported is different from the Thing supporting?

Phil. So that something distinct from, and exclusive of Extension, is supposed to be the *Substratum* of Extension.

Hyl. Just so.

Phil. Answer me, *Hylas*. Can a Thing be spread without Extension? or is not the Idea of Extension necessarily included in *Spreading*?

Hyl. It is.

Phil. Whatsoever therefore you suppose spread under any thing, must have in itself an Extension distinct from the Extension of that Thing under which it is spread.

Hyl. It must.

Phil. Consequently every corporeal Substance being the *Substratum* of Extension, must have in itself another Extension by which it is qualified to be a *Substratum*: And

And ſo on to Infinity. And I ask whether this be not abſurd in itſelf, and repugnant to what you granted juſt now, to wit, that the *Subſtratum* was ſomething diſtinct from, and excluſive of Extenſion.

Hyl. Ay but, *Philonous*, you take me wrong. I do not mean that Matter is *ſpread* in a groſs literal Senſe under Extenſion. The Word *Subſtratum* is uſed only to expreſs in general the ſame thing with *Subſtance.*

Phil. Well then, let us examine the Relation implied in the Term *Subſtance.* Is it not that it ſtands under Accidents?

Hyl. The very ſame.

Phil. But that one thing may ſtand under or ſupport another, muſt it not be extended?

Hyl. It muſt.

Phil. Is not therefore this Suppoſition liable to the ſame Abſurdity with the former?

Hyl. You ſtill take Things in a ſtrict literal Senſe: That is not fair, *Philonous.*

Phil. I am not for impoſing any Senſe on your Words: You are at Liberty to explain them as you pleaſe. Only I beſeech you, make me underſtand ſomething by them. You tell me, Matter ſupports or ſtands under Accidents. How! is it as your Legs ſupport your Body?

Hyl. No; that is the literal Senſe.

Phil. Pray let me know any Senſe, literal or not literal, that you underſtand it in.——How long muſt I wait for an Anſwer, *Hylas?*

Hyl. I declare I know not what to ſay. I once thought I underſtood well enough what was meant by Matter's ſupporting Accidents. But now the more I think on it, the leſs can I comprehend it; in ſhort, I find that I know nothing of it.

Phil. It ſeems then you have no Idea at all, neither relative nor poſitive of Matter; you know neither what it is in itſelf, nor what Relation it bears to Accidents.

Hyl. I acknowledge it.

Phil. And yet you aſſerted, that you could not conceive how Qualities or Accidents ſhould really exiſt, without conceiving at the ſame time a material Support of them.

Hyl. I did.

Phil. That is to ſay, when you conceive the real Exiſtence of Qualities, you do withal conceive ſomething which you cannot conceive.

Hyl. It was wrong I own. But ſtill I fear there is ſome Fallacy or other. Pray what think you of this? It is juſt come into my Head, that the Ground of all our Miſtake lies in your treating of each Quality

lity by itſelf. Now, I grant that each Quality cannot ſingly ſubſiſt without the Mind. Colour cannot without Extenſion, neither can Figure without ſome other ſenſible Quality. But as the ſeveral Qualities united or blended together form intire ſenſible Things, nothing hinders why ſuch Things may not be ſuppoſed to exiſt without the Mind.

Phil. Either, *Hylas*, you are jeſting, or have a very bad Memory. Though indeed we went through all the Qualities by Name one after another; yet my Arguments, or rather your Conceſſions no where tended to prove, that the Secondary Qualities did not ſubſiſt each alone by itſelf; but that they were not *at all* without the Mind. Indeed in treating of Figure and Motion, we concluded they could not exiſt without the Mind, becauſe it was impoſſible even in Thought to ſeparate them from all Secondary Qualities, ſo as to conceive them exiſting by themſelves. But then this was not the only Argument made uſe of upon that Occaſion. But (to paſs by all that hath been hitherto ſaid, and reckon it for nothing, if you will have it ſo) I am content to put the whole upon this Iſſue. If you can conceive it poſſible for any Mixture or Combination of Qualities, or any ſenſible Object whatever, to exiſt without the Mind, then I will grant it actually to be so.

Hyl. If it comes to that, the Point will soon be decided. What more easy than to conceive a Tree or House existing by itself, independent of, and unperceived by any Mind whatsoever? I do at this present time conceive them existing after that manner.

Phil. How say you, *Hylas*, can you see a thing which is at the same time unseen?

Hyl. No, that were a Contradiction.

Phil. Is it not as great a Contradiction to talk of *conceiving* a thing which is *unconceived?*

Hyl. It is.

Phil. The Tree or House therefore which you think of, is conceived by you.

Hyl. How should it be otherwise?

Phil. And what is conceived, is surely in the Mind.

Hyl. Without question, that which is conceived is in the Mind.

Phil. How then came you to say, you conceived a House or Tree existing independent and out of all Minds whatsoever?

Hyl. That was I own an Oversight; but stay, let me consider what led me into it.— It is a pleasant Mistake enough. As I was thinking of a Tree in a solitary Place, where no one was present to see it, methought

thought that was to conceive a Tree as existing unperceived or unthought of, not considering that I myself conceived it all the while. But now I plainly see, that all I can do is to frame Ideas in my own Mind. I may indeed conceive in my own Thoughts the Idea of a Tree, or a House, or a Mountain, but that is all. And this is far from proving, that I can conceive them *existing out of the Minds of all Spirits*.

Phil. You acknowledge then that you cannot possibly conceive, how any one corporeal sensible Thing should exist otherwise than in a Mind.

Hyl. I do.

Phil. And yet you will earnestly contend for the Truth of that which you cannot so much as conceive.

Hyl. I profess I know not what to think, but still there are some Scruples remain with me. Is it not certain I see Things at a Distance? Do we not perceive the Stars and Moon, for Example, to be a great way off? Is not this, I say, manifest to the Senses?

Phil. Do you not in a Dream too perceive those or the like Objects?

Hyl. I do.

Phil. And have they not then the same Appearance of being distant?

Hyl.

Hyl. They have.

Phil. But you do not thence conclude the Apparitions in a Dream to be without the Mind?

Hyl. By no means.

Phil. You ought not therefore to conclude that ſenſible Objects are without the Mind, from their Appearance or Manner wherein they are perceived.

Hyl. I acknowledge it. But doth not my Senſe deceive me in thoſe Caſes?

Phil. By no means. The Idea or Thing which you immediately perceive, neither Senſe nor Reaſon inform you that it actually exiſts without the Mind. By Senſe you only know that you are affected with ſuch certain Senſations of Light and Colours, &c. And theſe you will not ſay are without the Mind.

Hyl. True: But beſide all that, do you not think the Sight ſuggeſts ſomething of *Outneſs* or *Diſtance*?

Phil. Upon approaching a diſtant Object, do the viſible Size and Figure change perpetually, or do they appear the ſame at all Diſtances?

Hyl. They are in a continual Change.

Phil. Sight therefore doth not ſuggeſt or any way inform you, that the viſible Object you immediately perceive, exiſts at

a

a Diſtance *, or will be perceived when you advance farther onward, there being a continued Series of viſible Objects ſucceeding each other, during the whole time of your Approach.

Hyl. It doth not; but ſtill I know, upon ſeeing an Object, what Object I ſhall perceive after having paſſed over a certain Diſtance: No matter whether it be exactly the ſame or no: There is ſtill ſomething of Diſtance ſuggeſted in the Caſe.

Phil. Good *Hylas*, do but reflect a little on the Point, and then tell me whether there be any more in it than this. From the Ideas you actually perceive by Sight, you have by Experience learned to collect what other Ideas you will (according to the ſtanding Order of Nature) be affected with, after ſuch a certain Succeſſion of Time and Motion.

Hyl. Upon the whole, I take it to be nothing elſe.

Phil. Now is it not plain, that if we ſuppoſe a Man born blind was on a ſudden made to ſee, he could at firſt have no Experience of what may be ſuggeſted by Sight.

Hyl. It is.

* See the Eſſay towards a new Theory of Viſion; And its Vindication.

Phil.

Phil. He would not then according to you have any Notion of Diſtance annexed to the Things he ſaw; but would take them for a new Set of Senſations exiſting only in his Mind.

Hyl. It is undeniable.

Phil. But to make it ſtill more plain: Is not *Diſtance* a Line turned endwiſe to the Eye?

Hyl. It is.

Phil. And can a Line ſo ſituated be perceived by Sight?

Hyl. It cannot.

Phil. Doth it not therefore follow that Diſtance is not properly and immediately perceived by Sight?

Hyl. It ſhould ſeem ſo.

Phil. Again, is it your Opinion that Colours are at a Diſtance?

Hyl. It muſt be acknowledged, they are only in the Mind.

Phil. But do not Colours appear to the Eye as coexiſting in the ſame place with Extenſion and Figures?

Hyl. They do.

Phil. How can you then conclude from Sight, that Figures exiſt without, when you acknowledge Colours do not; the ſenſible Appearance being the very ſame with regard to both?

Hyl. I know not what to anſwer.

Phil.

Phil. But allowing that Diſtance was truly and immediately perceived by the Mind, yet it would not thence follow it exiſted out of the Mind. For whatever is immediately perceived is an Idea: And can any *Idea* exiſt out of the Mind?

Hyl. To ſuppoſe that, were abſurd: But inform me, *Philonous*, can we perceive or know nothing beſide our Ideas?

Phil. As for the rational deducing of Cauſes from Effects, that is beſide our Inquiry. And by the Senſes you can beſt tell, whether you perceive any thing which is not immediately perceived. And I ask you, whether the Things immediately perceived, are other than your own Senſations or Ideas? You have indeed more than once, in the Courſe of this Converſation, declared yourſelf on thoſe Points; but you ſeem by this laſt Queſtion to have departed from what you then thought.

Hyl. To ſpeak the Truth, *Philonous*, I think there are two Kinds of Objects, the one perceived immediately, which are likewiſe called *Ideas*; the other are real Things or external Objects perceived by the Mediation of Ideas, which are their Images and Repreſentations. Now I own, Ideas do not exiſt without the Mind; but the latter ſort of Objects do. I am ſorry I did not think of this Diſtinction ſooner;

it

it would probably have cut ſhort your Diſcourſe.

Phil. Are thoſe external Objects perceived by Senſe, or by ſome other Faculty?

Hyl. They are perceived by Senſe.

Phil. How! is there any thing perceived by Senſe, which is not immediately perceived?

Hyl. Yes, *Philonous*, in ſome ſort there is. For Example, when I look on a Picture or Statue of *Julius Cæſar*, I may be ſaid after a manner to perceive him (though not immediately) by my Senſes.

Phil. It ſeems then, you will have our Ideas, which alone are immediately perceived, to be Pictures of external Things: And that theſe alſo are perceived by Senſe, inaſmuch as they have a Conformity or Reſemblance to our Ideas.

Hyl. That is my Meaning.

Phil. And in the ſame way that *Julius Cæſar*, in himſelf inviſible, is nevertheleſs perceived by Sight; real Things in themſelves imperceptible, are perceived by Senſe.

Hyl. In the very ſame.

Phil. Tell me, *Hylas*, when you behold the Picture of *Julius Cæſar*, do you ſee with your Eyes any more than ſome Colours and Figures with a certain Symmetry and Compoſition of the whole?

Hyl. Nothing elſe.

Phil.

Phil. And would not a Man, who had never known any thing of *Julius Cæſar*, ſee as much?

Hyl. He would.

Phil. Conſequently he hath his Sight, and the Uſe of it, in as perfect a Degree as you.

Hyl. I agree with you.

Phil. Whence comes it then that your Thoughts are directed to the *Roman* Emperor, and his are not? This cannot proceed from the Senſations or Ideas of Senſe by you then perceived; ſince you acknowledge you have no Advantage over him in that reſpect. It ſhould ſeem therefore to proceed from Reaſon and Memory: ſhould it not?

Hyl. It ſhould.

Phil. Conſequently it will not follow from that Inſtance, that any thing is perceived by Senſe which is not immediately perceived. Though I grant we may in one Acceptation be ſaid to perceive ſenſible Things mediately by Senſe: That is, when from a frequently perceived Connexion, the immediate Perception of Ideas by one Senſe ſuggeſts to the Mind others perhaps belonging to another Senſe, which are wont to be connected with them. For inſtance, when I hear a Coach drive along the Streets, immediately I perceive only the Sound;

Sound; but from the Experience I have had that ſuch a Sound is connected with a Coach, I am ſaid to hear the Coach. It is nevertheleſs evident, that in truth and ſtrictneſs, nothing can be *heard* but *Sound:* And the Coach is not then properly perceived by Senſe, but ſuggeſted from Experience. So likewiſe when we are ſaid to ſee a red-hot Bar of Iron; the Solidity and Heat of the Iron are not the Objects of Sight, but ſuggeſted to the Imagination by the Colour and Figure, which are properly perceived by that Senſe. In ſhort, thoſe Things alone are actually and ſtrictly perceived by any Senſe, which would have been perceived, in caſe that ſame Senſe had then been firſt conferred on us. As for other Things, it is plain they are only ſuggeſted to the Mind by Experience grounded on former Perceptions. But to return to your Compariſon of *Cæſar*'s Picture, it is plain, if you keep to that, you muſt hold the real Things or Archetypes of our Ideas are not perceived by Senſe, but by ſome internal Faculty of the Soul, as Reaſon or Memory. I would therefore fain know, what Arguments you can draw from Reaſon for the Exiſtence of what you call *real Things* or *material Objects.* Or whether you remember to have ſeen them formerly as they are in themſelves?

or

or if you have heard or read of any one that did.

Hyl. I ſee, *Philonous*, you are diſpoſed to Rallery; but that will never convince me.

Phil. My Aim is only to learn from you, the way to come at the Knowledge of *material Beings*. Whatever we perceive, is perceived either immediately or mediately: By Senſe, or by Reaſon and Reflexion. But as you have excluded Senſe, pray ſhew me what Reaſon you have to believe their Exiſtence; or what *medium* you can poſſibly make uſe of, to prove it either to mine or your own Underſtanding.

Hyl. To deal ingenuouſly, *Philonous*, now I conſider the Point, I do not find I can give you any good Reaſon for it. But thus much ſeems pretty plain, that it is at leaſt poſſible ſuch Things may really exiſt. And as long as there is no Abſurdity in ſuppoſing them, I am reſolved to believe as I did, till you bring good Reaſons to the contrary.

Phil. What! is it come to this, that you only believe the Exiſtence of material Objects, and that your Belief is founded barely on the Poſſibility of its being true? Then you will have me bring Reaſons againſt it: Though another would think it reaſonable, the Proof ſhould lie on him who holds the Affirmative. And after all, this very Point which you are now reſolved to maintain without any Reaſon, is in effect what you have more than once during this Diſcourſe ſeen good Reaſon to give up. But to paſs over all this; if I underſtand you rightly, you ſay our Ideas do not exiſt without the Mind; but that they are Copies, Images, or Repreſentations of certain Originals that do.

Hyl. You take me right.

Phil. They are then like external Things.

Hyl. They are.

Phil. Have thoſe Things a ſtable and permanent Nature independent of our Senſes; or are they in a perpetual Change, upon our producing any Motions in our Bodies, ſuſpending, exerting, or altering our Faculties or Organs of Senſe.

Hyl. Real Things, it is plain, have a fixed and real Nature, which remains the ſame, notwithſtanding any Change in our Senſes, or in the Poſture and Motion of our Bodies; which indeed may affect the Ideas in our Minds, but it were abſurd to think they had the ſame Effect on Things exiſting without the Mind.

Phil. How then is it poſſible, that Things perpetually fleeting and variable as our Ideas, ſhould be Copies or Images of

any

any thing fixed and conſtant? Or in other Words, ſince all ſenſible Qualities, as Size, Figure, Colour, *&c.* that is, our Ideas are continually changing upon every Alteration in the Diſtance, Medium, or Inſtruments of Senſation; how can any determinate material Objects be properly repreſented or painted forth by ſeveral diſtinct Things, each of which is ſo different from and unlike the reſt? Or if you ſay it reſembles ſome one only of our Ideas, how ſhall we be able to diſtinguiſh the true Copy from all the falſe ones?

Hyl. I profeſs, *Philonous*, I am at a loſs. I know not what to ſay to this.

Phil. But neither is this all. Which are material Objects in themſelves, perceptible or imperceptible?

Hyl. Properly and immediately nothing can be perceived but Ideas. All material Things therefore are in themſelves inſenſible, and to be perceived only by their Ideas.

Phil. Ideas then are ſenſible, and their Archetypes or Originals inſenſible.

Hyl. Right.

Phil. But how can that which is ſenſible be like that which is inſenſible? Can a real thing in itſelf *inviſible* be like a *Colour*; or a real thing which is not *audible*, be like a *Sound?* In a word, can any thing be like a Senſation or Idea, but another Senſation or Idea?

Hyl. I muſt own, I think not.

Phil. Is it poſſible there ſhould be any doubt in the Point? Do you not perfectly know your own Ideas?

Hyl. I know them perfectly; ſince what I do not perceive or know, can be no part of my Idea.

Phil. Conſider therefore, and examine them, and then tell me if there be any thing in them which can exiſt without the Mind: or if you can conceive any thing like them exiſting without the Mind.

Hyl. Upon Inquiry, I find it is impoſſible for me to conceive or underſtand how any thing but an Idea can be like an Idea. And it is moſt evident, that *no Idea can exiſt without the Mind.*

Phil. You are therefore by your Principles forced to deny the Reality of ſenſible Things, ſince you made it to conſiſt in an abſolute Exiſtence exterior to the Mind. That is to ſay, you are a downright *Sceptic.* So I have gained my Point, which was to ſhew your Principles led to Scepticiſm.

Hyl. For the preſent I am, if not intirely convinced, at leaſt ſilenced.

Phil.

Phil. I would fain know what more you would require in order to a perfect Conviction. Have you not had the Liberty of explaining yourself all manner of ways? Were any little Slips in Discourse laid hold and insisted on? Or were you not allowed to retract or reinforce any thing you had offered, as best served your Purpose? Hath not every thing you could say been heard and examined with all the Fairness imaginable? In a word, have you not in every Point been convinced out of your own Mouth? And if you can at present discover any Flaw in any of your former Concessions, or think of any remaining Subterfuge, any new Distinction, Colour, or Comment whatsoever, why do you not produce it?

Hyl. A little Patience, *Philonous.* I am at present so amazed to see myself ensnared, and as it were imprisoned in the Labyrinths you have drawn me into, that on the sudden it cannot be expected I should find my way out. You must give me time to look about me, and recollect myself.

Phil. Hark; is not this the College-Bell?

Hyl. It rings for Prayers.

Phil. We will go in then if you please, and meet here again to Morrow Morning. In the mean time you may employ your

Thoughts on this Morning's Diſcourſe, and try if you can find any Fallacy in it, or invent any new means to extricate yourſelf.

Hyl. Agreed.

THE

THE SECOND DIALOGUE.

HYLAS.

I BEG your Pardon, *Philonous*, for not meeting you sooner. All this Morning my Head was so filled with our late Conversation, that I had not leisure to think of the Time of the Day, or indeed of any thing else.

Philonous. I am glad you were so intent upon it, in Hopes if there were any Mistakes in your Concessions, or Fallacies in my Reasonings from them, you will now discover them to me

Hyl. I assure you, I have done nothing ever since I saw you, but search after Mistakes and Fallacies, and with that View have minutely examined the whole Series of Yesterday's Discourse: but all in vain, for the Notions it led me into, upon Review appear still more clear and evident; and the more I consider them, the more irresistibly do they force my Assent.

Phil. And is not this, think you, a Sign that they are genuine, that they proceed from Nature, and are conformable to right Reason? Truth and Beauty are in this alike, that the strictest Survey sets them both off to Advantage. While the false Lustre of Error and Disguise cannot endure being reviewed, or too nearly inspected.

Hyl. I own there is a great deal in what you say. Nor can any one be more intirely satisfied of the Truth of those odd Consequences, so long as I have in View the Reasonings that lead to them. But when these are out of my Thoughts, there seems on the other hand something so satisfactory, so natural and intelligible in the modern way of explaining Things, that I profess I know not how to reject it.

Phil. I know not what way you mean.

Hyl. I mean the way of accounting for our Sensations or Ideas.

Phil. How is that?

Hyl. It is supposed the Soul makes her Residence in some part of the Brain, from which the Nerves take their rise, and are thence

thence extended to all Parts of the Body: And that outward Objects by the different Impressions they make on the Organs of Sense, communicate certain vibrative Motions to the Nerves; and these being filled with Spirits, propagate them to the Brain or Seat of the Soul, which according to the various Impressions or Traces thereby made in the Brain, is variously affected with Ideas.

Phil. And call you this an Explication of the manner whereby we are affected with Ideas?

Hyl. Why not, *Philonous*, have you any thing to object against it?

Phil. I would first know whether I rightly understand your Hypothesis. You make certain Traces in the Brain to be the Causes or Occasions of our Ideas. Pray tell me, whether by the *Brain* you mean any sensible Thing?

Hyl. What else think you I could mean?

Phil. Sensible Things are all immediately perceivable; and those Things which are immediately perceivable, are Ideas; and these exist only in the Mind. Thus much you have, if I mistake not, long since agreed to.

Hyl. I do not deny it.

Phil. The Brain therefore you speak of, being a sensible Thing, exists only in the Mind.

Mind. Now, I would fain know whether you think it reaſonable to ſuppoſe, that one Idea or Thing exiſting in the Mind, occaſions all other Ideas. And if you think ſo, pray how do you account for the Origin of that Primary Idea or Brain itſelf?

Hyl. I do not explain the Origin of our Ideas by that Brain which is perceivable to Senſe, this being itſelf only a Combination of ſenſible Ideas, but by another which I imagine.

Phil. But are not Things imagined as truly in the Mind as Things perceived?

Hyl. I muſt confeſs they are.

Phil. It comes therefore to the ſame thing; and you have been all this while accounting for Ideas, by certain Motions or Impreſſions in the Brain, that is, by ſome Alterations in an Idea, whether ſenſible or imaginable, it matters not.

Hyl. I begin to ſuſpect my Hypotheſis.

Phil. Beſide Spirits, all that we know or conceive are our own Ideas. When therefore you ſay, all Ideas are occaſioned by Impreſſions in the Brain, do you conceive this Brain or no? If you do, then you talk of Ideas imprinted in an Idea, cauſing that ſame Idea, which is abſurd. If you do not conceive it, you talk unintelligibly, inſtead of forming a reaſonable Hypotheſis.

Hyl.

Hyl. I now clearly ſee it was a mere Dream. There is nothing in it.

Phil. You need not be much concerned at it: for after all, this way of explaining Things, as you called it, could never have ſatisfied any reaſonable Man. What Connexion is there between a Motion in the Nerves, and the Senſations of Sound or Colour in the Mind? or how is it poſſible theſe ſhould be the Effect of that?

Hyl. But I could never think it had ſo little in it, as now it ſeems to have.

Phil. Well then, are you at length ſatisfied that no ſenſible Things have a real Exiſtence; and that you are in truth an arrant *Sceptic?*

Hyl. It is too plain to be denied.

Phil. Look! are not the Fields covered with a delightful Verdure? Is there not ſomething in the Woods and Groves, in the Rivers and clear Springs that ſooths, that delights, that tranſports the Soul? At the Proſpect of the wide and deep Ocean, or ſome huge Mountain whoſe Top is loſt in the Clouds, or of an old gloomy Foreſt, are not our Minds filled with a pleaſing Horror? Even in Rocks and Deſerts, is there not an agreeable Wildneſs? How ſincere a Pleaſure is it to behold the natural Beauties of the Earth! To preſerve and renew our Reliſh for them, is not the

Veil

Veil of Night alternately drawn over her Face, and doth ſhe not change her Dreſs with the Seaſons? How aptly are the Elements diſpoſed? What Variety and Uſe in the meaneſt Productions of Nature? What Delicacy, what Beauty, what Contrivance in animal and vegetable Bodies? How exquiſitely are all Things ſuited, as well to their particular Ends, as to conſtitute appoſite Parts of the Whole! And while they mutually aid and ſupport, do they not alſo ſet off and illuſtrate each other? Raiſe now your Thoughts from this Ball of Earth, to all thoſe glorious Luminaries that adorn the high Arch of Heaven. The Motion and Situation of the Planets, are they not admirable for Uſe and Order? Were thoſe (miſcalled *Erratique*) Globes ever known to ſtray, in their repeated Journeys through the pathleſs Void? Do they not meaſure Areas round the Sun ever proportioned to the Times? So fixed, ſo immutable are the Laws by which the unſeen Author of Nature actuates the Univerſe. How vivid and radiant is the Luſtre of the fixed Stars! How magnificent and rich that negligent Profuſion, with which they appear to be ſcattered throughout the whole Azure Vault! Yet if you take the Teleſcope, it brings into your Sight a new Hoſt of Stars that eſcape the naked Eye. Here they ſeem

ſeem contiguous and minute, but to a nearer View immenſe Orbs of Light at various Diſtances, far ſunk in the Abyſs of Space. Now you muſt call Imagination to your Aid. The feeble narrow Senſe cannot deſcry innumerable Worlds revolving round the central Fires; and in thoſe Worlds the Energy of an all-perfect Mind diſplayed in endleſs Forms. But neither Senſe nor Imagination are big enough to comprehend the boundleſs Extent with all its glittering Furniture. Though the labouring Mind exert and ſtrain each Power to its utmoſt reach, there ſtill ſtands out ungraſped a Surpluſage immeaſurable. Yet all the vaſt Bodies that compoſe this mighty Frame, how diſtant and remote ſoever, are by ſome ſecret Mechaniſm, ſome divine Art and Force linked in a mutual Dependence and Intercourſe with each other, even with this Earth, which was almoſt ſlipt from my Thoughts, and loſt in the Croud of Worlds. Is not the whole Syſtem immenſe, beautiful, glorious beyond Expreſſion and beyond Thought! What treatment then do thoſe Philoſophers deſerve, who would deprive theſe noble and delightful Scenes of all Reality? How ſhould thoſe Principles be entertained, that lead us to think all the viſible Beauty of the Creation a falſe imaginary Glare? To be plain, can

can you expect this Scepticism of yours will not be thought extravagantly absurd by all Men of Sense?

Hyl. Other Men may think as they please: But for your part you have nothing to reproach me with. My Comfort is, you are as much a *Sceptic* as I am.

Phil. There, *Hylas*, I must beg leave to differ from you.

Hyl. What! have you all along agreed to the Premises, and do you now deny the Conclusion, and leave me to maintain those Paradoxes by myself which you led me into? This surely is not fair.

Phil. I deny that I agreed with you in those Notions that led to Scepticism. You indeed said, the Reality of sensible Things consisted in an *absolute Existence* out of the Minds of Spirits, or distinct from their being perceived. And pursuant to this Notion of Reality, you are obliged to deny sensible Things any real Existence: That is, according to your own Definition, you profess yourself a *Sceptic*. But I neither said nor thought the Reality of sensible Things was to be defined after that manner. To me it is evident, for the Reasons you allow of, that sensible Things cannot exist otherwise than in a Mind or Spirit. Whence I conclude, not that they have no real Existence, but that seeing they depend

not

not on my Thought, and have an Exiſtence diſtinct from being perceived by me, *there muſt be ſome other Mind wherein they exiſt.* As ſure therefore as the ſenſible World really exiſts, ſo ſure is there an infinite omnipreſent Spirit who contains and ſupports it.

Hyl. What! this is no more than I and all Chriſtians hold; nay, and all others too who believe there is a God, and that he knows and comprehends all Things.

Phil. Ay, but here lies the Difference. Men commonly believe that all Things are known or perceived by God, becauſe they believe the Being of a God, whereas I on the other ſide, immediately and neceſſarily conclude the Being of a God, becauſe all ſenſible Things muſt be perceived by him.

Hyl. But ſo long as we all believe the ſame thing, what matter is it how we come by that Belief?

Phil. But neither do we agree in the ſame Opinion. For Philoſophers, though they acknowledge all corporeal Beings to be perceived by God, yet they attribute to them an abſolute Subſiſtence diſtinct from their being perceived by any Mind whatever, which I do not. Beſides, is there no Difference between ſaying, *There is a God, therefore he perceives all Things:* and ſaying, *Senſible Things do really exiſt: and if they*

they really exiſt, they are neceſſarily perceived by an infinite Mind: therefore there is an infinite Mind, or God. This furniſhes you with a direct and immediate Demonſtration, from a moſt evident Principle, of the *Being of a God.* Divines and Philoſophers had proved beyond all Controverſy, from the Beauty and Uſefulneſs of the ſeveral Parts of the Creation, that it was the Workmanſhip of God. But that ſetting aſide all Help of Aſtronomy and natural Philoſophy, all Contemplation of the Contrivance, Order, and Adjuſtment of Things, an infinite Mind ſhould be neceſſarily inferred from the bare Exiſtence of the ſenſible World, is an Advantage peculiar to them only who have made this eaſy Reflexion: That the ſenſible World is that which we perceive by our ſeveral Senſes; and that nothing is perceived by the Senſes beſide Ideas; and that no Idea or Archetype of an Idea can exiſt otherwiſe than in a Mind. You may now, without any laborious ſearch into the Sciences, without any Subtilty of Reaſon, or tedious Length of Diſcourſe, oppoſe and baffle the moſt ſtrenuous Advocate for Atheiſm. Thoſe miſerable Refuges, whether in an eternal Succeſſion of unthinking Cauſes and Effects, or in a fortuitous Concourſe of Atoms; thoſe wild Imaginations of *Vanini,*

Hobbes,

Hobbes, and *Spinosa*; in a word the whole System of Atheism, is it not intirely overthrown by this single Reflexion on the Repugnancy included in supposing the Whole, or any Part, even the most rude and shapeless of the visible World, to exist without a Mind? Let any one of those Abettors of Impiety but look into his own Thoughts, and there try if he can conceive how so much as a Rock, a Desert, a Chaos, or confused Jumble of Atoms; how any thing at all, either sensible or imaginable, can exist independent of a Mind, and he need go no farther to be convinced of his Folly. Can any thing be fairer than to put a Dispute on such an Issue, and leave it to a Man himself to see if he can conceive, even in Thought, what he holds to be true in Fact, and from a notional to allow it a real Existence?

Hyl. It cannot be denied, there is something highly serviceable to Religion in what you advance. But do you not think it looks very like a Notion entertained by some eminent Moderns, of *seeing all things in God*?

Phil. I would gladly know that Opinion; pray explain it to me.

Hyl. They conceive that the Soul being immaterial, is incapable of being united with material Things, so as to perceive them in themſelves, but that ſhe perceives them by her Union with the Subſtance of God, which being ſpiritual is therefore purely intelligible, or capable of being the immediate Object of a Spirit's Thought. Beſides, the Divine Eſſence contains in it Perfections correſpondent to each created Being; and which are for that Reaſon proper to exhibit or repreſent them to the Mind.

Phil. I do not underſtand how our Ideas, which are Things altogether paſſive and inert, can be the Eſſence, or any Part (or like any Part) of the Eſſence or Subſtance of God, who is an impaſſive, indiviſible, purely active Being. Many more Difficulties and Objections there are, which occur at firſt View againſt this Hypotheſis; but I ſhall only add that it is liable to all the Abſurdities of the common Hypotheſes, in making a created World exiſt otherwiſe than in the Mind of a Spirit. Beſide all which it hath this peculiar to itſelf; that it makes that material World ſerve to no Purpoſe. And if it paſs for a good Argument againſt other Hypotheſes in the Sciences, that they ſuppoſe Nature or the Divine Wiſdom to make ſomething in vain, or do that by tedious round-about Methods, which might have been performed in a much more eaſy and compendious

dious way, what ſhall we think of that Hypotheſis which ſuppoſes the whole World made in vain?

Hyl. But what ſay you, are not you too of Opinion that we ſee all Things in God? If I miſtake not, what you advance comes near it.

Phil. Few Men think, yet all will have Opinions. Hence Mens Opinions are ſuperficial and confuſed. It is nothing ſtrange that Tenets, which in themſelves are ever ſo different, ſhould nevertheleſs be confounded with each other by thoſe who do not conſider them attentively. I ſhall not therefore be ſurpriſed, if ſome Men imagine that I run into the Enthuſiaſm of *Malbranche*, though in truth I am very remote from it. He builds on the moſt abſtract general Ideas, which I intirely diſclaim. He aſſerts an abſolute external World, which I deny. He maintains that we are deceived by our Senſes, and know not the real Natures or the true Forms and Figures of extended Beings; of all which I hold the direct contrary. So that upon the whole there are no Principles more fundamentally oppoſite than his and mine. It muſt be owned I intirely agree with what the holy Scripture ſaith, *That in God we live, and move, and have our Being.* But that we ſee Things in his Eſſence after the

 manner

manner above ſet forth, I am far from believing. Take here in brief my Meaning. It is evident that the Things I perceive are my own Ideas, and that no Idea can exiſt unleſs it be in a Mind. Nor is it leſs plain that theſe Ideas or Things by me perceived, either themſelves or their Archetypes, exiſt independently of my Mind, ſince I know myſelf not to be their Author, it being out of my power to determine at pleaſure, what particular Ideas I ſhall be affected with upon opening my Eyes or Ears. They muſt therefore exiſt in ſome other Mind, whoſe Will it is they ſhould be exhibited to me. The Things, I ſay, immediately perceived, are Ideas or Senſations, call them which you will. But how can any Idea or Senſation exiſt in, or be produced by, any thing but a Mind or Spirit? This indeed is inconceivable; and to aſſert that which is inconceivable, is to talk Nonſenſe: Is it not?

Hyl. Without doubt.

Phil. But on the other hand, it is very conceivable that they ſhould exiſt in, and be produced by, a Spirit; ſince this is no more than I daily experience in myſelf, inaſmuch as I perceive numberleſs Ideas; and by an Act of my Will can form a great Variety of them, and raiſe them up in my Imagination: Though it muſt be confeſſed, theſe

theſe Creatures of the Fancy are not altogether ſo diſtinct, ſo ſtrong, vivid, and permanent, as thoſe perceived by my Senſes, which latter are called *Real Things*. From all which I conclude, *there is a Mind which affects me every Moment with all the ſenſible Impreſſions I perceive*. And from the Variety, Order, and Manner of theſe, I conclude the Author of them to be *wiſe, powerful, and good, beyond comprehenſion*. Mark it well; I do not ſay, I ſee Things by perceiving that which repreſents them in the intelligible Subſtance of God. This I do not underſtand; but I ſay, The Things by me perceived are known by the Underſtanding, and produced by the Will, of an infinite Spirit. And is not all this moſt plain and evident? Is there any more in it, than what a little Obſervation of our own Minds, and that which paſſes in them not only enableth us to conceive, but alſo obligeth us to acknowledge?

Hyl. I think I underſtand you very clearly; and own the Proof you give of a Deity ſeems no leſs evident, than it is ſurpriſing. But allowing that God is the Supreme and Univerſal Cauſe of all Things, yet may not there be ſtill a Third Nature beſides Spirits and Ideas? May we not admit a ſubordinate and limited Cauſe of our

Ideas? In a word, may there not for all that be *Matter?*

Phil. How often must I inculcate the same thing? You allow the Things immediately perceived by Sense to exist no where without the Mind: But there is nothing perceived by Sense, which is not perceived immediately: therefore there is nothing sensible that exists without the Mind. The Matter therefore which you still insist on, is something intelligible, I suppose; something that may be discovered by Reason, and not by Sense.

Hyl. You are in the right.

Phil. Pray let me know what Reasoning your Belief of Matter is grounded on; and what this Matter is in your present Sense of it.

Hyl. I find myself affected with various Ideas, whereof I know I am not the Cause; neither are they the Cause of themselves, or of one another, or capable of subsisting by themselves, as being altogether inactive, fleeting, dependent Beings. They have therefore some Cause distinct from me and them: Of which I pretend to know no more, than that it is *the Cause of my Ideas.* And this thing, whatever it be, I call Matter.

Phil. Tell me, *Hylas,* hath every one a Liberty to change the current proper Signification

nification annexed to a common Name in any Language? For Example, ſuppoſe a Traveller ſhould tell you, that in a certain Country Men might paſs unhurt through the Fire; and, upon explaining himſelf, you found he meant by the Word *Fire* that which others call *Water*: Or if he ſhould aſſert there are Trees which walk upon two Legs, meaning Men by the Term *Trees*. Would you think this reaſonable?

Hyl. No; I ſhould think it very abſurd. Common Cuſtom is the Standard of Propriety in Language. And for any Man to affect ſpeaking improperly, is to pervert the Uſe of Speech, and can never ſerve to a better purpoſe, than to protract and multiply Diſputes where there is no Difference in Opinion.

Phil. And doth not *Matter*, in the common current Acceptation of the Word, ſignify an extended, ſolid, moveable, unthinking, inactive Subſtance?

Hyl. It doth.

Phil. And hath it not been made evident, that no ſuch Subſtance can poſſibly exiſt? And though it ſhould be allowed to exiſt, yet how can that which is *inactive* be a *Cauſe*; or that which is *unthinking* be a *Cauſe of Thought*? You may indeed, if you pleaſe, annex to the Word *Matter* a contrary Meaning to what is vulgarly receiv-ed; and tell me you underſtand by it an unextended, thinking, active Being, which is the Cauſe of our Ideas. But what elſe is this, than to play with Words, and run into that very Fault you juſt now con-demned with ſo much Reaſon? I do by no means find fault with your Reaſoning, in that you collect a Cauſe from the *Phæ-nomena*: But I deny that the Cauſe de-ducible by Reaſon can properly be termed *Matter*.

Hyl. There is indeed ſomething in what you ſay. But I am afraid you do not thoroughly comprehend my Meaning. I would by no means be thought to deny that God or an Infinite Spirit is the Su-preme Cauſe of all things. All I contend for, is, that ſubordinate to the Supreme A-gent there is a Cauſe of a limited and in-ferior Nature, which concurs in the Pro-duction of our Ideas, not by any Act of Will or Spiritual Efficiency, but by that Kind of Action which belongs to Matter, *viz. Motion.*

Phil. I find, you are at every Turn re-lapſing into your old exploded Conceit, of a moveable and conſequently an extend-ed Subſtance exiſting without the Mind. What! Have you already forgot you were convinced, or are you willing I ſhould re-peat

peat what has been ſaid on that Head? In truth this is not fair Dealing in you, ſtill to ſuppoſe the Being of that which you have ſo often acknowledged to have no Being. But not to inſiſt farther on what has been ſo largely handled, I ask whether all your Ideas are not perfectly paſſive and inert, including nothing of Action in them?

Hyl. They are.

Phil. And are ſenſible Qualities any thing elſe but Ideas?

Hyl. How often have I acknowledged that they are not?

Phil. But is not Motion a ſenſible Quality?

Hyl. It is.

Phil. Conſequently it is no Action.

Hyl. I agree with you. And indeed it is very plain, that when I ſtir my Finger, it remains paſſive; but my Will which produced the Motion, is active.

Phil. Now I deſire to know in the firſt place, whether Motion being allowed to be no Action, you can conceive any Action beſides Volition: And in the ſecond place, whether to ſay ſomething and conceive nothing be not to talk Nonſenſe: And laſtly, whether having conſidered the Premiſes, you do not perceive that to ſuppoſe any efficient or active Cauſe of our Ideas, other than *Spirit*, is highly abſurd and unreaſonable?

Hyl.

Hyl. I give up the Point intirely. But though Matter may not be a Cauſe, yet what hinders its being an *Inſtrument* ſubſervient to the Supreme Agent in the Production of our Ideas?

Phil. An Inſtrument, ſay you; pray what may be the Figure, Springs, Wheels, and Motions of that Inſtrument?

Hyl. Thoſe I pretend to determine nothing of, both the Subſtance and its Qualities being intirely unknown to me.

Phil. What? You are then of Opinion, it is made up of unknown Parts, that it hath unknown Motions, and an unknown Shape.

Hyl. I do not believe it hath any Figure or Motion at all, being already convinced, that no ſenſible Qualities can exiſt in an unperceiving Subſtance.

Phil. But what Notion is it poſſible to frame of an Inſtrument void of all ſenſible Qualities, even Extenſion itſelf?

Hyl. I do not pretend to have any Notion of it.

Phil. And what reaſon have you to think, this unknown, this inconceivable Somewhat doth exiſt? Is it that you imagine God cannot act as well without it, or that you find by Experience the Uſe of ſome ſuch thing, when you form Ideas in your own Mind?

Hyl.

Hyl. You are always teizing me for Reasons of my Belief. Pray what Reasons have you not to believe it?

Phil. It is to me a sufficient Reason not to believe the Existence of any thing, if I see no Reason for believing it. But not to insist on Reasons for believing, you will not so much as let me know what it is you would have me believe, since you say you have no manner of Notion of it. After all, let me intreat you to consider whether it be like a Philosopher, or even like a Man of common Sense, to pretend to believe you know not what, and you know not why.

Hyl. Hold, *Philonous.* When I tell you Matter is an *Instrument*, I do not mean altogether Nothing. It is true, I know not the particular Kind of Instrument; but however I have some Notion of *Instrument in general*, which I apply to it.

Phil. But what if it should prove that there is something, even in the most general Notion of *Instrument*, as taken in a distinct Sense from *Cause*, which makes the Use of it inconsistent with the Divine Attributes?

Hyl. Make that appear, and I shall give up the Point.

Phil. What mean you by the general Nature or Notion of *Instrument*?

Hyl.

Hyl. That which is common to all particular Inſtruments, compoſeth the general Notion.

Phil. Is it not common to all Inſtruments, that they are applied to the doing thoſe things only, which cannot be performed by the mere Act of our Wills? Thus for inſtance, I never uſe an Inſtrument to move my Finger, becauſe it is done by a Volition. But I ſhould uſe one, if I were to remove part of a Rock, or tear up a Tree by the Roots. Are you of the ſame Mind? Or can you ſhew any Example where an Inſtrument is made uſe of in producing an Effect immediately depending on the Will of the Agent?

Hyl. I own, I cannot.

Phil. How therefore can you ſuppoſe, that an All-perfect Spirit, on whoſe Will all things have an abſolute and immediate Dependence, ſhould need an Inſtrument in his Operations, or not needing it make uſe of it? Thus it ſeems to me that you are obliged to own the Uſe of a lifeleſs inactive Inſtrument, to be incompatible with the Infinite Perfection of God; that is, by your own Confeſſion, to give up the Point.

Hyl. It doth not readily occur what I can anſwer you.

Phil.

Phil. But methinks you ſhould be ready to own the Truth, when it hath been fairly proved to you. We indeed, who are Beings of Finite Powers, are forced to make uſe of Inſtruments. And the Uſe of an Inſtrument ſheweth the Agent to be limited by Rules of another's Preſcription, and that he cannot obtain his End, but in ſuch a Way and by ſuch Conditions. Whence it ſeems a clear Conſequence, that the ſupreme unlimited Agent uſeth no Tool or Inſtrument at all. The Will of an Omnipotent Spirit is no ſooner exerted than executed, without the Application of Means, which, if they are employed by inferior Agents, it is not upon account of any real Efficacy that is in them, or neceſſary Aptitude to produce any Effect, but merely in compliance with the Laws of Nature, or thoſe Conditions preſcribed to them by the firſt Cauſe, who is Himſelf above all Limitation or Preſcription whatſoever.

Hyl. I will no longer maintain that Matter is an Inſtrument. However, I would not be underſtood to give up its Exiſtence neither; ſince, notwithſtanding what hath been ſaid, it may ſtill be an *Occaſion.*

Phil. How many Shapes is your Matter to take? Or how often muſt it be

proved

proved not to exiſt, before you are content to part with it? But to ſay no more of this (though by all the Laws of Diſputation I may juſtly blame you for ſo frequently changing the Signification of the principal Term) I would fain know what you mean by affirming that Matter is an Occaſion, having already denied it to be a Cauſe. And when you have ſhewn in what Senſe you underſtand *Occaſion*, pray in the next place be pleaſed to ſhew me what Reaſon induceth you to believe there is ſuch an Occaſion of our Ideas.

Hyl. As to the firſt Point: By *Occaſion* I mean an inactive unthinking Being, at the Preſence whereof God excites Ideas in our Minds.

Phil. And what may be the Nature of that inactive unthinking Being?

Hyl. I know nothing of its Nature.

Phil. Proceed then to the ſecond Point, and aſſign ſome Reaſon why we ſhould allow an Exiſtence to this inactive, unthinking, unknown thing.

Hyl. When we ſee Ideas produced in our Minds after an orderly and conſtant manner, it is natural to think they have ſome fixed and regular Occaſions, at the Preſence of which they are excited.

Phil.

Phil. You acknowledge then God alone to be the Caufe of our Ideas, and that he caufes them at the Prefence of thofe Occafions.

Hyl. That is my Opinion.

Phil. Thofe Things which you fay are prefent to God, whithout doubt He perceives.

Hyl. Certainly; otherwife they could not be to Him an Occafion of acting.

Phil. Not to infift now on your making Senfe of this Hypothefis, or anfwering all the puzzling Queftions and Difficulties it is liable to: I only ask whether the Order and Regularity obfervable in the Series of our Ideas, or the Courfe of Nature, be not fufficiently accounted for by the Wifdom and Power of God; and whether it doth not derogate from thofe Attributes, to fuppofe He is influenced, directed, or put in mind, when and what He is to act, by any unthinking Subftance. And laftly whether, in cafe I granted all you contend for, it would make any thing to your purpofe, it not being eafy to conceive how the external or abfolute Exiftence of an unthinking Subftance, diftinct from its being perceived, can be inferred from my allowing that there are certain things perceived by the Mind of God, which are to to Him the Occaſion of producing Ideas in us.

Hyl. I am perfectly at a loſs what to think, this Notion of *Occaſion* ſeeming now altogether as groundleſs as the reſt.

Phil. Do you not at length perceive, that in all theſe different Acceptations of *Matter*, you have been only ſuppoſing you know not what, for no manner of Reaſon, and to no kind of Uſe?

Hyl. I freely own my ſelf leſs fond of my Notions, ſince they have been ſo accurately examined. But ſtill, methinks I have ſome confuſed Perception that there is ſuch a thing as *Matter*.

Phil. Either you perceive the Being of Matter immediately, or mediately. If immediately, pray inform me by which of the Senſes you perceive it. If mediately, let me know by what Reaſoning it is inferred from thoſe Things which you perceive immediately. So much for the Perception. Then for the Matter it ſelf, I ask whether it is Object, *Subſtratum*, Cauſe, Inſtrument, or Occaſion? You have already pleaded for each of theſe, ſhifting your Notions, and making Matter to appear ſometimes in one Shape, then in another. And what you have offered hath been diſapproved and rejected by your ſelf. If you

you have any thing new to advance, I would gladly hear it.

Hyl. I think I have already offered all I had to ſay on thoſe Heads. I am at a loſs what more to urge.

Phil. And yet you are loth to part with your old Prejudice. But to make you quit it more eaſily, I deſire that, beſide what has been hitherto ſuggeſted, you will farther conſider whether, upon ſuppoſition that Matter exiſts, you can poſſibly conceive how you ſhould be affected by it? Or ſuppoſing it did not exiſt, whether it be not evident you might for all that be affected with the ſame Ideas you now are, and conſequently have the very ſame reaſons to believe its Exiſtence that you now can have?

Hyl. I acknowledge it is poſſible we might perceive all things juſt as we do now, though there was no Matter in the World; neither can I conceive, if there be Matter, how it ſhould produce any Idea in our Minds. And I do farther grant, you have intirely ſatisfied me, that it is impoſſible there ſhould be ſuch a thing as Matter in any of the foregoing Acceptations. But ſtill I cannot help ſuppoſing that there is *Matter* in ſome ſenſe or other. What that is I do not indeed pretend to determine.

Phil. I do not expect you should define exactly the Nature of that unknown Being. Only be pleased to tell me, whether it is a Substance: And if so, whether you can suppose a Substance without Accidents; or in case you suppose it to have Accidents or Qualities, I desire you will let me know what those Qualities are, at least what is meant by Matter's supporting them.

Hyl. We have already argued on those Points. I have no more to say to them. But to prevent any farther Questions, let me tell you, I at present understand by *Matter* neither Substance nor Accident, thinking nor extended Being, neither Cause, Instrument, nor Occasion, but something intirely unknown, distinct from all these.

Phil. It seems then you include in your present Notion of Matter, nothing but the general abstract Idea of *Entity.*

Hyl. Nothing else, save only that I superadd to this general Idea the Negation of all those particular Things, Qualities, or Ideas that I perceive, imagine, or in any wise apprehend.

Phil. Pray where do you suppose this unknown Matter to exist?

Hyl. Oh *Philonous!* now you think you have entangled me; for if I say it exists in Place, then you will infer that it exists in the Mind, since it is agreed, that Place or Extension

Extenſion exiſts only in the Mind: But I am not aſhamed to own my Ignorance. I know not where it exiſts; only I am ſure it exiſts not in Place. There is a negative Anſwer for you: And you muſt expect no other to all the Queſtions you put for the future about Matter.

Phil. Since you will not tell me where it exiſts, be pleaſed to inform me after what Manner you ſuppoſe it to exiſt, or what you mean by its *Exiſtence.*

Hyl. It neither thinks nor acts, neither perceives, nor is perceived.

Phil. But what is there poſitive in your abſtracted Notion of its Exiſtence?

Hyl. Upon a nice Obſervation, I do not find I have any poſitive Notion or Meaning at all. I tell you again I am not aſhamed to own my Ignorance. I know not what is meant by its *Exiſtence*, or how it exiſts.

Phil. Continue, good *Hylas*, to act the ſame ingenuous Part, and tell me ſincerely whether you can frame a diſtinct Idea of Entity in general, preſcinded from and excluſive of all thinking and corporeal Beings, all particular things whatſoever.

Hyl. Hold, let me think a little —— I profeſs, *Philonous*, I do not find that I can. At firſt Glance methought I had ſome dilute and airy Notion of pure Entity in Abſtract; but upon cloſer Attention it hath quite vaniſhed out of Sight. The more I think on it, the more am I confirmed in my prudent Reſolution of giving none but negative Anſwers, and not pretending to the leaſt Degree of any poſitive Knowledge or Conception of Matter, its *Where*, its *How*, its *Entity*, or any thing belonging to it.

Phil. When therefore you ſpeak of the Exiſtence of Matter, you have not any Notion in your Mind.

Hyl. None at all.

Phil. Pray tell me if the Caſe ſtands not thus: At firſt, from a Belief of Material Subſtance you would have it that the immediate Objects exiſted without the Mind; then that their Archetypes; then Cauſes; next Inſtruments; then Occaſions: Laſtly, *ſomething in general*, which being interpreted proves *nothing*. So Matter comes to nothing. What think you, *Hylas*, is not this a fair Summary of your whole Proceeding?

Hyl. Be that as it will, yet I ſtill inſiſt upon it, that our not being able to conceive a Thing, is no Argument againſt its Exiſtence.

Phil. That from a Cauſe, Effect, Operation, Sign, or other Circumſtance, there may reaſonably be inferred the Exiſtence of a Thing not immediately perceived, and

that

that it were absurd for any Man to argue against the Existence of that Thing, from his having no direct and positive Notion of it, I freely own. But where there is nothing of all this; where neither Reason nor Revelation induce us to believe the Existence of a Thing; where we have not even a relative Notion of it; where an Abstraction is made from perceiving and being perceived, from Spirit and Idea: Lastly, where there is not so much as the most inadequate or faint Idea pretended to: I will not indeed thence conclude against the Reality of any Notion or Existence of any thing: But my Inference shall be, that you mean nothing at all: That you imploy words to no manner of Purpose, without any Design or Signification whatsoever. And I leave it to you to consider how mere Jargon should be treated.

Hyl. To deal frankly with you, *Philonous*, your Arguments seem in themselves unanswerable, but they have not so great an Effect on me as to produce that intire Conviction, that hearty Acquiescence which attends Demonstration. I find myself still relapsing into an obscure Surmise of I know not what, *Matter*.

Phil. But are you not sensible, *Hylas*, that two Things must concur to take away all Scruple, and work a plenary Assent in the Mind? Let a visible Object be set in never so clear a Light, yet if there is any Imperfection in the Sight, or if the Eye is not directed towards it, it will not be distinctly seen. And though a Demonstration be never so well grounded and fairly proposed, yet if there is withal a Stain of Prejudice, or a wrong Bias on the Understanding, can it be expected on a sudden to perceive clearly and adhere firmly to the Truth? No, there is need of Time and Pains: The Attention must be awakened and detained by a frequent Repetition of the same Thing placed oft in the same, oft in different Lights. I have said it already, and find I must still repeat and inculcate, that it is an unaccountable Licence you take in pretending to maintain you know not what, for you know not what Reason, to you know not what Purpose? Can this be paralleled in any Art or Science, any Sect or Profession of Men? Or is there any thing so barefacedly groundless and unreasonable to be met with even in the lowest of common Conversation? But perhaps you will still say, Matter may exist, though at the same time you neither know what is meant by *Matter*, or by its *Existence*. This indeed is surprizing, and the more so because it is altogether voluntary, you not being led to it by any one Reason; for I challenge you

to

to ſhew me that Thing in Nature which needs Matter to explain or account for it.

Hyl. The Reality of Things cannot be maintained without ſuppoſing the Exiſtence of Matter. And is not this, think you, a good Reaſon why I ſhould be earneſt in its Defence?

Phil. The Reality of Things! What Things, ſenſible or intelligible?

Hyl. Senſible Things.

Phil. My Glove, for Example?

Hyl. That or any other thing perceived by the Senſes.

Phil. But to fix on ſome particular thing; is it not a ſufficient Evidence to me of the Exiſtence of this *Glove*, that I ſee it, and feel it, and wear it? Or if this will not do, how is it poſſible I ſhould be aſſured of the Reality of this Thing, which I actually ſee in this Place, by ſuppoſing that ſome unknown Thing which I never did or can ſee, exiſts after an unknown manner, in an unknown place, or in no place at all? How can the ſuppoſed Reality of that which is intangible, be a Proof that any thing tangible really exiſts? or of that which is inviſible, that any viſible thing, or in general of any thing which is imperceptible, that a Perceptible exiſts? Do but explain this, and I ſhall think nothing too hard for you.

Hyl. Upon the whole, I am content to own the Exiſtence of Matter is highly improbable; but the direct and abſolute Impoſſibility of it does not appear to me.

Phil. But granting Matter to be poſſible, yet upon that account merely it can have no more Claim to Exiſtence, than a Golden Mountain or a Centaur.

Hyl. I acknowledge it; but ſtill you do not deny it is poſſible; and that which is poſſible, for ought you know, may actually exiſt.

Phil. I deny it to be poſſible; And have, if I miſtake not, evidently proved from your own Conceſſions that it is not. In the common Senſe of the Word *Matter*, is there any more implied, than an extended, ſolid, figured, moveable Subſtance exiſting without the Mind? And have not you acknowledged over and over, that you have ſeen evident Reaſon for denying the Poſſibility of ſuch a Subſtance?

Hyl. True, but that is only one Senſe of the Term *Matter*.

Phil. But is it not the only proper genuine received Senſe? And if Matter in ſuch a Senſe be proved impoſſible, may it not be thought with good Grounds abſolutely impoſſible? Elſe how could any thing be proved impoſſible? Or indeed how could there be any Proof at all one way or o-

ther,

ther, to a Man who takes the Liberty to unſettle and change the common Signification of Words?

Hyl. I thought Philoſophers might be allowed to ſpeak more accurately than the Vulgar, and were not always confined to the common Acceptation of a Term.

Phil. But this now mentioned is the common received Senſe among Philoſophers themſelves. But not to inſiſt on that, have you not been allowed to take Matter in what Senſe you pleaſed? And have you not uſed this Privilege in the utmoſt Extent, ſometimes intirely changing, at others leaving out or putting into the Definition of it whatever for the preſent beſt ſerved your Deſign, contrary to all the known Rules of Reaſon and Logick? And hath not this ſhifting unfair Method of yours ſpun out our Diſpute to an unneceſſary Length; Matter having been particularly examined, and by your own Confeſſion refuted in each of thoſe Senſes? And can any more be required to prove the abſolute Impoſſibility of a Thing, than the proving it impoſſible in every particular Senſe, that either you or any one elſe underſtands it in?

Hyl. But I am not ſo thoroughly ſatisfied that you have proved the Impoſſibility of Matter

Matter in the laſt moſt obſcure abſtracted and indefinite Senſe.

Phil. When is a thing ſhewn to be impoſſible?

Hyl. When a Repugnancy is demonſtrated between the Ideas comprehended in its Definition.

Phil. But where there are no Ideas, there no Repugnancy can be demonſtrated between Ideas.

Hyl. I agree with you.

Phil. Now in that which you call the obſcure indefinite Senſe of the Word *Matter*, it is plain, by your own Confeſſion, there was included no Idea at all, no Senſe except an unknown Senſe, which is the ſame thing as none. You are not therefore to expect I ſhould prove a Repugnancy between Ideas where there are no Ideas; or the Impoſſibility of Matter taken in an *unknown* Senſe, that is no Senſe at all. My buſineſs was only to ſhew, you meant *nothing*; and this you were brought to own. So that in all your various Senſes, you have been ſhewed either to mean nothing at all, or if any thing, an Abſurdity. And if this be not ſufficient to prove the Impoſſibility of a Thing, I deſire you will let me know what is.

Hyl. I acknowledge you have proved that Matter is impoſſible; nor do I ſee what

more

more can be ſaid in defence of it. But at the ſame time that I give up this, I ſuſpect all my other Notions. For ſurely none could be more ſeemingly evident than this once was: And yet it now ſeems as falſe and abſurd as ever it did true before. But I think we have diſcuſſed the Point ſufficiently for the preſent. The remaining Part of the Day I would willingly ſpend, in running over in my Thoughts the ſeveral Heads of this Morning's Converſation, and to Morrow ſhall be glad to meet you here again about the ſame time.

Phil. I will not fail to attend you.

THE THIRD DIALOGUE.

PHILONOUS.

TELL me, *Hylas*, What are the Fruits of Yeſterday's Meditation? Hath it confirmed you in the ſame Mind you were in at parting? or have you ſince ſeen Cauſe to change your Opinion?

Hyl. Truly my Opinion is, that all our Opinions are alike vain and uncertain. What we appove to day, we condemn to morrow. We keep a Stir about Knowledge, and ſpend our Lives in the Purſuit of it, when, alas! we know nothing all the while: nor do I think it poſſible for us ever to know any thing in this Life. Our Faculties are too narrow

narrow and too few. Nature certainly never intended us for Speculation.

Phil. What! ſay you we can know nothing, *Hylas*?

Hyl. There is not that ſingle thing in the World, whereof we can know the real Nature, or what it is in itſelf.

Phil. Will you tell me I do not really know what Fire or Water is?

Hyl. You may indeed know that Fire appears hot, and Water fluid: But this is no more than knowing what Senſations are produced in your own Mind, upon the Application of Fire and Water to your Organs of Senſe. Their internal Conſtitution, their true and real Nature, you are utterly in the dark as to *that*.

Phil. Do I not know this to be a real Stone that I ſtand on, and that which I ſee before my Eyes to be a real Tree?

Hyl. Know? No, it is impoſſible you or any Man alive ſhould know it. All you know, is, that you have ſuch a certain Idea or Appearance in your own Mind. But what is this to the real Tree or Stone? I tell you, that Colour, Figure, and Hardneſs, which you perceive, are not the real Natures of thoſe Things, or in the leaſt like them. The ſame may be ſaid of all other real Things or corporeal Subſtances which compoſe the World. They have none

none of them any thing in themſelves, like thoſe ſenſible Qualities by us perceived. We ſhould not therefore pretend to affirm or know any thing of them, as they are in their own Nature.

Phil. But ſurely, *Hylas*, I can diſtinguiſh Gold, for Example, from Iron: And how could, this be if I knew not what either truly was?

Hyl. Believe me, *Philonous*, you can only diſtinguiſh between your own Ideas. That Yellowneſs, that Weight, and other ſenſible Qualities, think you they are really in the Gold? They are only relative to the Senſes, and have no abſolute Exiſtence in Nature. And in pretending to diſtinguiſh the Species of real Things, by the Appearances in your Mind, you may perhaps act as wiſely as he that ſhould conclude two Men were of a different Species, becauſe their Clothes were not of the ſame Colour.

Phil. It ſeems then we are altogether put off with the Appearances of Things, and thoſe falſe ones too. The very Meat I eat, and the Cloth I wear, have nothing in them like what I ſee and feel.

Hyl. Even ſo.

Phil. But is it not ſtrange the whole World ſhould be thus impoſed on, and ſo fooliſh as to believe their Senſes? And yet I know not how it is, but Men eat, and drink,

drink, and ſleep, and perform all the Offices of Life as comfortably and conveniently, as if they really knew the Things they are converſant about.

Hyl. They do ſo: But you know ordinary Practice does not require a Nicety of ſpeculative Knowledge. Hence the Vulgar retain their Miſtakes, and for all that, make a Shift to buſtle through the Affairs of Life. But Philoſophers know better things.

Phil. You mean, they know that they *know nothing*.

Hyl. That is the very Top and Perfection of Humane Knowledge.

Phil. But are you all this while in earneſt, *Hylas*; and are you ſeriouſly perſuaded that you know nothing real in the World? Suppoſe you are going to write, would you not call for Pen, Ink, and Paper, like another Man; and do you not know what it is you call for?

Hyl. How often muſt I tell you, that I know not the real Nature of any one thing in the Univerſe? I may indeed upon Occaſion make uſe of Pen, Ink, and Paper. But what any one of them is in its own true Nature, I declare poſitively I know not. And the ſame is true with regard to every other corporeal thing. And, what is more, we are not only ignorant of the true and

real

real Nature of Things, but even of their Existence. It cannot be denied that we perceive such certain Appearances or Ideas; but it cannot be concluded from thence that Bodies really exist. Nay, now I think on it, I must agreeably to my former Concessions farther declare, that it is impossible any real corporeal Thing should exist in Nature.

Phil. You amaze me. Was ever any thing more wild and extravagant than the Notions you now maintain: And is it not evident you are led into all these Extravagancies by the Belief of *material Substance?* This makes you dream of those unknown Natures in every thing. It is this occasions your distinguishing between the Reality and sensible Appearances of Things. It is to this you are indebted for being ignorant of what every Body else knows perfectly well. Nor is this all: You are not only ignorant of the true Nature of every Thing, but you know not whether any thing really exists, or whether there are any true Natures at all; forasmuch as you attribute to your material Beings an absolute or external Existence, wherein you suppose their Reality consists. And as you are forced in the end to acknowledge such an Existence means either a direct Repugnancy, or nothing at all, it follows that you are obliged

to

to pull down your own Hypothesis of material Substance, and positively to deny the real Existence of any Part of the Universe. And so you are plunged into the deepest and most deplorable *Scepticism* that ever Man was. Tell me, *Hylas*, is it not as I say?

Hyl. I agree with you. *Material Substance* was no more than an Hypothesis, and a false and groundless one too. I will no longer spend my Breath in defence of it. But whatever Hypothesis you advance, or whatsoever Scheme of Things you introduce in its stead, I doubt not it will appear every whit as false: Let me but be allowed to question you upon it. That is, suffer me to serve you in your own kind, and I warrant it shall conduct you through as many Perplexities and Contradictions, to the very same State of Scepticism that I my self am in at present.

Phil. I assure you, *Hylas*, I do not pretend to frame any Hypothesis at all. I am of a vulgar Cast, simple enough to believe my Senses, and leave Things as I find them. To be plain, it is my Opinion, that the real Things are those very Things I see and feel, and perceive by my Senses. These I know, and finding they answer all the Necessities and Purposes of Life, have no reason to be ſolicitous about any other unknown Beings. A Piece of ſenſible Bread, for Inſtance, would ſtay my Stomach better than ten thouſand times as much of that inſenſible, unintelligible, real Bread you ſpeak of. It is likewiſe my Opinion, that Colours and other ſenſible Qualities are on the Objects. I cannot for my Life help thinking that Snow is white, and Fire hot. You indeed, who by *Snow* and *Fire* mean certain external, unperceived, unperceiving Subſtances, are in the right to deny Whiteneſs or Heat to be Affections inherent in them. But I, who underſtand by thoſe Words the Things I ſee and feel, am obliged to think like other Folks. And as I am no Sceptic with regard to the Nature of Things, ſo neither am I as to their Exiſtence. That a thing ſhould be really perceived by my Senſes, and at the ſame time not really exiſt, is to me a plain Contradiction; ſince I cannot preſcind or abſtract, even in Thought, the Exiſtence of a ſenſible Thing from its being perceived. Wood, Stones, Fire, Water, Fleſh, Iron, and the like Things, which I name and diſcourſe of, are Things that I know. And I ſhould not have known them, but that I perceived them by my Senſes; and Things perceived by the Senſes are immediately perceived; and Things immediately

immediately perceived are Ideas; and Ideas cannot exiſt without the Mind; their Exiſtence therefore conſiſts in being perceived; when therefore they are actually perceived, there can be no doubt of their Exiſtence. Away then with all that Scepticiſm, all thoſe ridiculous philoſophical Doubts. What a Jeſt is it for a Philoſopher to queſtion the Exiſtence of ſenſible Things, till he hath it proved to him from the Veracity of God: Or to pretend our Knowledge in this Point falls ſhort of Intuition or Demonſtration? I might as well doubt of my own Being, as of the Being of thoſe Things I actually ſee and feel.

Hyl. Not ſo faſt, *Philonous:* you ſay you cannot conceive how ſenſible Things ſhould exiſt without the Mind. Do you not?

Phil. I do.

Hyl. Suppoſing you were annihilated, cannot you conceive it poſſible, that Things perceivable by Senſe may ſtill exiſt?

Phil I can; but then it muſt be in another mind. When I deny ſenſible Things an Exiſtence out of the Mind, I do not mean my Mind in particular, but all Minds. Now it is plain they have an Exiſtence exterior to my Mind, ſince I find them by Experience to be independent of it. There is therefore ſome other Mind wherein they exiſt, during the Intervals between the Times of my perceiving them: As likewiſe they did before my Birth, and would do after my ſuppoſed Annihilation. And as the ſame is true, with regard to all other finite created Spirits; it neceſſarily follows, there is an *Omnipreſent Eternal Mind*, which knows and comprehends all things, and exhibits them to our View in ſuch a manner, and according to ſuch Rules as He Himſelf hath ordained, and are by us termed the *Laws of Nature*.

Hyl. Anſwer me, *Philonous*. Are all our Ideas perfectly inert Beings? Or have they any Agency included in them?

Phil. They are altogether paſſive and inert.

Hyl. And is not God an Agent, a Being purely active?

Phil. I acknowledge it.

Hyl. No Idea therefore can be like unto, or repreſent the Nature of God.

Phil. It cannot.

Hyl. Since therefore you have no Idea of the Mind of God, how can you conceive it poſſible, that things ſhould exiſt in his Mind? Or, if you can conceive the Mind of God without having an Idea of it, it, why may not I be allowed to conceive the Exiſtence of Matter, notwithſtanding that I have no Idea of it?

Phil. As to your firſt Queſtion; I own I have properly no Idea, either of God or any other Spirit; for theſe being active, cannot be repreſented by things perfectly inert, as our Ideas are. I do nevertheleſs know, that I who am a Spirit or thinking Subſtance, exiſt as certainly, as I know my Ideas exiſt. Farther, I know what I mean by the Terms *I* and *Myſelf*; and I know this immediately, or intuitively, though I do not perceive it as I perceive a Triangle, a Colour, or a Sound. The Mind, Spirit or Soul, is that indiviſible unextended Thing, which thinks, acts, and perceives. I ſay *indiviſible*, becauſe unextended; and *unextended*, becauſe extended, figured, moveable Things, are Ideas; and that which perceives Ideas, which thinks and wills, is plainly it ſelf no Idea, nor like an Idea. Ideas are Things inactive, and perceived: And Spirits a ſort of Beings altogether different from them. I do not therefore ſay my Soul is an Idea, or like an Idea. However, taking the Word *Idea* in a large Senſe, my Soul may be ſaid to furniſh me with an Idea, that is, an Image, or Likeneſs of God, though indeed extremely in-

 adequate.

adequate. For all the Notion I have of God, is obtained by reflecting on my own Soul heightning its Powers, and removing its Imperfections. I have therefore, though not an inactive Idea, yet in my self some sort of an active thinking Image of the Deity. And though I perceive Him not by Sense, yet I have a Notion of Him, or know Him by Reflexion and Reasoning. My own Mind and my own Ideas I have an immediate Knowledge of; and by the help of these, do mediately apprehend the Possibility of the Existence of other Spirits and Ideas. Farther, from my own Being, and from the Dependency I find in my self and my Ideas, I do by an Act of Reason, necessarily infer the Existence of a God, and of all created Things in the Mind of God. So much for your first Question. For the second: I suppose by this time you can answer it your self. For you neither perceive Matter objectively, as you do an inactive Being or Idea, nor know it, as you do your self by a reflex Act: Neither do you mediately apprehend it by Similitude of the one or the other: Nor yet collect it by Reasoning from that which you know immediately. All which makes the Case of *Matter* widely different from that of the *Deity*.

Hyl.

Hyl. You ſay your own Soul ſupplies you with ſome ſort of an Idea or Image of God. But at the ſame time you acknowledge you have, properly ſpeaking, no Idea of your own Soul. You even affirm that Spirits are a ſort of Beings altogether different from Ideas. Conſequently that no Idea can be like a Spirit. We have therefore no Idea of any Spirit. You admit nevertheleſs that there is ſpiritual Subſtance, although you have no Idea of it; while you deny there can be ſuch a thing as material Subſtance, becauſe you have no Notion or Idea of it. Is this fair Dealing? To act conſiſtently, you muſt either admit Matter or reject Spirit. What ſay you to this?

Phil. I ſay in the firſt place, that I do not deny the Exiſtence of material Subſtance, merely becauſe I have no Notion of it, but becauſe the Notion of it is inconſiſtent, or in other words, becauſe it is repugnant that there ſhould be a Notion of it. Many things, for ought I know, may exiſt, whereof neither I nor any other Man hath or can have any Idea or Notion whatſoever. But then thoſe things muſt be poſſible, that is, nothing inconſiſtent muſt be included in their Definition. I ſay ſecondly, that although we believe things to exiſt which we do not perceive; yet we may not believe that any particular thing exiſts, without ſome reaſon for ſuch Belief: But I have no reaſon for believing the Exiſtence of Matter. I have no immediate Intuition thereof: neither can I mediately from my Senſations, Ideas, Notions, Actions or Paſſions, infer an unthinking, unperceiving, inactive Subſtance, either by probable Deduction, or neceſſary Conſequence. Whereas the Being of my ſelf, that is, my own Soul, Mind or thinking Principle, I evidently know by Reflexion. You will forgive me if I repeat the ſame things in anſwer to the ſame Objections. In the very Notion or Definition of material Subſtance, there is included a manifeſt Repugnance and Inconſiſtency. But this cannot be ſaid of the Notion of Spirit. That Ideas ſhould exiſt in what doth not perceive, or be produced by what doth not act, is repugnant. But it is no Repugnancy to ſay, that a perceiving Thing ſhould be the Subject of Ideas, or an active Thing the Cauſe of them. It is granted we have neither an immediate Evidence nor a demonſtrative Knowledge of the Exiſtence of other finite Spirits; but it will not thence follow that ſuch Spirits are on a foot with material Subſtances: if to ſuppoſe the one be inconſiſtent, and it be not inconſiſtent to ſuppoſe the other; if the one can be inferred

ferred by no Argument, and there is a Probability for the other; if we see Signs and Effects indicating distinct finite Agents like our selves, and see no Sign or Symptom whatever that leads to a rational Belief of Matter. I say lastly, that I have a Notion of Spirit, though I have not, strictly speaking, an Idea of it. I do not perceive it as an Idea or by Means of an Idea, but know it by Reflexion.

Hyl. Notwithstanding all you have said, to me it seems, that according to your own way of thinking, and in consequence of your own Principles, it should follow that you are only a System of floating Ideas, without any Substance to support them. Words are not to be used without a meaning. And as there is no more Meaning in spiritual Substance than in material Substance, the one is to be exploded as well as the other.

Phil. How often must I repeat, that I know or am conscious of my own Being; and that I my self am not my Ideas, but somewhat else, a thinking active Principle that perceives, knows, wills, and operates about Ideas. I know that I, one and the same self, perceive both Colours and Sounds: that a Colour cannot perceive a Sound, nor a Sound a Colour: That I am therefore one individual Principle,

ciple, diſtinct from Colour and Sound; and, for the ſame reaſon, from all other ſenſible things and inert Ideas. But I am not in like manner conſcious either of the Exiſtence or Eſſence of Matter. On the contrary, I know that nothing inconſiſtent can exiſt, and that the Exiſtence of Matter implies an Inconſiſtency. Farther, I know what I mean, when I affirm that there is a ſpiritual Subſtance or Support of Ideas, that is, That a Spirit knows and perceives Ideas. But I do not know what is meant, when it is ſaid, that an unperceiving Subſtance hath inherent in it and ſupports either Ideas or the Archetypes of Ideas. There is therefore upon the whole no parity of caſe between Spirit and Matter.

Hyl. I own my ſelf ſatisfied in this point. But do you in earneſt think, the real Exiſtence of ſenſible things conſiſts in their being actually perceived? If ſo; How comes it that all Mankind diſtinguiſh between them? Ask the firſt Man you meet, and he ſhall tell you, *to be perceived* is one thing, and *to exiſt* is another.

Phil. I am content, *Hylas*, to appeal to the common Senſe of the World for the Truth of my Notion. Ask the Gardiner, why he thinks yonder Cherry-Tree exiſts in the Garden, and he ſhall tell you, be-

cauſe

cauſe he ſees and feels it; in a word, becauſe he perceives it by his Senſes. Ask him, why he thinks an Orange-Tree not to be there, and he ſhall tell you, becauſe he does not perceive it. What he perceives by Senſe, that he terms a real Being, and ſaith it *is*, or *exiſts*; but that which is not perceivable, the ſame, he ſaith, hath no Being.

Hyl. Yes, *Philonous*, I grant the Exiſtence of a ſenſible thing conſiſts in being perceivable, but not in being actually perceived.

Phil. And what is perceivable but an Idea? And can an Idea exiſt without being actually perceived? Theſe are Points long ſince agreed between us.

Hyl. But be your opinion never ſo true, yet ſurely you will not deny it is ſhocking, and contrary to the common Senſe of Men. Ask the Fellow, whether yonder Tree hath an Exiſtence out of his Mind: What Anſwer think you he would make?

Phil. The ſame that I ſhould my ſelf, to wit, That it doth exiſt out of his Mind. But then to a Chriſtian it cannot ſurely be ſhocking to ſay, The real Tree exiſting without his Mind is truly known and comprehended by (that is, *exiſts in)* the infinite Mind of God. Probably he may not at firſt glance be aware of the direct

and

and immediate Proof there is of this, inasmuch as the very Being of a Tree, or any other ſenſible Thing, implies a Mind wherein it is. But the Point it ſelf he cannot deny. The Queſtion between the Materialiſts and me is not, whether Things have a real Exiſtence out of the Mind of this or that Perſon, but whether they have an abſolute Exiſtence, diſtinct from being perceived by God, and exterior to all Minds. This indeed ſome Heathens and Philoſophers have affirmed, but whoever entertains Notions of the Deity ſuitable to the Holy Scriptures, will be of another Opinion.

Hyl. But according to your Notions, what Difference is there between real Things, and Chimeras formed by the Imagination, or the Viſions of a Dream, ſince they are all equally in the Mind?

Phil. The Ideas formed by the Imagination are faint and indiſtinct; they have beſides an intire Dependence on the Will. But the Ideas perceived by Senſe, that is, real Things, are more vivid and clear, and being imprinted on the Mind by a Spirit diſtinct from us, have not a like Dependence on our Will. There is therefore no Danger of confounding theſe with the foregoing: and there is as little of confounding them with the Viſions of a Dream, which are

are dim, irregular, and confuſed. And though they ſhould happen to be never ſo lively and natural, yet by their not being connected, and of a piece with the preceding and ſubſequent Tranſactions of our Lives, they might eaſily be diſtinguiſhed from Realities. In ſhort, by whatever Method you diſtinguiſh *Things* from *Chimeras* on your own Scheme, the ſame, it is evident, will hold alſo upon mine. For it muſt be, I preſume, by ſome perceived Difference, and I am not for depriving you of any one thing that you perceive.

Hyl. But ſtill, *Philonous*, you hold, there is nothing in the World but Spirits and Ideas. And this, you muſt needs acknowledge, ſounds very odly.

Phil. I own the Word *Idea*, not being commonly uſed for *Thing*, ſounds ſomething out of the way. My Reaſon for uſing it was, becauſe a neceſſary Relation to the Mind is underſtood to be implied by that Term; and it is now commonly uſed by Philoſophers, to denote the immediate Objects of the Underſtanding. But however odly the Propoſition may ſound in Words, yet it includes nothing ſo very ſtrange or ſhocking in its Senſe, which in effect amounts to no more than this, to wit, that there are only Things per-

perceiving, and Things perceived; or that every unthinking Being is neceſſarily, and from the very Nature of its Exiſtence, perceived by ſome Mind; if not by any finit created Mind, yet certainly by the infinite Mind of God, in whom *we live, and move, and have our Being*. Is this as ſtrange as to ſay, The ſenſible Qualities are not on the Objects: Or, That we cannot be ſure of the Exiſtence of Things, or know any thing of their real Natures, though we both ſee and feel them, and perceive them by all our Senſes?

Hyl. And in Conſequence of this, muſt we not think there are no ſuch Things as Phyſical or Corporeal Cauſes; but that a Spirit is the immediate Cauſe of all the *Phænomena* in Nature? Can there be any thing more extravagant than this?

Phil. Yes, it is infinitely more extravagant to ſay, A thing which is inert, operates on the Mind, and which is unperceiving, is the Cauſe of our Perceptions. Beſides, that which to you, I know not for what Reaſon, ſeems ſo extravagant, is no more than the Holy Scriptures aſſert in a hundred Places. In them God is repreſented as the ſole and immediate Author of all thoſe Effects, which ſome Heathens and Philoſophers are wont to aſcribe to Nature, Matter, Fate, or the like unthinking

ing Principle. This is ſo much the conſtant Language of Scripture, that it were needleſs to confirm it by Citations.

Hyl. You are not aware, *Philonous*, that in making God the immediate Author of all the Motions in Nature, you make him the Author of Murder, Sacrilege, Adultery, and the like heinous Sins.

Phil. In Anſwer to that, I obſerve firſt, that the Imputation of Guilt is the ſame, whether a Perſon commits an Action with or without an Inſtrument. In caſe therefore you ſuppoſe God to act by the Mediation of an Inſtrument, or Occaſion, called *Matter*, you as truly make Him the Author of Sin as I, who think Him the immediate Agent in all thoſe Operations vulgarly aſcribed to Nature. I farther obſerve, that Sin or moral Turpitude doth not conſiſt in the outward Phyſical Action or Motion, but in the internal Deviation of the Will from the Laws of Reaſon and Religion. This is plain, in that the killing an Enemy in a Battle, or putting a Criminal legally to Death, is not thought ſinful, though the outward Act be the very ſame with that in the Caſe of Murder. Since therefore Sin doth not conſiſt in the Phyſical Action, the making God an immediate Cauſe of all ſuch Actions, is not making him the Author of Sin. Laſtly, I

I have no where ſaid that God is the only Agent who produces all the Motions in Bodies. It is true, I have denied there are any other Agents beſide Spirits: But this is very conſiſtent with allowing to Thinking Rational Beings, in the Production of Motions, the Uſe of limited Powers, ultimately indeed derived from God, but immediately under the Direction of their own Wills, which is ſufficient to intitle them to all the Guilt of their Actions.

Hyl. But the denying Matter, *Philonous*, or corporeal Subſtance; there is the Point. You can never perſuade me that this is not repugnant to the univerſal Senſe of Mankind. Were our Diſpute to be determined by moſt Voices, I am confident you would give up the Point, without gathering the Votes.

Phil. I wiſh both our Opinions were fairly ſtated and ſubmitted to the Judgment of Men who had plain common Senſe, without the Prejudices of a learned Education. Let me be repreſented as one who truſts his Senſes, who thinks he knows the Things he ſees and feels, and entertains no Doubts, of their Exiſtence; and you fairly ſet forth with all your Doubts, your Paradoxes, and your Scepticiſm about you, and I ſhall willingly acquieſce in the Determination of any indifferent Perſon. That there

there is no Subſtance wherein Ideas can exiſt beſide Spirit, is to me evident. And that the Objects immediately perceived are Ideas, is on all Hands agreed. And that ſenſible Qualities are Objects immediately perceived, no one can deny. It is therefore evident there can be no *Subſtratum* of thoſe Qualities but Spirit, in which they exiſt, not by way of Mode or Property, but as a thing perceived in that which perceives it. I deny therefore that there is any unthinking *Subſtratum* of the Objects of Senſe, and in that Acceptation that there is any material Subſtance. But if by *material Subſtance* is meant only ſenſible Body, that which is ſeen and felt, (and the unphiloſophical Part of the World, I dare ſay, mean no more) then I am more certain of Matter's Exiſtence than you, or any other Philoſopher, pretend to be. If there be any thing which makes the Generality of Mankind averſe from the Notions I eſpouſe, it is a Miſapprehenſion that I deny the Reality of ſenſible Things: But as it is you who are guilty of that and not I, it follows that in truth their Averſion is againſt your Notions, and not mine. I do therefore aſſert that I am as certain as of my own Being, that there are Bodies or corporeal Subſtances, (meaning the Things I perceive by my Senſes) and that granting this, the

Bulk of Mankind will take no Thought about, nor think themſelves at all concern-ed in the Fate of thoſe unknown Natures, and Philoſophical Quiddities, which ſome Men are ſo fond of.

Hyl. What ſay you to this? Since, ac-cording to you, Men judge of the Reality of Things by their Senſes, how can a Man be miſtaken in thinking the Moon a plain lucid Surface, about a Foot in Diameter; or a ſquare Tower, ſeen at a diſtance, round; or an Oar, with one End in the Water, crooked?

Phil. He is not miſtaken with regard to the Ideas he actually perceives; but in the Inferences he makes from his preſent Per-ceptions. Thus in the Caſe of the Oar, what he immediately perceives by Sight is certainly crooked; and ſo far he is in the right. But if he thence conclude, that up-on taking the Oar out of the Water he ſhall perceive the ſame Crookedneſs; or that it would affect his Touch, as crook-ed things are wont to do: In that he is miſtaken. In like mannner, if he ſhall conclude from what he perceives in one Station, that in caſe he advances toward the Moon or Tower, he ſhould ſtill be affected with the like Ideas, he is miſtaken. But his Miſtake lies not in what he per-ceives immediately and at preſent, (it being

a

a maniſeſt Contradiction to ſuppoſe he ſhould err in reſpect of that) but in the wrong Judgment he makes concerning the Ideas he apprehends to be connected with thoſe immediately perceived: Or concerning the Ideas that, from what he perceives at preſent, he imagines would be perceived in other Circumſtances. The Caſe is the ſame with regard to the *Copernican* Syſtem. We do not here perceive any Motion of the Earth: But it were erroneous thence to conclude, that in caſe we were placed at as great a Diſtance from that, as we are now from the other Planets, we ſhould not then perceive its Motion.

Hyl. I underſtand you; and muſt needs own you ſay things plauſible enough: But give me leave to put you in mind of one thing. Pray, *Philonous*, were you not formerly as poſitive that Matter exiſted, as you are now that it does not?

Phil. I was. But here lies the Difference. Before, my Poſitiveneſs was founded without Examination, upon Prejudice; but now, after Inquiry, upon Evidence.

Hyl. After all, it ſeems our Diſpute is rather about Words than Things. We agree in the Thing, but differ in the Name. That we are affected with Ideas from without is evident; and it is no leſs evident, that there muſt be (I will not ſay Archetypes, but) Powers without the Mind, corresponding to those Ideas. And as these Powers cannot subsist by themselves, there is some Subject of them necessarily to be admitted, which I call *Matter*, and you call *Spirit*. This is all the Difference.

Phil. Pray, *Hylas*, is that powerful Being, or Subject of Powers, extended?

Hyl. It hath not Extension; but it hath the Power to raise in you the Idea of Extension.

Phil. It is therefore itself unextended.

Hyl. I grant it.

Phil. Is it not also active?

Hyl. Without doubt: Otherwise, how could we attribute Powers to it?

Phil. Now let me ask you Two Questions: *First*, Whether it be agreeable to the Usage either of Philosophers or others, to give the Name *Matter* to an unextended active Being? And *Secondly*, Whether it be not ridiculously absurd to misapply Names contrary to the common Use of Language?

Hyl. Well then, let it not be called Matter, since you will have it so, but some *Third Nature* distinct from Matter and Spirit. For, what reason is there why you should call it Spirit? does not the Notion of of Spirit imply, that it is thinking as well as active and unextended?

Phil. My Reason is this: because I have a mind to have some Notion or Meaning in what I say; but I have no Notion of any Action distinct from Volition, neither can I conceive Volition to be any where but in a Spirit: therefore when I speak of an active Being, I am obliged to mean a Spirit. Beside, what can be plainer than that a thing which hath no Ideas in itself, cannot impart them to me; and if it hath Ideas, surely it must be a Spirit. To make you comprehend the Point still more clearly if it be possible: I assert as well as you, that since we are affected from without, we must allow Powers to be without in a Being distinct from ourselves. So far we are agreed. But then we differ as to the Kind of this powerful Being. I will have it to be Spirit, you Matter, or I know not what (I may add too, you know not what) Third Nature. Thus I prove it to be Spirit. From the Effects I see produced, I conclude there are Actions; and because Actions, Volitions; and because there are Volitions, there must be a Will. Again, the Things I perceive must have an Existence, they or their Archetypes, out of my Mind: But being Ideas, neither they nor their Archetypes can exist otherwiſe than in an Underſtanding: There is therefore an Underſtanding. But Will and Underſtanding conſtitute in the ſtricteſt Senſe a Mind or Spirit. The powerful Cauſe therefore of my Ideas, is in ſtrict Propriety of Speech a *Spirit.*

Hyl. And now I warrant you think you have made the Point very clear, little ſuſpecting that what you advance leads directly to a Contradiction. Is it not an Abſurdity to imagine any Imperfection in God?

Phil. Without doubt.

Hyl. To ſuffer Pain is an Imperfection.

Phil. It is.

Hyl. Are we not ſometimes affected with Pain and Uneaſineſs by ſome other Being?

Phil. We are.

Hyl. And have you not ſaid that Being is a Spirit, and is not that Spirit God?

Phil. I grant it.

Hyl. But you have aſſerted, that whatever Ideas we perceive from without, are in the Mind which affects us. The Ideas threfore of Pain and Uneaſineſs are in God; or in other words, God ſuffers Pain: That is to ſay, there is an Imperfection in the Divine Nature, which you acknowledged was abſurd. So you are caught in a plain Contradiction.

Phil.

Phil. That God knows or underſtands all things, and that He knows among other things what Pain is, even every ſort of painful Senſation, and what it is for His Creatures to ſuffer Pain, I make no queſtion. But that God, though He knows and ſometimes cauſes painful Senſations in us, can Himſelf ſuffer Pain, I poſitively deny. We who are limited and dependent Spirits, are liable to Impreſſions of Senſe, the Effects of an external Agent, which being produced againſt our Wills, are ſometimes painful and uneaſy. But God, whom no external Being can affect, who perceives nothing by Senſe as we do, whoſe Will is abſolute and independent, cauſing all things, and liable to be thwarted or reſiſted by nothing; it is evident, ſuch a Being as this can ſuffer nothing, nor be affected with any painful Senſation, or indeed any Senſation at all. We are chained to a Body, that is to ſay, our Perceptions are connected with corporeal Motions. By the Law of our Nature we are affected upon every Alteration in the nervous Parts of our ſenſible Body: Which ſenſible Body rightly conſidered, is nothing but a Complexion of ſuch Qualities or Ideas, as have no Exiſtence diſtinct from being perceived by a Mind: So that this Connexion of Senſations with corporeal Motions, means no more than a Correſpondence in the Order of Nature between two Sets of Ideas, or Things immediately perceivable. But God is a pure Spirit, disengaged from all such Sympathy or natural Ties. No corporeal Motions are attended with the Sensations of Pain or Pleasure in his Mind. To know every thing knowable is certainly a Perfection; but to endure, or suffer, or feel any thing by Sense, is an Imperfection. The former, I say, agrees to God, but not the latter. God knows or hath Ideas; but His Ideas are not convey'd to Him by Sense, as ours are. Your not Distinguishing where there is so manifest a Difference, makes you fancy you see an Absurdity where there is none.

Hyl. But all this while you have not considered, that the Quantity of Matter hath been demonstrated to be proportional to the Gravity of Bodies. And what can withstand Demonstration?

Phil. Let me see how you demonstrate that Point.

Hyl. I lay it down for a Principle, that the Moments or Quantities of Motion in Bodies, are in a direct compounded Reason of the Velocities and Quantities of Matter contained in them. Hence, where the Velocities are equal, it follows, the Moments are directly as the Quantity of Matter in each. But it is found by Experience, that all Bodies (bating the small Inequalities, arising

arising from the Resistance of the Air) descend with an equal Velocity; the Motion therefore of descending Bodies, and consequently their Gravity, which is the Cause or Principle of that Motion, is proportional to the Quantity of Matter: which was to be demonstrated.

Phil. You lay it down as a self-evident Principle, that the Quantity of Motion in any Body, is proportional to the Velocity and *Matter* taken together: And this is made use of to prove a Proposition, from whence the Existence of *Matter* is inferred. Pray is not this arguing in a Circle?

Hyl. In the Premise I only mean, that the Motion is proportional to the Velocity, jointly with the Extension and Solidity.

Phil. But allowing this to be true, yet it will not thence follow, that Gravity is proportional to *Matter*, in your Philosophic Sense of the Word; except you take it for granted, that unknown *Substratum*, or whatever else you call it, is proportional to those sensible Qualities; which to suppose, is plainly begging the Question. That there is Magnitude and Solidity, or Resistance, perceived by Sense, I readily grant; as likewise that Gravity may be proportional to those Qualities, I will

not

not diſpute. But that either theſe Qualities as perceived by us, or the Powers producing them do exiſt in a *material Subſtratum*; this is what I deny, and you indeed affirm, but notwithſtanding your Demonſtration, have not yet proved.

Hyl. I ſhall inſiſt no longer on that Point. Do you think however, you ſhall perſuade me the natural Philoſophers have been dreaming all this while; pray what becomes of all their Hypotheſes and Explications of the *Phænomena*, which ſuppoſe the Exiſtence of Matter?

Phil. What mean you, *Hylas*, by the *Phænomena*?

Hyl. I mean the Appearances which I perceive by my Senſes.

Phil. And the Appearances perceived by Senſe, are they not Ideas?

Hyl. I have told you ſo a hundred times.

Phil. Therefore, to explain the *Phænomena*, is to ſhew how we come to be affected with Ideas, in that Manner and Order wherein they are imprinted on our Senſes. Is it not?

Hyl. It is.

Phil. Now if you can prove, that any Philoſopher hath explained the Production of any one Idea in our Minds by the Help of *Matter*, I ſhall for ever acquieſce, and look on all that hath been ſaid againſt

it

it as nothing: But if you cannot, it is in vain to urge the Explication of *Phænomena*. That a Being endowed with Knowledge and Will, ſhould produce or exhibit Ideas, is eaſily underſtood. But that a Being which is utterly deſtitute of theſe Faculties ſhould be able to produce Ideas, or in any ſort to affect an Intelligence, this I can never underſtand. This I ſay, though we had ſome poſitive Conception of Matter, though we knew its Qualities, and could comprehend its Exiſtence, would yet be ſo far from explaining things, that it is it ſelf the moſt inexplicable thing in the World. And yet for all this, it will not follow, that Philoſophers have been doing nothing; for by obſerving and reaſoning upon the Connexion of Ideas, they diſcover the Laws and Methods of Nature, which is a part of Knowledge both uſeful and entertaining.

Hyl. After all, can it be ſuppoſed God would deceive all Mankind? Do you imagine, He would have induced the whole World to believe the Being of Matter, if there was no ſuch thing?

Phil. That every epidemical Opinion ariſing from Prejudice, or Paſſion, or Thoughtleſneſs, may be imputed to God, as the Author of it, I believe you will not affirm. Whatſoever Opinion we father on Him,

Him, it muſt be either becauſe He has diſcovered it to us by ſupernatural Revelation, or becauſe it is ſo evident to our natural Faculties, which were framed and given us by God, that it is impoſſible we ſhould withhold our Aſſent from it. But where is the Revelation? or where is the Evidence that extorts the Belief of Matter? Nay, how does it appear, that Matter taken for ſomething diſtinct from what we perceive by our Senſes, is thought to exiſt by all Mankind, or indeed by any except a few Philoſophers, who do not know what they would be at? Your Queſtion ſuppoſes theſe Points are clear; and when you have cleared them, I ſhall think my ſelf obliged to give you another Anſwer. In the mean time let it ſuffice that I tell you, I do not ſuppoſe God has deceived Mankind at all.

Hyl. But the Novelty, *Philonous*, the Novelty! There lies the Danger. New Notions ſhould always be diſcountenanced; they unſettle Mens Minds, and no body knows where they will end.

Phil. Why the rejecting a Notion that hath no Foundation either in Senſe or in Reaſon, or in Divine Authority, ſhould be thought to unſettle the Belief of ſuch Opinions as are grounded on all or any of theſe, I cannot imagine. That Innova-

tions

tions in Government and Religion, are dangerous, and ought to be diſcountenanced, I freely own. But is there the like Reaſon why they ſhould be diſcouraged in Philoſophy? The making any thing known which was unknown before, is an Innovation in Knowledge: And if all ſuch Innovations had been forbidden, Men would have made a notable Progreſs in the Arts and Sciences. But it is none of my buſineſs to plead for Novelties and Paradoxes. That the Qualities we perceive, are not on the Objects: That we muſt not believe our Senſes: That we know nothing of the real Nature of Things, and can never be aſſured even of their Exiſtence: That real Colours and Sounds are nothing but certain unknown Figures and Motions: That Motions are in themſelves neither ſwift nor ſlow: That there are in Bodies abſolute Extenſions, without any particular Magnitude or Figure: That a Thing ſtupid, thoughtleſs and inactive, operates on a Spirit: That the leaſt Particle of a Body, contains innumerable extended Parts. Theſe are the Novelties, theſe are the ſtrange Notions which ſhock the genuine uncorrupted Judgment of all Mankind; and being once admitted, embarraſs the Mind with endleſs Doubts and Difficulties. And it is againſt theſe and the like

Innova-

Innovations, I endeavour to vindicate common Senſe. It is true, in doing this, I may perhaps be obliged to uſe ſome *Ambages*, and ways of Speech not common. But if my Notions are once thorowly underſtood, that which is moſt ſingular in them, will in effect be found to amount to no more than this: That it is abſolutely impoſſible, and a plain Contradiction to ſuppoſe, any unthinking Being ſhould exiſt without being perceived by a Mind. And if this Notion be ſingular, it is a ſhame it ſhould be ſo at this time of day, and in a Chriſtian Country.

Hyl. As for the Difficulties other Opinions may be liable to, thoſe are out of the Queſtion. It is your Buſineſs to defend your own Opinion. Can any thing be plainer, than that you are for changing all things into Ideas? You, I ſay, who are not aſhamed to charge me with *Scepticiſm*. This is ſo plain, there is no denying it.

Phil. You miſtake me. I am not for changing Things into Ideas, but rather Ideas into Things; ſince thoſe immediate Objects of Perception, which according to you, are only Appearances of Things, I take to be the real Things themſelves.

Hyl. Things! you may pretend what you pleaſe; but it is certain, you leave

us

us nothing but the empty Forms of Things, the Outside only which strikes the Senses.

Phil. What you call the empty Forms and Outside of Things, seems to me the very Things themselves. Nor are they empty or incomplete otherwise, than upon your Supposition, that Matter is an essential Part of all corporeal Things. We both therefore agree in this, that we perceive only sensible Forms: But herein we differ, you will have them to be empty Appearances, I real Beings. In short you do not trust your Senses, I do.

Hyl. You say you believe your Senses; and seem to applaud your self that in this you agree with the Vulgar. According to you therefore, the true Nature of a Thing is discovered by the Senses. If so, whence comes that Disagreement? Why is not the same Figure, and other sensible Qualities, perceived all manner of Ways? and why should we use a Microscope, the better to discover the true Nature of a Body, if it were discoverable to the naked Eye?

Phil. Strictly speaking, *Hylas*, we do not see the same Object that we feel; neither is the same Object perceived by the Microscope, which was by the naked Eye. But in case every Variation was

was thought ſufficient to conſtitute a new Kind or Individual, the endleſs Number or Confuſion of Names would render Language impracticable. Therefore to avoid this as well as other Inconveniencies which are obvious upon a little Thought, Men combine together ſeveral Ideas, apprehended by divers Senſes, or by the ſame Senſe at different times, or in different Circumſtances, but obſerved however to have ſome Connexion in Nature, either with reſpect to Coexiſtence or Succeſſion ; all which they refer to one Name, and conſider as one Thing. Hence it follows that when I examine by my other Senſes a Thing I have ſeen, it is not in order to underſtand better the ſame Object which I had perceived by Sight, the Object of one Senſe not being perceived by the other Senſes. And when I look through a Microſcope, it is not that I may perceive more clearly what I perceived already with my bare Eyes, the Object perceived by the Glaſs being quite different from the former. But in both caſes my Aim is only to know what Ideas are connected together ; and the more a Man knows of the Connexion of Ideas, the more he is ſaid to know of the Nature of Things. What therefore if our Ideas are variable ; what if our Senſes are not in all Circum-

ſtances

ſtances affected with the ſame Appearances? It will not thence follow, they are not to be truſted, or that they are inconſiſtent either with themſelves or any thing elſe, except it be with your preconceived Notion of (I know not what) one ſingle, unchanged, unperceivable, real Nature, marked by each Name: Which Prejudice ſeems to have taken its Riſe from not rightly underſtanding the common Language of Men ſpeaking of ſeveral diſtinct Ideas, as united into one thing by the Mind. And indeed there is Cauſe to ſuſpect ſeveral erroneous Conceits of the Philoſophers are owing to the ſame Original: While they began to build their Schemes, not ſo much on Notions as Words, which were framed by the Vulgar, merely for Conveniency and Diſpatch in the common Actions of Life, without any regard to Speculation.

Hyl. Methinks I apprehend your Meaning.

Phil. It is your Opinion, the Ideas we perceive by our Senſes are not real Things, but Images, or Copies of them. Our Knowledge therefore is no farther real, than as our Ideas are the true Repreſentations of thoſe Originals. But as theſe ſuppoſed Originals are in themſelves unknown, it is impoſſible to know how far our Ideas resemble them; or whether they resemble them at all. We cannot therefore be sure we have any real Knowledge. Farther, as our Ideas are perpetually varied, without any Change in the supposed real Things, it necessarily follows they cannot all be true Copies of them: Or if some are, and others are not, it is impossible to distinguish the former from the latter. And this plunges us yet deeper in Uncertainty. Again, when we consider the Point, we cannot conceive how any Idea, or any thing like an Idea, should have an absolute Existence out of a Mind: Nor consequently, according to you, how there should be any real thing in Nature. The Result of all which is, that we are thrown into the most hopeless and abandoned *Scepticism*. Now give me leave to ask you, *First*, Whether your referring Ideas to certain absolutely existing unperceived Substances, as their Originals, be not the Source of all this *Scepticism*? *Secondly*, Whether you are informed, either by Sense or Reason, of the Existence of those unknown Originals? And in case you are not, Whether it be not absurd to suppose them? *Thirdly*, Whether, upon Inquiry, you find there is any thing distinctly conceived or meant by the *absolute or external Existence of unperceiving Substances*?

ſtances? *Laſtly*, Whether the Premiſes conſidered, it be not the wiſeſt way to follow Nature, truſt your Senſes, and laying aſide all anxious Thought about unknown Natures or Subſtances, admit with the Vulgar thoſe for real Things, which are perceived by the Senſes?

Hyl. For the preſent, I have no Inclination to the anſwering Part. I would much rather ſee how you can get over what follows. Pray are not the Objects perceived by the Senſes of one, likewiſe perceivable to others preſent? If there were an hundred more here, they would all ſee the Garden, the Trees, and Flowers as I ſee them. But they are not in the ſame manner affected with the Ideas I frame in my Imagination. Does not this make a Difference between the former ſort of Objects and the latter?

Phil. I grant it does. Nor have I ever denied a Difference between the Objects of Senſe and thoſe of Imagination. But what would you infer from thence? You cannot ſay that ſenſible Objects exiſt unperceived, becauſe they are perceived by many.

Hyl. I own, I can make nothing of that Objection: But it hath led me into another. Is it not your Opinion that by our Senſes we perceive only the Ideas exiſting in our Minds?

Phil. It is.

Hyl. But the ſame Idea which is in my Mind, cannot be in yours, or in any other Mind. Doth it not therefore follow from your Principles, that no Two can ſee the ſame thing? And is not this highly abſurd?

Phil. If the Term *ſame* be taken in the vulgar Acceptation, it is certain, (and not at all repugnant to the Principles I maintain) that different Perſons may perceive the ſame Thing; or the ſame Thing or Idea exiſt in different Minds. Words are of arbitrary Impoſition; and ſince Men are uſed to apply the Word *ſame* where no Diſtinction or Variety is perceived, and I do not pretend to alter their Perceptions, it follows, that as Men have ſaid before, *ſeveral ſaw the ſame thing*, ſo they may upon like Occaſions ſtill continue to uſe the ſame Phraſe, without any Deviation either from Propriety of Language, or the Truth of Things. But if the Term *ſame* be uſed in the Acceptation of Philoſophers, who pretend to an abſtracted Notion of Identity, then, according to their ſundry Definitions of this Notion, (for it is not yet agreed wherein that Philoſophic Identity conſiſts) it may or may not

not be possible for divers Persons to perceive the same thing. But whether Philosophers shall think fit to call a thing the *same* or no, is, I conceive, of small Importance. Let us suppose several Men together, all endued with the same Faculties, and consequently affected in like sort by their Senses, and who had yet never known the Use of Language; they would without question agree in their Perceptions. Though perhaps, when they came to the Use of Speech, some regarding the Uniformness of what was perceived, might call it the *same* thing: Others especially regarding the Diversity of Persons who perceived, might choose the Denomination of different things. But who sees not that all the Dispute is about a Word? to wit, Whether what is perceived by different Persons, may yet have the Term *same* applied to it? Or suppose a House, whose Walls or outward Shell remaining unaltered, the Chambers are all pulled down, and new ones built in their place; and that you should call this the *same*, and I should say it was not the *same* House: Would we not for all this perfectly agree in our Thoughts of the House, considered in it self? and would not all the Difference consist in a Sound? If you should say, We differed in our Notions; for that you ſuperadded to your Idea of the Houſe the ſimple abſtracted Idea of Identity, whereas I did not; I would tell you I know not what you mean by that *abſtracted Idea of Identity*; and ſhould deſire you to look into your own Thoughts, and be ſure you underſtood your ſelf.------ Why ſo ſilent, *Hylas*? Are you not yet ſatisfied, Men may diſpute about Identity and Diverſity, without any real Difference in their Thoughts and Opinions, abſtracted from Names? Take this farther Reflexion with you: That whether Matter be allowed to exiſt or no, the Caſe is exactly the ſame as to the Point in hand. For the Materialiſts themſelves acknowledge what we immediately perceive by our Senſes, to be our own Ideas. Your Difficulty therefore, that no two ſee the ſame thing, makes equally againſt the Materialiſts and me.

Hyl. But they ſuppoſe an external Archetype, to which referring their ſeveral Ideas, they may truly be ſaid to perceive the ſame thing.

Phil. And (not to mention your having diſcarded thoſe Archetypes) ſo may you ſuppoſe an external Archetype on my Principles; *external*, I mean, to your own Mind; though indeed it muſt be ſuppoſed to exiſt in that Mind which comprehends all things; but then this ſerves all the Ends of Identity,

tity, as well as if it existed out of a Mind. And I am sure you yourself will not say, It is less intelligible.

Hyl. You have indeed clearly satisfied me, either that there is no Difficulty at bottom in this Point; or if there be, that it makes equally against both Opinions.

Phil. But that which makes equally against two contradictory Opinions, can be a Proof against neither.

Hyl. I acknowledge it. But after all, *Philonous*, when I consider the Substance of what you advance against *Scepticism*, it amounts to no more than this. We are sure that we really see, hear, feel; in a word, that we are affected with sensible Impressions.

Phil. And how are we concerned any farther? I see this *Cherry*, I feel it, I taste it: And I am sure *nothing* cannot be seen, or felt, or tasted: It is therefore *real*. Take away the Sensations of Softness, Moisture, Redness, Tartness, and you take away the *Cherry*. Since it is not a Being distinct from Sensations; a *Cherry*, I say, is nothing but a Congeries of sensible Impressions, or Ideas perceived by various Senses: Which Ideas are united into one thing (or have one Name given them) by the Mind; because they are observed to attend each other. Thus when the Palate is affected with ſuch a particular Taſte, the Sight is affected with a red Colour, the Touch with Roundneſs, Softneſs, *&c.* Hence, when I ſee, and feel, and taſte, in ſundry certain manners, I am ſure the *Cherry* exiſts, or is real; its Reality being in my Opinion nothing abſtracted from thoſe Senſations. But if by the Word *Cherry* you mean an unknown Nature diſtinct from all thoſe ſenſible Qualities, and by its Exiſtence ſomething diſtinct from its being perceived; then indeed I own, neither you nor I, nor any one elſe can be ſure it exiſts.

Hyl. But what would you ſay, *Philonous*, if I ſhould bring the very ſame Reaſons againſt the Exiſtence of ſenſible Things in a Mind, which you have offered againſt their exiſting in a material *Subſtratum*?

Phil. When I ſee your Reaſons, you ſhall hear what I have to ſay to them.

Hyl. Is the Mind extended or unextended?

Phil. Unextended, without doubt.

Hyl. Do you ſay the Things you perceive are in your Mind?

Phil. They are.

Hyl. Again, have I not heard you ſpeak of ſenſible Impreſſions?

Phil. I believe you may.

Hyl.

Hyl. Explain to me now, O *Philonous!* how it is possible there should be room for all those Trees and Houses to exist in your Mind. Can extended Things be contained in that which is unextended? Or are we to imagine Impressions made on a Thing void of all Solidity? You cannot say Objects are in your Mind, as Books in your Study: Or that Things are imprinted on it, as the Figure of a Seal upon Wax. In what Sense therefore are we to understand those Expressions? Explain me this if you can: And I shall then be able to answer all those Queries you formerly put to me about my *Substratum.*

Phil. Look you, *Hylas,* when I speak of Objects as existing in the Mind or imprinted on the Senses; I would not be understood in the gross literal Sense, as when Bodies are said to exist in a place, or a Seal to make an Impression upon Wax. My Meaning is only that the Mind comprehends or perceives them; and that it is affected from without, or by some Being distinct from itself. This is my Explication of your Difficulty; and how it can serve to make your Tenet of an unperceiving material *Substratum* intelligible, I would fain know.

Hyl. Nay, if that be all, I confeſs I do not ſee what Uſe can be made of it. But are you not guilty of ſome Abuſe of Language in this?

Phil. None at all: It is no more than common Cuſtom, which you know is the Rule of Language, hath authorized: Nothing being more uſual, than for Philoſophers to ſpeak of the immediate Objects of the Underſtanding as Things exiſting in the Mind. Nor is there any thing in this, but what is conformable to the general Analogy of Language; moſt part of the mental Operations being ſignified by Words borrowed from ſenſible Things; as is plain in the Terms *Comprehend*, *Reflect*, *Diſcourſe*, *&c.* which being applied to the Mind, muſt not be taken in their groſs original Senſe.

Hyl. You have, I own, ſatisfied me in this Point: But there ſtill remains one great Difficulty, which I know not how you will get over. And indeed it is of ſuch Importance, that if you could ſolve all others, without being able to find a Solution for this, you muſt never expect to make me a Proſelyte to your Principles.

Phil. Let me know this mighty Difficulty.

Hyl.

Hyl. The Scripture Account of the Creation, is what appears to me utterly irreconcileable with your Notions. *Moses* tells us of a Creation: A Creation of what? of Ideas? No certainly, but of Things, of real Things, solid corporeal Substances. Bring your Principles to agree with this, and I shall perhaps agree with you.

Phil. Moses mentions the Sun, Moon, and Stars, Earth and Sea, Plants and Animals: That all these do really exist, and were in the Beginning created by God, I make no question. If by *Ideas*, you mean Fictions and Fancies of the Mind, then these are no Ideas. If by *Ideas*, you mean immediate Objects of the Understanding, or sensible Things which cannot exist unperceived, or out of a Mind, then these Things are Ideas. But whether you do, or do not call them *Ideas*, it matters little. The Difference is only about a Name. And whether that Name be retained or rejected, the Sense, the Truth and Reality of Things continues the same. In common Talk, the Objects of our Senses are not termed *Ideas* but *Things*. Call them so still: Provided you do not attribute to them any absolute external Existence, and I shall never quarrel with you for a Word. The Creation therefore I allow to have been a Creation of Things, of of *Real* Things. Neither is this in the least inconſiſtent with my Principles, as is evident from what I have now ſaid; and would have been evident to you without this, if you had not forgotten what had been ſo often ſaid before. But as for ſolid corporeal Subſtances, I deſire you to ſhew where *Moſes* makes any mention of them; and if they ſhould be mentioned by him, or any other inſpired Writer, it would ſtill be incumbent on you to ſhew thoſe Words were not taken in the vulgar Acceptation, for things falling under our Senſes, but in the Philoſophic Acceptation, for Matter, or an unknown Quiddity, with an abſolute Exiſtence. When you have proved theſe Points, then (and not till then) may you bring the Authority of *Moſes* into our Diſpute.

Hyl. It is in vain to diſpute about a Point ſo clear. I am content to refer it to your own Conſcience. Are you not ſatisfied there is ſome peculiar Repugnancy between the *Moſaic* Account of the Creation, and your Notions?

Phil. If all poſſible Senſe, which can be put on the firſt Chapter of *Geneſis*, may be conceived as conſiſtently with my Principles as any other, then it has no peculiar Repugnancy with them. But there is no Senſe you may not as well conceive,

believing

believing as I do. Since, beside Spirits, all you conceive are Ideas; and the Existence of these I do not deny. Neither do you pretend they exist without the Mind.

Hyl. Pray let me see any Sense you can understand it in.

Phil. Why, I imagine that if I had been present at the Creation, I should have seen Things produced into Being; that is, become perceptible, in the Order described by the Sacred Historian. I ever before believed the *Mosaic* Account of the Creation, and now find no Alteration in my Manner of believing it. When Things are said to begin or end their Existence, we do not mean this with regard to God, but His Creatures. All Objects are eternally known by God, or which is the same thing, have an Eternal Existence in his Mind: But when Things before imperceptible to Creatures, are by a Decree of God, made perceptible to them; then are they said to begin a relative Existence, with respect to created Minds. Upon reading therefore the *Mosaic* Account of the Creation, I understand that the several Parts of the World became gradually perceiveable to finite Spirits, endowed with proper Faculties; so that whoever such were present, they were in truth perceived by them.

This

This is the literal obvious Senſe ſuggeſted to me, by the Words of the Holy Scripture: In which is included no Mention or no Thought, either of *Subſtratum*, Inſtrument, Occaſion, or abſolute Exiſtence. And upon Inquiry, I doubt not, it will be found, that moſt plain honeſt Men, who believe the Creation, never think of thoſe things any more than I. What metaphyſical Senſe you may underſtand it in, you only can tell.

Hyl. But, *Philonous*, you do not ſeem to be aware, that you allow created Things in the Beginning, only a relative, and conſequently hypothetical Being: That is to ſay, upon Suppoſition there were Men to perceive them, without which they have no Actuality of abſolute Exiſtence, wherein Creation might terminate. Is it not therefore according to you plainly impoſſible, the Creation of any inanimate Creatures ſhould precede that of Man? And is not this directly contrary to the *Moſaic* Account?

Phil. In Anſwer to that I ſay, *Firſt*, Created Beings might begin to exiſt in the Mind of other created Intelligences, beſide Men. You will not therefore be able to prove any Contradiction between *Moſes* and my Notions, unleſs you firſt ſhew, there was no other Order of finite created

created Spirits in Being before Man. I ſay farther, in caſe we conceive the Creation, as we ſhould at this time a Parcel of Plants or Vegetables of all ſorts, produced by an inviſible Power, in a Deſert where no body was preſent: That this Way of explaining or conceiving it, is conſiſtent with my Principles, ſince they deprive you of nothing, either ſenſible or imaginable: That it exactly ſuits with the common, natural, undebauched Notions of Mankind: That it manifeſts the Dependence of all Things on God; and conſequently hath all the good Effect or Influence, which it is poſſible that important Article of our Faith ſhould have in making Men humble, thankful, and reſigned to their Creator. I ſay moreover, that in this naked Conception of Things, diveſted of Words, there will not be found any Notion of what you call the *Actuality of abſolute Exiſtence.* You may indeed raiſe a Duſt with thoſe Terms, and ſo lengthen our Diſpute to no purpoſe. But I intreat you calmly to look into your own Thoughts, and then tell me if they are not an uſeleſs and unintelligible Jargon.

Hyl. I own, I have no very clear Notion annexed to them. But what ſay you to this? Do you not make the Exiſtence of of ſenſible Things conſiſt in their being in a Mind? And were not all Things eternally in the Mind of God? Did they not therefore exiſt from all Eternity, according to you? And how could that which was Eternal, be created in Time? Can any thing be clearer or better connected than this?

Phil. And are not you too of Opinion, that God knew all Things from Eternity?

Hyl. I am.

Phil. Conſequently they always had a Being in the Divine Intellect.

Hyl. This I acknowledge.

Phil. By your own Confeſſion therefore, nothing is New, or begins to be, in reſpect of the Mind of God. So we are agreed in that Point.

Hyl. What ſhall we make then of the Creation?

Phil. May we not underſtand it to have been intirely in reſpect of finite Spirits; ſo that Things, with regard to us, may properly be ſaid to begin their Exiſtence, or be created, when God decreed they ſhould become perceptible to intelligent Creatures, in that Order and Manner which He then eſtabliſhed, and we now call the Laws of Nature? You may call this a *relative*, or *hypothetical Exiſtence* if you pleaſe. But ſo ſo long as it ſupplies us with the moſt natural, obvious, and literal Senſe of the *Moſaic* Hiſtory of the Creation; ſo long as it anſwers all the religious Ends of that great Article; in a word, ſo long as you can aſſign no other Senſe or Meaning in its ſtead; why ſhould we reject this? Is it to comply with a ridiculous Sceptical Humour of making every thing Nonſenſe and Unintelligible? I am ſure you cannot ſay, it is for the Glory of God. For allowing it to be a thing poſſible and conceivable, that the corporeal World ſhould have an abſolute Subſiſtence extrinſical to the Mind of God, as well as to the Minds of all created Spirits: Yet how could this ſet forth either the Immenſity or Omniſcience of the Deity, or the neceſſary and immediate Dependence of all things on Him? Nay, would it not rather ſeem to derogate from thoſe Attributes?

Hyl. Well, but as to this Decree of God's, for making Things perceptible: What ſay you, *Philonous*, is it not plain, God did either execute that Decree from all Eternity, or at ſome certain time began to will what He had not actually willed before, but only deſigned to will. If the former, then there could be no Creation or Beginning of Exiſtence in finite Things. If the latter, then we muſt acknowledge ſomething new to befal the Deity; which implies a ſort of Change: and all Change argues Imperfection.

Phil. Pray conſider what you are doing. Is it not evident, this Objection concludes equally againſt a Creation in any Senſe; nay, againſt every other Act of the Deity, diſcoverable by the Light of Nature? None of which can we conceive, otherwiſe than as performed in Time, and having a Beginning. God is a Being of tranſcendent and unlimited Perfections: His Nature therefore is incomprehenſible to finite Spirits. It is not therefore to be expected, that any Man, whether *Materialiſt* or *Immaterialiſt*, ſhould have exactly juſt Notions of the Deity, His Attributes, and ways of Operation. If then you would infer any thing againſt me, your Difficulty muſt not be drawn from the Inadequateneſs of our Conceptions of the Divine Nature, which is unavoidable on any Scheme; but from the Denial of Matter, of which there is not one Word, directly or indirectly, in what you have now objected.

Hyl. I muſt acknowledge, the Difficulties you are concerned to clear, are ſuch only as ariſe from the Non-exiſtence of Matter, and are peculiar to that Notion. So far you are in the right. But I cannot by any means bring my ſelf to think there

there is no ſuch peculiar Repugnancy between the Creation and your Opinion; though indeed where to fix it, I do not diſtinctly know.

Phil. What would you have! do I not acknowledge a twofold State of Things, the one Ectypal or Natural, the other Archetypal and Eternal? The former was created in Time; the latter exiſted from Everlaſting in the Mind of God. Is not this agreeable to the common Notions of Divines? or is any more than this neceſſary in order to conceive the Creation? But you ſuſpect ſome peculiar Repugnancy, though you know not where it lies. To take away all Poſſibility of Scruple in the caſe, do but conſider this one Point. Either you are not able to conceive the Creation on any Hypotheſis whatſoever; and if ſo, there is no ground for Diſlike or Complaint againſt my particular Opinion on that Score: Or you are able to conceive it; and if ſo, why not on my Principles, ſince thereby nothing conceivable is taken away? You have all along been allowed the full Scope of Senſe, Imagination, and Reaſon. Whatever therefore you could before apprehend, either immediately or mediately by your Senſes, or by Ratiocination from your Senſes; whatever you could perceive, imagine or underſtand, remains ſtill with you. If therefore the Notion you have of the Creation by other Principles be intelligible, you have it ſtill upon mine; if it be not intelligible, I conceive it to be no Notion at all; and ſo there is no Loſs of it. And indeed it ſeems to me very plain, that the Suppoſition of Matter, that is, a thing perfectly unknown and inconceivable, cannot ſerve to make us conceive any thing. And I hope, it need not be proved to you, that if the Exiſtence of Matter doth not make the Creation conceivable, the Creation's being without it inconceivable, can be no Objection againſt its Non-Exiſtence.

Hyl. I confeſs, *Philonous*, you have almoſt ſatisfied me in this Point of the Creation.

Phil. I would fain know why you are not quite ſatisfied. You tell me indeed of a Repugnancy between the *Moſaic* Hiſtory and Immaterialiſm: But you know not where it lies. Is this reaſonable, *Hylas*? Can you expect I ſhould ſolve a Difficulty without knowing what it is? But to paſs by all that, would not a Man think you were aſſured there is no Repugnancy between the received Notions of Materialiſts and the inſpired Writings?

Hyl. And ſo I am.

Phil. Ought the Hiſtorical Part of Scripture to be underſtood in a plain obvious

vious Senſe, or in a Senſe which is metaphyſical, and out of the way?

Hyl. In the plain Senſe, doubtleſs.

Phil. When *Moſes* ſpeaks of Herbs, Earth, Water, &c. as having been created by God; think you not the ſenſible Things, commonly ſignified by thoſe Words, are ſuggeſted to every unphiloſophical Reader?

Hyl. I cannot help thinking ſo.

Phil. And are not all Ideas, or Things perceived by Senſe, to be denied a real Exiſtence by the Doctrine of the Materialiſts?

Hyl. This I have already acknowledged.

Phil. The Creation therefore, according to them, was not the Creation of Things ſenſible, which have only a relative Being, but of certain unknown Natures, which have an abſolute Being, wherein Creation might terminate.

Hyl. True.

Phil. Is it not therefore evident, the Aſſerters of Matter deſtroy the plain obvious Senſe of *Moſes*, with which their Notions are utterly inconſiſtent; and inſtead of it obtrude on us I know not what, ſomething equally unintelligible to themſelves and me?

Hyl. I cannot contradict you.

Phil. *Moſes* tells us of a Creation. A Creation of what? of unknown Quiddities,

 of

of Occasions, or *Substratums*? No certainly; but of Things obvious to the Senses. You must first reconcile this with your Notions, if you expect I should be reconciled to them.

Hyl. I see you can assault me with my own Weapons.

Phil. Then as to *absolute Existence*; was there ever known a more jejune Notion than that? Something it is, so abstracted and unintelligible, that you have frankly owned you could not conceive it, much less explain any thing by it. But allowing Matter to exist, and the Notion of absolute Existence to be as clear as Light; yet was this ever known to make the Creation more credible? Nay hath it not furnished the *Atheists* and *Infidels* of all Ages, with the most plausible Argument against a Creation? That a corporeal Substance, which hath an absolute Existence without the Minds of Spirits, should be produced out of nothing by the mere Will of a Spirit, hath been looked upon as a thing so contrary to all Reason, so impossible and absurd, that not only the most celebrated among the Ancients, but even divers Modern and Christian Philosophers have thought Matter coeternal with the Deity. Lay these things together, and then judge you whether Materialism disposes Men to believe the Creation of Things.

Hyl.

Hyl. I own, *Philonous*, I think it does not. This of the *Creation* is the last Objection I can think of; and I must needs own it hath been sufficiently answered as well as the rest. Nothing now remains to be overcome, but a sort of unaccountable Backwardness that I find in my self toward your Notions.

Phil. When a Man is swayed, he knows not why, to one Side of a Question; Can this, think you, be any thing else but the Effect of Prejudice, which never fails to attend old and rooted Notions? And indeed in this respect I cannot deny the Belief of Matter to have very much the Advantage over the contrary Opinion, with Men of a learned Education.

Hyl. I confess it seems to be as you say.

Phil. As a Balance therefore to this Weight of Prejudice, let us throw into the Scale the great Advantages that arise from the Belief of Immaterialism, both in regard to Religion and Humane Learning. The Being of a God, and Incorruptibility of the Soul, those great Articles of Religion, are they not proved with the clearest and most immediate Evidence? When I say the Being of a *God*, I do not mean an obscure general Cause of Things, whereof we have no Conception, but *God*, in the strict and proper Sense of the Word.

A Being whoſe Spirituality, Omnipreſence, Providence, Omniſcience, Infinite Power and Goodneſs, are as conſpicuous as the Exiſtence of ſenſible Things, of which (notwithſtanding the fallacious Pretences and affected Scruples of *Scepticks*) there is no more reaſon to doubt, than of our own Being. Then with relation to Humane Sciences; in Natural Philoſophy, what Intricacies, what Obſcurities, what Contradictions, hath the Belief of Matter led Men into! To ſay nothing of the numberleſs Diſputes about its Extent, Continuity, Homogeneity, Gravity, Diviſibility, *&c.* do they not pretend to explain all things by Bodies operating on Bodies, according to the Laws of Motion? and yet, are they able to comprehend how any one Body ſhould move another? Nay, admitting there was no Difficulty in reconciling the Notion of an inert Being with a Cauſe; or in conceiving how an Accident might paſs from one Body to another; yet by all their ſtrained Thoughts and extravagant Suppoſitions, have they been able to reach the mechanical Production of any one Animal or Vegetable Body? Can they account by the Laws of Motion, for Sounds, Taſtes, Smells, or Colours, or for the regular Courſe of Things? Have they accounted by Phyſical Principles for the Aptitude and

and Contrivance, even of the moſt inconſiderable Parts of the Univerſe? But laying aſide Matter and corporeal Cauſes, and admitting only the Efficiency of an All-perfect Mind, are not all the Effects of Nature eaſy and intelligible? If the *Phænomena* are nothing elſe but *Ideas*; God is a *Spirit*, but Matter an unintelligent, unperceiving Being. If they demonſtrate an unlimited Power in their Cauſe; God is Active and Omnipotent, but Matter an inert Maſs. If the Order, Regularity, and Uſefulneſs of them, can never be ſufficiently admired; God is infinitely Wiſe and Provident, but Matter deſtitute of all Contrivance and Deſign. Theſe ſurely are great Advantages in *Phyſics*. Not to mention that the Apprehenſion of a diſtant Deity, naturally diſpoſes Men to a Negligence in their *moral* Actions, which they would be more cautious of, in caſe they thought Him immediately preſent, and acting on their Minds without the Interpoſition of Matter, or unthinking Second Cauſes. Then in *Metaphyſics*; what Difficulties concerning Entity in Abſtract, Subſtantial Forms, Hylarchic Principles, Plaſtic Natures, Subſtance and Accident Principle of Individuation, Poſſibility of Matter's thinking, Origin of Ideas, the Manner how two independent Subſtances, ſo widely

widely different as *Spirit* and *Matter*, should mutually operate on each other? What Difficulties, I say, and endless Disquisitions concerning these and innumerable other the like Points, do we escape by supposing only Spirits and Ideas? Even the *Mathematicks* themselves, if we take away the absolute Existence of extended Things, become much more clear and easy; the most shocking Paradoxes and intricate Speculations in those Sciences, depending on the infinite Divisibility of finite Extension, which depends on that Supposition. But what need is there to insist on the particular Sciences? Is not that Opposition to all Science whatsoever, that Phrensy of the ancient and modern *Scepticks*, built on the same Foundation? Or can you produce so much as one Argument against the Reality of corporeal Things, or in behalf of that avowed utter Ignorance of their Natures, which doth not suppose their Reality to consist in an external absolute Existence? Upon this Supposition indeed, the Objections from the Change of Colours in a Pigeon's Neck, or the Appearances of a broken Oar in the Water, must be allowed to have Weight. But those and the like Objections vanish, if we do not maintain the Being of absolute external Originals, but place the Reality of

Things

Things in Ideas, fleeting indeed, and changeable; however not changed at random, but according to the fixed Order of Nature. For herein consists that Constancy and Truth of Things, which secures all the Concerns of Life, and distinguishes that which is *real* from the irregular Visions of the Fancy.

Hyl. I agree to all you have now said, and must own that nothing can incline me to embrace your Opinion, more than the Advantages I see it is attended with. I am by Nature lazy; and this would be a mighty Abridgment in Knowledge. What Doubts, what Hypotheses, what Labyrinths of Amusement, what Fields of Disputation, what an Ocean of false Learning, may be avoided by that single Notion of *Immaterialism*?

Phil. After all, is there any thing farther remaining to be done? You may remember you promised to embrace that Opinion, which upon Examination should appear most agreeable to common Sense, and remote from *Scepticism*. This by your own Confession is that which denies Matter, or the absolute Existence of corporeal Things. Nor is this all; The same Notion has been proved several Ways, viewed in different Lights, pursued in its Consequences, and all Objections against it it cleared. Can there be a greater Evidence of its Truth? or is it poſſible it ſhould have all the Marks of a true Opinion, and yet be falſe?

Hyl. I own my ſelf intirely ſatisfied for the preſent in all reſpects. But what Security can I have that I ſhall ſtill continue the ſame full Aſſent to your Opinion, and that no unthought-of Objection or Difficulty will occur hereafter?

Phil. Pray, *Hylas,* do you in other Caſes, when a Point is once evidently proved, withhold your Aſſent on account of Objections or Difficulties it may be liable to? Are the Difficulties that attend the Doctrine of incommenſurable Quantities, of the Angle of Contact, of the Aſymptotes to Curves or the like, ſufficient to make you hold out againſt Mathematical Demonſtration? Or will you disbelieve the Providence of God, becauſe there may be ſome particular things which you know not how to reconcile with it? If there are Difficulties attending Immaterialiſm, there are at the ſame time direct and evident Proofs for it. But for the Exiſtence of Matter, there is not one Proof, and far more numerous and inſurmountable Objections lie againſt it. But where are thoſe mighty Difficulties you inſiſt on? Alas! you know not where or what they are; ſomething which may poſſibly occur hereafter. If this be be a ſufficient Pretence for withholding your full Aſſent, you ſhould never yield it to any Propoſition, how free ſoever from Exceptions, how clearly and ſolidly ſoever demonſtrated.

Hyl. You have ſatisfied me, *Philonous.*

Phil. But to arm you againſt all future Objections, do but conſider, That which bears equally hard on two contradictory Opinions, can be a Proof againſt neither. Whenever therefore any Difficulty occurs, try if you can find a Solution for it on the Hypotheſis of the *Materialiſts.* Be not deceived by Words; but ſound your own Thoughts. And in caſe you cannot conceive it eaſier by the help of *Materialiſm*, it is plain it can be no Objection againſt *Immaterialiſm.* Had you proceeded all along by this Rule, you would probably have ſpared yourſelf abundance of trouble in objecting; ſince of all your Difficulties I challenge you to ſhew one that is explained by Matter; nay, which is not more unintelligible with, than without that Suppoſition, and conſequently makes rather *againſt* than *for* it. You ſhould conſider in each Particular, whether the Difficulty ariſes from the *Non-exiſtence of Matter*. If it doth not, you might as well argue from the infinite Diviſibility of Extenſion againſt the Divine Preſcience, as from ſuch a Difficulty againſt *Im-*

Immaterialiſm. And yet upon Recollection I believe you will find this to have been often, if not always the Caſe. You ſhould likewiſe take heed not to argue on a *petitio Principii.* One is apt to ſay, The unknown Subſtances ought to be eſteemed real Things, rather than the Ideas in our Minds: And who can tell but the unthinking external Subſtance may concur as a Cauſe or Inſtrument in the Production of our Ideas? But is not this proceeding on a Suppoſition that there are ſuch external Subſtances? And to ſuppoſe this, is it not begging the Queſtion? But above all things you ſhould beware of impoſing on your ſelf by that vulgar Sophiſm, which is called *Ignoratio Elenchi.* You talked often as if you thought I maintained the Non-exiſtence of ſenſible Things: Whereas in truth no one can be more thorowly aſſured of their Exiſtence than I am: And it is you who doubt; I ſhould have ſaid, poſitively deny it. Every thing that is ſeen, felt, heard, or any way perceived by the Senſes, is on the Principles I embrace, a real Being, but not on yours. Remember, the Matter you contend for is an unknown ſomewhat, (if indeed it may be termed *ſomewhat)* which is quite ſtripped of all ſenſible Qualities, and can neither be perceived by Senſe, nor apprehended by the Mind. Remember, I ſay, that it is not

any

any Object which is hard or soft, hot or cold, blue or white, round or square, &c. For all these things I affirm do exist. Though indeed I deny they have an Existence distinct from being perceived; or that they exist out of all Minds whatsoever. Think on these Points; let them be attentively considered and still kept in view. Otherwise you will not comprehend the State of the Question; without which your Objections will always be wide of the Mark, and instead of mine, may possibly be directed (as more than once they have been) against your own Notions.

Hyl. I must needs own, *Philonous*, nothing seems to have kept me from agreeing with you more than this same *mistaking the Question*. In denying Matter, at first glimpse I am tempted to imagine you deny the things we see and feel; but upon Reflexion find there is no Ground for it. What think you therefore of retaining the Name *Matter*, and applying it to sensible Things? This may be done without any Change in your Sentiments: And believe me it would be a Means of reconciling them to some Persons, who may be more shocked at an Innovation in Words than in Opinion.

Phil. With all my heart: Retain the Word *Matter*, and apply it to the Objects of of Senſe, if you pleaſe, provided you do not attribute to them any Subſiſtence diſtinct from their being perceived. I ſhall never quarrel with you for an Expreſſion. *Matter*, or *material Subſtance*, are Terms introduced by Philoſophers; and as uſed by them, imply a ſort of Independency, or a Subſiſtence diſtinct from being perceived by a Mind: But are never uſed by common People; or if ever, it is to ſignify the immediate Objects of Senſe. One would think therefore, ſo long as the Names of all particular Things, with the Terms *ſenſible*, *Subſtance*, *Body*, *Stuff*, and the like, are retained, the Word *Matter* ſhould be never miſſed in common Talk. And in Philoſophical Diſcourſes it ſeems the beſt way to leave it quite out; ſince there is not perhaps any one thing that hath more favoured and ſtrengthned the depraved Bent of the Mind toward *Atheiſm*, than the Uſe of that general confuſed Term.

Hyl. Well but, *Philonous*, ſince I am content to give up the Notion of an unthinking Subſtance exterior to the Mind, I think you ought not to deny me the Privilege of uſing the Word *Matter* as I pleaſe, and annexing it to a Collection of ſenſible Qualities ſubſiſting only in the Mind. I freely own there is no other Subſtance in a ſtrict Senſe, than *Spirit*. But I have been

been ſo long accuſtomed to the Term *Matter*, that I know not how to part with it. To ſay, There is no *Matter* in the World, is ſtill ſhocking to me. Whereas to ſay, There is no *Matter*, if by that Term be meant an unthinking Subſtance exiſting without the Mind: But if by *Matter* is meant ſome ſenſible Thing, whoſe Exiſtence conſiſts in being perceived, then there is *Matter*: This Diſtinction gives it quite another Turn: And Men will come into your Notions with ſmall Difficulty, when they are propoſed in that manner. For after all, the Controverſy about *Matter* in the ſtrict Acceptation of it, lies altogether between you and the Philoſophers; whoſe Principles, I acknowledge, are not near ſo natural, or ſo agreeable to the common Senſe of Mankind, and Holy Scripture, as yours. There is nothing we either deſire or ſhun, but as it makes, or is apprehended to make ſome Part of our Happineſs or Miſery. But what hath Happineſs or Miſery, Joy or Grief, Pleaſure or Pain, to do with abſolute Exiſtence, or with unknown Entities, abſtracted from all Relation to us? It is evident, Things regard us only as they are pleaſing or diſpleaſing: And they can pleaſe or diſpleaſe, only ſo far forth as they are perceived. Farther therefore we are not concerned; and thus far you leave things as you found them. Yet ſtill there is ſomething new in this Doctrine. It is plain, I do not now think with the Philoſophers, nor yet altogether with the Vulgar. I would know how the Caſe ſtands in that reſpect: Preciſely, what you have added to, or altered in my former Notions.

Phil. I do not pretend to be a Setter-up of *New Notions.* My Endeavours tend only to unite and place in a clearer Light that Truth, which was before ſhared between the Vulgar and the Philoſophers: The former being of Opinion, that *thoſe Things they immediately perceive are the real Things*; and the latter, that *the Things immediately perceived, are Ideas which exiſt only in the Mind.* Which Two Notions put together, do in effect conſtitute the Subſtance of what I advance.

Hyl. I have been a long time diſtruſting my Senſes; methought I ſaw things by a dim Light, and through falſe Glaſſes. Now the Glaſſes are removed, and a new Light breaks in upon my Underſtanding. I am clearly convinced that I ſee things in their native Forms; and am no longer in Pain about their unknown Natures or abſolute Exiſtence. This is the State I find my ſelf in at preſent: Though indeed the Courſe that brought me to it, I do do not yet thorowly comprehend. You ſet out upon the ſame Principles that *Academicks*, *Carteſians*, and the like Sects, uſually do; and for a long time it looked as if you were advancing their Philoſophical *Scepticiſm*; but in the End your Concluſions are directly oppoſite to theirs.

Phil. You ſee, *Hylas*, the Water of yonder Fountain, how it is forced upwards, in a round Column, to a certain Height; at which it breaks and falls back into the Baſon from whence it roſe: Its Aſcent as well as Deſcent, proceeding from the ſame uniform Law or Principle of *Gravitation*. Juſt ſo, the ſame Principles which at firſt View lead to *Scepticiſm*, purſued to a certain Point, bring Men back to common Senſe.

FINIS.